Managing

■ ■ ■

SCHOOL LEADERSHIP AND MANAGEMENT SERIES

Series Editors: Brent Davies and John West-Burnham

Managing Learning for Achievement

■ ■ ■

Strategies for Raising Achievement Through Effective Learning

Edited by

Christopher Bowring-Carr

and

John West-Burnham

Pearson
Education

PEARSON EDUCATION LIMITED

Head Office:
Edinburgh Gate
Harlow CM20 2JE
Tel: +44 (0)1279 623623
Fax: +44 (0)1279 431059

London Office:
128 Long Acre
London WC2E 9AN
Tel: +44 (0)20 7447 2000
Fax: +44 (0)20 7240 5771
Website: www.business-minds.com

First published in Great Britain 1999

ISBN 0 273 63989 7

British Library Cataloguing in Publication Data
A CIP catalogue record for this book can be obtained from the British Library.

10 9 8 7 6 5 4

Typeset by Pantek Arts, Maidstone, Kent.
Printed and bound in Great Britain by Bookcraft (Bath) Ltd, Midsomer Norton, Somerset

The Publishers' policy is to use paper manufactured from sustainable forests.

About the editors

■   ■   ■

Christopher Bowring-Carr is a Visiting Fellow at the International Educational Leadership and Management Centre, Lincoln University campus. He has worked as a school teacher and Principal, and was an HMI. He is an associate lecturer with the Open University and the University of Leicester.

Professor John West-Burnham, co-editor of this series, jointly runs the International MBA in Educational Leadership and Management at the Lincoln University campus. He has been a teacher, a Principal Lecturer in Education Management at a College of Higher Education, and an LEA officer.

Contents

■ ■ ■

Part 4
TECHNOLOGIES OF LEARNING

Part 5
CREATING A LEARNING CULTURE

Part 6
THE FUTURE

Contributors

■ ■ ■

Kevan Bleach is senior teacher, Sneyd School, Walsall.

Gillian Boyd is headteacher, Foyleview Special School, Northern Ireland.

Max Coates is headteacher, Bourne Community College, West Sussex.

Ann Cockerham is headteacher, Ratton School, Eastbourne.

Steve Davis is assistant headteacher, Sydney Smith School, Hull.

Richard S. Fawcett is headteacher, Thurston Upper School, Suffolk.

Robert Gwynne is Principal of Longsands Community College, St Neots, Cambridgeshire.

Steven Hales is headteacher, Beaupré Primary School, Wisbech, Cambridgeshire.

Phyllis Harris was principal of Washington Accelerated Learning Centre, Pasadena, California and is now a doctoral student at the University of Cambridge.

Graham Harrison is a teacher at Queen Elizabeth's Grammar School, Gainsborough, Lincolnshire.

Howard Kennedy was headteacher of Holy Family R.C. School, on the outskirts of Slough, and is now deputy director, London Leadership Centre.

Kath Lee is deputy headteacher, King Edward VII Upper School, Melton Mowbray.

Trevor Male is senior lecturer in educational leadership, International Educational Leadership Centre, Lincoln University campus.

Ian McKenzie is principal of Endeavour Hills Campus, Eumemmerring Secondary College, Victoria, Australia.

Suzanne Nexhip is vice principal of Endeavour Hills Campus, Eumemmerring Secondary College, Victoria, Australia.

Carrie Sabin-Young is director of Raising Achievements, Effective Learning Centre, Holmshill, Borehamwood.

Julia Shahid is director, ACT Academy, Texas, USA.

George Thomas is headteacher, Kesgrave High School, Ipswich, Suffolk.

Eric Tope is headteacher, St Thomas the Apostle College, London.

John Versey is headteacher, Goffs School, Essex.

Linda White is headteacher, Eastwood Infant and Nursery School, Nottingham.

Preface

■ ■ ■

This collection of case studies grows out of the publication of *Effective Learning in Schools* (1997, Financial Times Prentice Hall). The responses to that book have led to our being involved in a wide range of conferences, workshops and school-based activities. We became aware of a number of initiatives, many of which exemplified the principles and approaches we had discussed in *Effective Learning in Schools*. It became obvious that many schools are becoming increasingly interested in the notion of strategies which are focused on young people's learning rather than on effective teaching or the delivery of the curriculum.

One of the most significant features of the case studies in this book is that they demonstrate the richness, diversity and creativity of school-based improvement strategies. In spite of the increasing burden of highly specific and directive government policies, schools with effective leadership are still able to be innovative and generate strategies which are valid and appropriate to their own students. Equally, the teachers and leaders in the schools represented demonstrate a movement away from reactive compliance and mechanical implementation to innovation based on an understanding of trends and issues which transcend instrumental and reductionist accountability-driven models.

We therefore decided to collect a number of case studies to publicise, demonstrate and make available a range of innovative and successful strategies. None of the writers would claim uniqueness or best practice. Equally, we know that there are many examples of radical and innovative practice that we are not aware of. However, the positive response to *Reengineering and Total Quality in Schools* (1996, Financial Times Prentice Hall) convinces us of the importance of making innovative approaches available to a wider audience. One of the major problems with the current organisation of schools is that they provide very few opportunities to share and disseminate effective practice within schools and between schools. The opportunity to get access to, to understand, and then to apply as appropriate, alternative strategies which are of proven success is a major source of innovation and effective change management. This book seeks to provide a platform for a wide range of educationalists to describe the strategies that are significant in their own schools.

We have encouraged the contributors to write in the style that suits them best. We have deliberately avoided a formally structured approach or a quasi-academic presentation. Instead, the contributors were encouraged to tell the story of their school's approach in the style that is most appropriate to them. One of the most salutary aspects of designing and delivering professional development activities is that often the most highly valued aspects of the programme are the formal and informal opportunities for teachers to talk, discuss and share experiences. We hope that this collection replicates this aspect of professional learning.

This book aims to provide a range of insights to encourage individual and team reflection, to offer reassurance and challenge, and to identify a range of possible strategies growing out of professional practice in schools. We have sought to set the various studies in context. Chapter 1 provides a summary of the current state of understanding about the nature of learning. We have divided the case studies into three sections, each of which concludes with a review. Chapter 19 describes the strategies appropriate to school and classroom-based innovation. Chapter 20 is a review of the book as a whole which we have included to reinforce our belief that all learning experiences should make review and reflection implicit.

We are grateful to Trevor Male, senior lecturer in educational leadership, International Educational Leadership Centre, Lincoln University campus for agreeing to write the critical review. We are also grateful to the contributors for the time they gave to preparing and writing their contributions, often under significant pressure. Finally, we are grateful to Maureen Young for co-ordinating the production of the manuscript and to Karen Raynes, Julia Lee, and Kirsty Baker for their word-processing skills.

Christopher Bowring-Carr
John West-Burnham

PART 1

■ ■ ■

What is learning?

1

■ ■ ■

What is learning?

CHRISTOPHER BOWRING-CARR AND JOHN WEST-BURNHAM

Throughout the major part of the history of the human race, what you learned by observing your father and mother, by listening to and obeying the elders of the tribe, by complying with the lore of the group, and, later in our history, through apprenticeships, was sufficient to inform the conduct of the rest of your life. What you learned as a young person was the basis for work, pleasure, social behaviour and worship, and constituted all that would be passed on to your children. As the centuries passed, there were certainly small changes or additions which were built in to the repertoire of activities and skills, but such additions did not in any way alter the fundamental structures. In other words, the boundaries of knowledge were limited. It was possible to learn all that there was to be learned. The wise men of a time not so long ago in terms of human history could be sure in their knowledge that nothing was left to be learned; all knowledge was theirs. Now there are virtually no boundaries. As we approach the 21st century, anyone believing that there is nothing else to be learned is as much out of step with the truths of the time as would have been the leader of a tribe 20 000 years ago saying that there are galaxies out there waiting to be explored.

Moreover, the learning that took place was underpinned by a set of transcendental values in which all in the tribe or village believed. The seed was sown not only – even perhaps not mainly – in order to have food for the following winter, but in order to placate a particular spirit. An animal was hunted in a ritualised way, with ceremonies before and after the hunt, and eaten according to long-established rules because, of course, there was enjoyment and nourishment, but just as importantly because a god would be honoured by so doing. The network of relationships was established and maintained because the sense of order, reflecting and reifying the spiritual order, was a vital part of making the society cohere.

Learning, therefore, was on two levels simultaneously, each reinforcing and giving meaning to the other. The learning that occurred did so because it was answering a need above that of merely eating a meal, or building a tribal meeting-house. The learning was embedded in the total life of the learner, took place all the time, was added to by every experience, was reinforced by every adult. Learning, living and worshipping were one.

The children in our schools today are, clearly, in a totally different world. Since the early 19th century, the rate of change has accelerated at an exponential rate, and increasingly change in one area of life has had unexpected impacts on other, seemingly unrelated areas. In the late-1940s, for example, it was thought that the total worldwide demand for computers was four or five. The computer was seen quite simply as a machine to crunch very large numbers, and would have no impact on any area outside that specialist mathematical field. The idea that every aspect of our lives, in a matter of some 40 years, would be in a greater or lesser way altered by the invasive computer was unthinkable.

Change is now rapid, and non-linear, and alters the basics in our lives so that we are having to adjust continuously to new approaches, new jobs, and new expectations. Our children will be doing jobs for which we do not at present have names; they will be using technologies that have not yet been invented; they will need to be able to cope with a world in which the absolute certainty of yesterday may be doubtful by tomorrow, and overturned next week. It is, after all, not so long ago that a leading maker of films said that people would most certainly not want to hear actors talk; a surgeon, in the late 1800s, stated firmly that the heart and the brain would be two areas into which the wise and compassionate surgeon would never venture; a director of IBM in the fifties said he believed that the weight of a computer might be brought down to 1.5 tons. The history of the past two centuries is strewn with examples of categorical statements that have been overturned.

Hence the emphasis that we put on learning in this book and in our previous one, *Effective Learning in Schools*. In the face of continuous change there is only one answer – keep learning. The idea that a person can rely on what has been learned in school and university to provide a sure bedrock for the rest of his or her working life is preposterous. An emphasis on the content of an arbitrary parcel of subjects is an anachronism. As we will be arguing in this chapter, and demonstrating in a number of the chapters that follow, what we need to be asking our schools is not: 'What have your students learned?' but: 'To what extent have you enabled and encouraged them to keep on learning for the rest of their lives?' What we are suggesting is the creation of a learning community, one in which everyone and all structures are dedicated to learning. Such a community would establish a culture of thoughtful learning, and that culture would be underpinned by shared values. Among the visible outcomes would be a passionate excitement about learning, and a total commitment to life-long learning.

Our schools today, as a direct result of many years of propaganda from central government, have to operate in a climate which says that education is essentially instrumental. It is the market place that provides the set of values by which schools are supposed to steer themselves. It is the market place, and its ideas of competition, that is supposed to provide the spur to school improvement. It is the market place that judges the worth and success of education. Such a view of education is impoverished and impoverishing. This book contains many examples of schools which have raised themselves above the poverty of the belief in a purely instrumental education, and we know that there are many others which we could have included if we had had the space. These schools have put the learning of the individual at the core of their vision. They have seen that having as a goal the acquisition of five GCSEs is a necessary starting-point but an insufficient long-term aim with which to create a culture of shared learning.

At this point it is worth raising the question as to the half-life of those GCSEs which are used as a marker for a school's success: what is their worth to the individual student after, say, 12 months? Is all that human effort, that spending of financial and material resources, to have a shelf life of so short a duration? Kenton (1996, p. 56) recounts the words of a university dean, speaking at the class reunion of a medical school. He said that the half-life of what is now taught in medical schools is 10–15 years. He said he knew when they graduated that half of what they had been taught would turn out to be wrong, but at the time of graduation he did not know which half. Kenton's friend muses:

> Next year ... I suspect that he will say that the half-life of medical information is down to six or seven years because of the accelerated rate at which things now change.

Furthermore, the use of examination grades as pointers to a school's success is fundamentally flawed because those grades are most uncertain markers of an individual's learning. These markers are then aggregated to provide performance indicators for an institution. Such aggregated numbers are used because competition is of importance to the survival of the school; however, they tell one nothing about whether an individual student learned as well and as variedly as he or she might, whether they saw learning as absorbing and exhilarating and of permanent value, and whether they have been equipped with the passion and the abilities to keep on learning for the rest of their lives. Central government, in its simplistic emphasis on the most frothy and evanescent of numbers, has created a system in which the individual's learning is of less importance than a dubious statistic which is supposed to indicate an institution's overall performance.

Furthermore, as we argue later in this chapter, the type of learning that is validated by public examinations is, by and large, the least permanent type of learning. The emphasis, repeated over and over again by the many teachers the authors meet, is on being under tremendous pressure to 'get through the material'. This need to cover the content goes against everything that is known about how individuals learn. It is ironic that the very values that inform the education system are values which are antithetical to true learning. As we said above, the goal of five GCSEs at grades A–C for the highest possible number of pupils can be looked upon as the kick-start to what will then turn into a far more penetrating examination of how to enable all children to learn most effectively with the maximum of excitement, and with retention. As has been proved so many times, the broader and the more individually experienced a curriculum is, the better the students will do in whatever type of examination is set.

We may well have lost the certainties of previous ages, but what is possible is a replacement of the mechanistic values imposed on education by successive governments by a transcendence which is based on a passionate belief in and devotion to learning. Such a shift implies putting at the heart of every school the absolute statement: 'All children can learn and learn to the highest levels.' The next section of this chapter will look at that statement and its implications.

All children can learn

There have always been individuals who have put that belief into practice. There have been teachers who have known, intellectually and emotionally, that by starting with where the child is, by keying in to the child's curiosity, and by encouraging a variety of learning approaches, children can learn, and to the highest levels.

However, institutions have not always put that belief at the core of their structures. Tests, IQ numbers, streaming, setting, tiered examinations, hierarchies of subjects, selective post-primary schools have all been part of structures which grade young people according to ill-founded expectations of their potential. Institutions and indeed individual teachers have been heard to say something to the effect that given these children and their background, very little in the way of learning can be expected.

All children can learn. A simple statement, but one which put at the heart of every deliberation can profoundly alter the way a school works. Every activity, every organisational structure, every decision, every notice or poster or letter to parents, every grouping of children and the times and resources allocated to them – every single facet of the life of a school has to be judged by that one unalterable, undiminishable statement.

We know of three school systems in the United States – one in a mainly rural state, another in a large city and the third in a smaller town – which have put that statement at the centre of their reforms. 'All children can learn, and at the highest levels' is the standard against which everything is judged, and that 'everything' includes political decisions, staffing and other resource levels, the accountability system, and the attainments which students are expected to achieve. Support networks have been created to help teachers, students and parents to achieve the challenging goals that have been set, and in one of the three systems, extra taxation was voted through the legislature in order to provide the extra resources needed. Nothing is allowed to diminish the integrity of the central statement.

We need at this point to give some definitions of intelligence, and make some statements of belief upon which this book is founded. First: intelligence is not fixed at birth and beyond alteration. Intelligence, as Bruner (1996, p. 132) says:

> ... reflects a micro-culture of praxis: the reference books one uses, the notes one habitually takes, the computer programs and databases one relies upon, and perhaps most important of all, the network of friends, colleagues, or mentors on whom one leans for feedback, help, advice, even just for company.

He goes on to say:

> Indeed, if you make science classrooms more like the quirky worlds of working scientists – full of the humour of wild hypotheses, the exhilaration of unconventional procedures – the dividends in better performance are quickly evident. Learning to be a scientist is not the same as 'learning science', it is learning a culture, with all the 'non-rational' meaning-making that goes with it.

Bruner's statements point to two essentials. The first is that the context for learning cannot be contained within the normal classroom. Ever since formal, state-organised education started, the tendency has been to believe that children can learn all that is needed to be learned within the school-house. Now, through technology, we can expand the time frame and the geographical frame within which learning takes place. The second essential is that the emphasis must be not only on the content, but also on the culture of the subject. As Bruner emphasises, the 'non-rational' has to go alongside the rational. The dichotomy found in too many of our schools disadvantages the learner by concentrating on only one part of the person.

Another definition of intelligence which underscores the idea that it is not a fixed quantity, but organic and dependent on context, is that of Robert Sternberg (1990, p. 6):

> *I define intelligence as consisting of those mental functions purposively employed for purposes of adaptation to, and shaping and selecting of, real-world environments.*

Again, such a definition takes us away from the boundaries of the school, and says that we can help intelligence to grow if we enable our students to interact with a range of environments situated in the real world. The problem for a long time has been, as the National Advisory Council on Creative and Cultural Education (1998) says, that 'the system is dominated by a confusion between intelligence and academic ability'. This confusion has led to the institutionalisation of the segregation of children into those who are believed to be able to learn, and those who are believed to be able to learn less. It has also led to a series of mistaken beliefs about what learning is.

Definitions of learning

Here we look at some definitions of learning and examine the difference between shallow and deep learning, and the consequences of these definitions for the way our schools and classrooms are organised.

Learning is constructive

The belief that learning is an interactive process undertaken in the triangle of learner, teacher and the discipline of the subject is central to this book. The opposite to this belief is the idea that there is a body of knowledge which we, as teachers, need to transmit to our students, who accept that knowledge without demur or question, and prove their acceptance of it by reproducing it when asked to do so in a test or examination. It is a stance which equates knowledge with 'reality', which is fixed, permanent, and 'out there' to be tapped by our students. However, knowledge is not a package to be delivered to the students.

Knowledge is mediated by human interests. The very form and structure of what we know are conditioned by our reasons for wanting to know ... the acquisition of knowledge is a moral pursuit, not merely a technical challenge. In the reforms now being implemented, knowledge is perceived and acquired as if it were inert and objective, like information methodically processed, refined and disseminated for its usefulness. (Strain, M., 1993)

If we believe that learning is constructive, then what we are saying is that each of us has to make our knowledge our own. Bruner, in Elliott (1998), says: 'most learning in most settings is a communal activity, a sharing of the culture. It is not just that the child must make his knowledge his own, but that he must make it his own in a community of those who share his sense of belonging to a culture.' That 'sharing of the culture' is a vital part of the transcendence to which we referred earlier.

What Bruner, Elliott and others stress is that constructive learning is a dialogue between the learner and the material, aided, fostered, encouraged by a teacher/mentor, a dialogue in which, as the student's experience increases, her stance shifts and develops. The student and the teacher/mentor together build the knowledge that the student takes to herself and makes her own. Experience, knowledge, emotions, and intrapersonal awareness combine to sift and resift what she meets so that learning becomes a continuum, a never-ending adaptation to the encountered world. There is the danger that such a statement will suggest to critics that what we are advocating is a personal house, built on sand. However, that is far from the truth. As we have suggested in *Effective Learning in Schools*, and as Elliott and Bruner have suggested above, learning occurs in a community, and a learning or thinking or interpretative community (the terms vary but the meaning is the same) is one which has among its highest priorities the establishment of an ethical code, a clear statement of its moral vision. That is the community within which the learner will be growing. Those are the values which inspire the learning.

Learning is incremental

So, learning is building. As far as the school is concerned, this belief means that not only does each teacher have to take previous learning into account when deciding on a learning plan for the individual child, but also that other issues, such as areas of experience, interests, areas about which the child is curious, emotional predispositions, learning styles, all have to be taken into account. Some schools have introduced the idea of the 'learning manager', someone with the express brief to get to know the individual child in order to make sure that what the school and other agencies have to offer match as closely as possible the previous experiences and current needs of the child.

Learning is co-operative

It follows absolutely from what has been said above that by and large we learn best in a community. There is some learning which is necessarily individual, which is a means to an end, and the end is the ability to build on our knowledge with and through other people. Within a learning community, the pleasures and uncertainties of learning are shared: tentative ideas are tested among trusted companions; the first expressions of mastery of part of a topic are celebrated by the community together; some learning will be stimulated by a group activity, and that learning will be demonstrated by the group. The culture of the group is affected by the learning that is taking place, and the learning in turn is influenced by the culture of the community.

> In the constructionist view, our perceptions, appreciations, and beliefs are rooted in worlds of our own making that we come to accept as reality ... Through countless acts of attention and inattention, aiming, sensemaking, boundary setting, and control, they make and maintain the worlds matched to their professional knowledge and know-how ... When practitioners respond to the indeterminate zones of practice by holding a reflective conversation with the materials of their situations, they remake a part of their practice world and thereby reveal the usually tacit processes of worldmaking that underlie all of their practice.
>
> (Schon, D. , 1987, p. 36)

Naturally, indeed essentially, the community to which we refer is the entire community of the school or college. Everyone is a learner. Roland Barth, in his book *Improving Schools from Within* (1990, p. 49–50), stresses the absolute need for all in the schoolhouse to be learners:

> Just as potters cannot teach others to craft in clay without setting their own hands to work at the wheel, so teachers cannot fully teach others the excitement, the difficulty, the patience, and the satisfaction that accompany learning without themselves engaging in the messy, frustrating, and rewarding 'clay' of learning ... For when teachers observe, examine, question, and reflect on their ideas and develop new practices that lead towards their ideals, students are alive. When teachers stop growing, so do their students.

Learning is regulated by the learner

Our aim, as we have said, is to enable students to become life-long, self-starting and self-sustaining learners. The autonomous learner must be the final outcome of all that goes on in schools and colleges. Only when he is autonomous can the learner contribute to the learning community. Consider the construction of a tall building. At first, there has to be a great deal of scaffolding to support and direct the building, but as the building takes on an integral strength of its own, the scaffolding can, and should, be steadily withdrawn. The scaffolding in the world of learning is the teacher in a variety of roles: teacher, instructor, mentor, coach, partner. The other elements in the structure are the other resources of the school, and the neighbourhood, and the larger community in which the school lives. The first steps in dismantling that scaffold has to be the enablement of the child to look at what is going on when she is learning. The child needs a language to talk about and investigate her learning. Metacognition is essential if the child is to have an understanding of and therefore a control of her learning. That metalanguage will contribute to the conversations between child and teacher as they search for the best way to move on to the next stage of learning. Obviously it will not be the only language between the two, but it will be an important one. There is a great deal of research to support this idea that being able to look at one's learning and discuss it with oneself and with others is a vital part of becoming a life-long learner, and an ability to discuss one's learning helps one to learn more easily and more deeply.

Learning needs a goal

Under this heading we return to what we were saying at the beginning of the chapter, namely that there is a need for a transcendent set of values for the learner to have a faith in and to act as a spur to his learning. At present it is very difficult to see any such set of values. Indeed, Elliott (1998, p. 31) suggests that the National Curriculum

> constitutes a denial of the social being of children in favour of turning them into possessive individuals ... As such, implementation will only reinforce the social alienation of children because it denies them the chance to develop a sense of what it means to participate with others in the construction of shared values and beliefs.

There is a deep malaise at the heart of the central bureaucracy which controls the education system; having started on the path of 'market forces rule all', there is an inability to see that the soul, the spirit, that inspiring

11

force which can lead all in schools and colleges to amazing achievements across the spectrum of what humans can do, is not inspired by the leaden demands of a purely instrumental curriculum.

Learning is contextual

One of the many problems facing schools is that, by the imposition of the National Curriculum, learning is fragmented. The factory model on which schools were created in the last century contained, *inter alia*, the notion of breaking down to the smallest parts the work that children and teachers have to do in parallel with the breaking down of work on the assembly line. We still have the utterly ludicrous notion that during a school day we obtain, at considerable cost and with the addition of an element of luck and complicity, the attention of a class of children on, say, a fictional character. At the end of 40 minutes, regardless of the state of understanding, commitment, enjoyment of some or all of the class on that topic, a bell rings and within five minutes that same class is expected to be equally involved and absorbed by a question of biology, or the machinations of a mediaeval king or whatever. There is no linkage between one item and the next or the preceding one, no recognition that one child is just starting to understand the main problem and that another child is ready to move on to a deeper question, no notice taken of the need for that group to get together to talk the topic through. The assembly line rules. What is the context for this happenstance of subjects? What is the context for the sequence of subjects through a school day? At what point in this school day is the child's context put first and then the threads of various topics woven into that? No adult would ever contemplate voluntarily undertaking that sort of rootless and jumbled learning.

Learning cannot be mandated

There is a curious idea abroad that a group of people sitting in Whitehall or wherever can say that this group of children will learn that topic by using this plan. Whether it is literacy – and it is interesting that there is no contemporary definition of the term – or numeracy, there is the belief that by putting together a 'teacher-proof' package, all the children in England will become 'literate', although we do not know what that word means. Deep learning is by its very nature unpredictable. It is not governed by a timetable; it does not start and stop with a particular teacher or textbook; it does not respond to marks in tests; it does not obey orders from people totally unconcerned with the process; it cannot be shaped by curricular material created by those who are uninterested in the individual.

Schon (1987, p. 89–90) gives a lengthy quotation from a talk given by Carl Rogers, an eminent American educator, to a group of teachers assembled at Harvard University:

> My experience has been that I cannot teach another person how to teach. To attempt it is for me, in the long run, futile. It seems to me that anything that can be taught to another is relatively inconsequential and has little or no significant influence on behaviour. That sounds so ridiculous that I cannot help but question it at the same time as I present it.
>
> I realise increasingly that I am only interested in learnings which significantly influence behaviour. Quite possibly this is simply a personal idiosyncrasy. I have come to feel that only learning which significantly influences behaviour is self-discovered, self-appropriated learning. Such self-discovered learning, truth that has been personally appropriated and assimilated in experience, cannot be directly communicated to another.
>
> When I try to teach, as I do sometimes, I am appalled by the results, which seem little more than inconsequential, because sometimes the teaching appears to succeed. When this happens, I find the results are damaging. It seems to cause the individual to distrust his own experience and stifle significant learning.
>
> ... I realise that I am only interested in being a learner, preferably learning things that matter, that have some significant influence on my own behaviour.
>
> I find that one of the best, but most difficult, ways for me to learn is to drop my own defensiveness, at least temporarily, and to try to understand the way in which this experience seems and feels to the other person. I find that another way of learning for me is to state my own uncertainties, to try to clarify my puzzlement, and thus get closer to the meaning that my experience actually seems to have.

Schon goes on to say (p. 92) that

> Rogers has not lost all interest in being a teacher, but that he has reframed teaching in a way that gives central importance to his own role as a learner. He elicits self-discovery in others, first by modelling for others, as a learner, the open expression of his own deepest reflections (however absurd they may seem) and then, when others criticise him, by refusing to become defensive. ... He believes that the very expression of thoughts and feelings usually withheld, manifestly divergent from one another, has the potential to promote self-discovery.

How far is that view of what learning is from the one promulgated by our successive education ministers. Their rigid belief in 'the centre knows best' is totally opposed to the humility and uncertainty expressed by Rogers.

Their view of teaching as being purely transmissive fits ill with all that we know about learners and how they learn. The teacher- and child-proof methodology that the government advocates ignores all uncertainties and defensiveness and, of course, it has been tried so often and failed an equal number of times, because of that ignoring.

Steps towards a learning community

First, there needs to be an agreement on what is meant by the word 'learning'. If some people in the school believe that learning is the receiving of packets of knowledge – that teaching, in other words, is transmissive – and others believe in the constructive nature of learning, there will be no chance of establishing a learning, thinking community. To learn is to change, and to change brings with it the evidence that knowledge changes. Knowledge is shaped by our experiences, and our experiences shape our knowledge. The transmissive mode does not allow for knowledge to be personally malleable. The learning institution is, above all else, one in which there is a continuous questioning to find out how things can be improved; it is a place in which uncertainty is an essential because only when there is uncertainty can there be change.

It is necessary to stress that there are key foundation stones in this building, this schoolhouse, about which there is no uncertainty: the transcendent values are not open to debate. The placing of learning at the heart; the certainty that all children can learn and to the highest levels; that all in the community can learn continuously. Those values are fixed. However, it is the means by which they are achieved that can always be examined, rethought, or adapted in the light of new ideas, new challenges, and the unexpected.

The students must enter into this debate on the meaning of 'learning'. It is very easy for students, because of their experience, to think that learning is receiving and remembering what the teacher and the text books tell them, and to be able to reproduce that material in much the same state as it was received on demand. We said earlier that from an early age students need to be able to develop a metalanguage with which to discuss their learning. This acquisition of such a language will wean them from the dependency culture into which the transmissive mode of teaching has led them.

In *Effective Learning in Schools* we discussed at some length the idea of the six levels of learning. At this point, we will merely summarise that discussion. Learning, at its most shallow, is the mere memorising of facts – a necessary precursor to other learning but not a demanding aspect of learning. Next, there is an increase of our knowledge about a topic, and then facts are acquired and retained so that they can be used when necessary. From this there can be a move on to the next three levels, which are deeper levels of learning. The first is the abstraction of meaning from a series of related facts, after which there can be a move to an interpretative process aimed at understanding and ordering our reality. The sixth and most important level is reached when the learning changes the individual as a person. If what a person has 'learned' leaves him or her exactly the same as before, then the learning has been superficial, and will, sooner or later, be rejected, forgotten or ignored. Deep learning means there is a change, the world is seen in a different way, and the perception of reality alters.

Second, and as a corollary to the first, the school (and whenever we write 'school' we mean everyone connected with it) needs to start on the never-ending process of looking at every aspect of the organisation to judge whether it helps strengthen learning. For example, can we do no better than divide a day into 45-minute chunks, each devoted to a topic which has little, if any, connection with what goes before or after? There is a great deal of research which says that humans learn in many different ways – 32 at least – but none of it says that it is best fostered by arbitrary time slots. Do children – not children in general but our children in this school – learn best in age-related groups? Can our children learn a topic best by spending a week on it, two weeks, a month? Why only one teacher at a time? Why are we so parsimonious with our palette – can we not let our students employ the whole spectrum of colours to illuminate a topic with which they are increasingly deeply involved? Do we have to start the school day at 08.30 and end at 15.50? And be closed at weekends?

These, of course, might not be the questions that you, the reader, need to ask in your school or college. What we are suggesting is that if there is to be change, then there can be no areas which are excluded from rigorous challenge.

Third, children, and adults of course, demonstrate a wide range of intelligence. Howard Gardner (1993) states that there are seven intelligences, or ways in which we see the world. Sternberg (1990), in comparing the definitions of intelligence given by two sets of contributors to two symposia, one held in 1921 and the other in 1986, lists 27 attributes used to define intelligence. He notes (pp. 50–1) that 'attributes such as adaptation to the environment, basic mental processes and higher order thinking were prominent in both listings', but then goes on to point to the many differences of emphasis and indeed the many attributes that were listed in one symposium but not in the other.

Gardner (1993, p. 12) goes on to say that

> *people do learn, represent, and utilise knowledge in many different ways ...*
> *these differences challenge an educational system that assumes that everyone*
> *can learn the same materials in the same way and that a universal measure suf-*
> *fices to test student learning.*

He continues by saying that students would learn more easily if the material were presented in a number of ways, to mesh with the particular intelligence which was the strongest in each student. He also makes the point that our assessment system is heavily weighted towards the linguistic mode, and to a lesser extent towards the logical-quantitative mode.

To become a learning community, therefore, demands that multiple ways of demonstrating learning be found. The student, or a group of students, together with the teacher(s) need to discuss how best some learning could be expressed, and then together they need to find what criteria would be needed to assess whether the learning was sound. There is a great deal of research which shows that the method of assessing students predicts the ways in which they will learn. If the assessment system gives high marks to giving a simple 'right' answer, the students will memorise those right answers but will not learn the material at any level deeper. If the assessment system emphasises the process, and shows an acceptance of a variety of approaches, then the students will begin to learn at a deeper level. Ramsden, in Willis (1993), puts the argument succinctly:

> *Evidence now exists to show students' interests, attitudes to studying, and*
> *approaches to academic tasks are strongly related to their experiences of teach-*
> *ing and assessment.*

Of course, it is not only the assessment system that needs to reflect the many intelligences that students can demonstrate. Every overt and hidden message that the school gives needs to reflect that every sort of attainment is of equal worth, not only those which traditionally have been seen to be 'academically' respectable.

Fourth, the school needs to look with urgency for ways to incorporate information and communication technology (ICT) in order to show that learning is not an activity confined to a certain time and to a certain set of rooms. There is a growing mass of evidence which shows that ICT, once brought into the mainstream and not seen as a bolt-on to do a little more easily what we have always done, can make permeable the previously watertight compartments of time, geography and people. Through ICT we can learn at any time, in any actual or virtual location, and with a range of people unimaginable a few years ago. Once our students experience that broad-based learning, the chances of their becoming life-long learners will increase greatly.

Our aim, in this book, is to give our readers a small sample of the many examples we could cite of those schools which have put at the heart of their activities the idea of the learning community. There is no single pattern; nor could there be because learning does not produce or depend on neat, formulaic approaches. Learning, and the ways to express that learning, are multifarious; learning organisations cannot be mass produced. Wheatley, in Gunter (1997, p. 83) says:

> *There are no recipes or formulae, no checklists or advice that describe 'reality'. There is only what we create through our engagement with others and with events. Nothing really transfers; everything is always new and different and unique to each of us.*

We have aimed in this book to provide some ideas and possibilities of engagement which might be the spark that could inspire some more schools to begin the process of becoming a unique learning community. The chapters that follow are testimonies to the many and varied approaches taken by schools to establish their learning communities.

References

Barth, R.S. (1990) *Improving Schools from Within*, San Francisco, Jossey-Bass.

Bowring-Carr, C. and West-Burnham, J. (1997) *Effective Learning in Schools*, London, Financial Times Pitman Publishing.

Bruner, J. (1996) *The Culture of Education*, Cambridge, Mass., Harvard University Press.

Elliott, J. (1998) *The Curriculum Experiment*, Buckingham, The Open University Press.

Gardner, H. (1993) *The Unschooled Mind*, London, Fontana.

Gunter, H. (1997) *Rethinking Education*, London, Cassell.

Kenton, L. (1996) *Passage to Power*, London, Vermillion.

Schon, D.A. (1987) *Educating the Reflective Practitioner*, San Francisco, Jossey-Bass.

Sternberg, R.J. (1990) *Metaphors of the Mind*, Cambridge University Press.

Strain, M. (1993) 'Education reform and defamiliarisation', *Educational Management and Administration*, 21(3).

Willis, D. (1993) 'Learning and assessment: exposing the inconconsistencies of theory and practice', *Oxford Review of Education*, 19(3).

PART 2

■ ■ ■

Whole-school approaches

This section provides examples of whole-school strategies which are focused on raising achievement through the adoption of systematic and integrated approaches developed in response to an awareness of the need for improvement. Although the approaches described are in response to very different forces, they all have, at their heart, the integrity of the experience of the individual student. All the strategies are derived from detailed and systematic analysis, are based on high levels of consultation and involvement, and are driven by highly effective leadership.

2

■ ■ ■

Total quality provision for able children in comprehensive schools

KEVAN BLEACH

There has been a curious reluctance on the part of some comprehensive schools to promote actively the opportunities and interests of their most able pupils. This lack of provision and failure to make high expectations has been a feature not missed by HMI and OFSTED in a significant minority of school inspection reports (HMI/DEF, 1992). What lies at the root of it, perhaps, is an ethical reservation about initiatives that could be construed as fostering 'elitism' or memories of the unfairness of the 11-plus and the selective system. I suspect there is also a tendency to assume that bright pupils will look after themselves, without extra help from teachers, by virtue of their natural ability.

Over the past decade, however, government reforms have created a more competitive environment in education. The emergence of city technology colleges (CTCs) and grant maintained (GM) schools, and the current plans to allow all schools to develop a 'magnet' curriculum status and select a proportion of their intake, is contributing to much greater diversity. In order to maintain high standards in parents' eyes, schools seek effective ways of maximising pupils' levels of performance. External levers, like the publication of OFSTED reports and league tables of National Curriculum assessment and public examination results, have made them much more accountable in the provision they offer. Contemporary concerns with school effectiveness, improvement and quality have contributed to the sharper environment in which schools now have to operate.

All these changes have created a framework in which the development and implementation of provision for able and talented children should take on greater significance in *all* comprehensive schools. In pursuit of this, I have been involved in two activities: introducing a programme for the most able pupils at Sneyd School, Walsall, and writing a policy document for Walsall LEA's Inspectorate that identifies a strategy by which all the borough's comprehensives can make quality provision for their most able children. (Bleach, 1997).

The purpose of this paper is to explore the extent to which the principles and processes of total quality could be applied to the implementation and management of provision for the most able. My strategy can be itemised in the following terms:

- identification of the educational outcomes and ethical issues relating to how such provision would affect able pupils
- exploration of what is understood by the term 'most able', in terms of various kinds of intelligence
- consideration of ways in which such ability can be identified, and recognised establishment of what different kinds of curriculum provision, strategies for classroom organisation and teaching methodology are appropriate to the needs of the most able
- awareness of the need for procedures to assess pupils' progress and monitor provision
- recognition of the roles of various school 'stake-holders' (senior management, governors, parents, department heads and teachers, and the local education authority) in responding to the needs of the most able pupils.

Definition and applicability

It is appropriate, before going further, to devote a few lines to exploring the meaning of 'total quality' (TQ) and how appropriate its application is to schools. TQ's pedigree originated in the total quality *management* preoccupations of business and industry in Japan and the USA. Its impact was not felt in Britain until the early eighties. A brief survey of literature from Juran (1964) to Deming (1982) to West-Burnham (1992, 1997) reveals total quality as meaning different things in different situations. It resembles much more a broad framework than a unitary model. However, the common denominators in TQ's guiding principles may be summed up as mission and culture, the collective role of leadership and team-based management, provision and measurement of quality customer service, and constant analysis and review of work processes involving all employees. Suitably refined to the situation and needs of any given organisational context, these different strands are harnessed to the pursuit of continuous improvement. The turn of this decade saw recognition of TQ's potential as a mechanism for school effectiveness and improvement.

In applying the principles of total quality to a public service like education, concerns have been expressed about the importation of business and manufacturing principles. What possible use could they be, given the gulf between mass-producing industrial components and satisfying the individual educational needs of young people? Cultures and day-to-day problems differ, but there are also similarities. Quality has always been important to school practitioners, even if the means for securing it have not been particularly well codified in the past. Quality issues are much more in the public domain nowadays as a result of the market context of competition and accountability in which schools have to operate, which in turn reflects wider economic pressures and changes. The adoption and *adaptation* of TQ's guiding principles, therefore, is perfectly feasible because of their complementary relationship to many of the practices internationally acknowledged by educational research to be valid and successful. The emphasis in school effectiveness literature on teamwork, shared decision making and creating a positive school culture, for instance, closely parallels Deming's philosophy (Weller, 1997, p. 194).

The extent to which different characteristics of total quality are relevant, singly and in an inter-related sense, to one key factor in school effectiveness, i.e. provision for the most able, is the subject of the remainder of this paper. Writers about TQ have grouped its components into various discrete but inter-related categories. For the purpose of discussion here, the four broad headings of *vision, people, prevention* and *customers* are used (West-Burnham, 1996).

Vision

Putting this heading first underlines the difference between 'total quality' and 'total quality management' approaches. Discarding the term 'management' enables one's emphasis to move from a purely transactional level – whereby short-term, controllable and attainable processes are subjected to regular review – to a more *transformational* plane, involving the communication of vision and commitment. It is one in which moral imperatives are paramount. How does that apply to a school? The core purpose of any educational establishment should be to offer an environment in which teaching and all-round expectations are of sufficient quality to have the maximum impact on pupils' learning and progress (Sammons, Hillman and Mortimore, 1995). A high quality school is one that clearly articulates such an over-arching purpose and then sets about meeting its goals, thus demonstrating that it is 'fit for its purpose'. This sense of mission becomes fulfilled by permeating and enthusing all aspects of strategic planning, thereby facilitating its *total* application within the institution. It must attract everyone's hearts and minds.

My belief that this kind of vision provides a moral basis for action led me to justify provision for able pupils in terms of helping them 'achieve their full potential by ensuring schools create learning environments in which they are able to progress as far and fast as they can'. This subsidiary view of where one should be going was set within two important contexts: first, the structural economic changes that require schools to nurture qualities of creative thinking, leadership and problem-solving appropriate to the 21st-century marketplace, and second, the fact that our Pacific Rim competitors in the globalised economy have specific policies for helping talented pupils that schools are *obliged* to implement. In addition, I urged that every school should have a policy statement acknowledging provision as an integral part of a wider commitment to quality teaching methods, classroom resources and learning styles. To ensure consistent application, this should be reflected in departmental policies for the most able.

There is also a need for leadership. Leaders are crucial in the implementation of any vision by virtue of their conviction that it is attainable, particularly in the time-lag between implementing developments and achieving improved results (Barber, 1995, p. ii). This is why I called for schools to appoint path-finding co-ordinators from within their senior management teams and, similarly, for the LEA to designate one member of the inspection team with responsibility for the more able. Their status will provide them with sufficient clout to prioritise, enthuse, resource, celebrate and generally 'make things happen'. Celebration is an important ingredient in motivating people: companies committed to TQ, for instance, make photographs and stories about quality improvements a strong feature of their in-house magazines (Stott, 1994, p. 200). From a quality *assurance* viewpoint, they have a further role in auditing and evaluating whether the provision programme is successfully achieving the aims set for it.

People

A total quality approach calls for the 'significance and responsibility of every employee' to be recognised in an organisation's pursuit of its mission (West-Burnham, 1997, p. 122). In that sense, *everyone* is a leader. A quality culture requires *all* of its members to take a personal responsibility for its delivery. Therefore, the greater the opportunities for every teacher – individually or on a team basis – to be involved in the production of his/her subject department's interpretation of the whole-school policy for bright children, the more likely one is to raise his/her awareness, promote a sense of ownership in the initiative, and foster a common approach, within the limits of acceptable diversity, to extending these pupils. There is always a danger that when one person has a named responsibility, others tend to think they need not be involved. A quality management approach will both invite and demand active participation at all levels (Hampton, 1994, p. 289). The ideal is that *all* teachers feel sufficiently confident that even if a young Mozart (or his female equivalent) started in Year 7, they would have a clear idea how to recognise, cater for and celebrate his talents.

Mention has been made of the ethical reservations some teachers might hold. Herein lies a possible problem for applying total quality principles to an organisation such as a school, that is characterised by 'phenomenological perspectives' (Davies and West-Burnham, 1997, p. 11). How, in this particular case, can greater consensus in outlook be worked for? My suggestion is that a programme for the most able be set in the context of equal opportunities for *all*. To be true to their name, comprehensives should foster a climate that recognises each child has equal value and *individual needs*. Just as pupils with special educational needs are catered for, so those with marked talents should be encouraged in their achievements.

One of the reasons for the needs of the most able remaining unconsidered in some schools is the popular belief that they are a very small minority. The notion that high ability is restricted to purely intellectual talents, however, has been questioned by research indicating that there are multiple intelligences by which children can learn effectively (Gardner, 1993; Perkins, 1995). Failure to provide teaching and learning opportunities that work through, and aim at, these different areas could be represented as neglecting the right of a sizeable proportion of one's 'customers' in the school population to optimise their potential. In getting away from the traditional equation of quality with exclusivity (Pfeffer and Coote, 1991), and making one's definitions of ability *inclusive*, teachers who are inclined to dismiss provision as 'elitist' because of the distinctiveness it confers on a small minority might well think again.

25

As with leadership, there is a quality assurance dimension to the creation of collegial structures. The more staff are trusted and involved in meeting the needs of the most able, the greater the devolution of responsibility to each of them for personally maintaining quality teaching and learning experiences.

Prevention

Much of what has been written about total quality concerns quality control, assurance, management, audit and assessment of the 'product' – in this case, the creation of an appropriate learning environment for able pupils. It is to do with specific techniques to help 'translate principle into practice – the abstract into concrete experience' (West-Burnham, 1997, p. 122). In defining the standards for a quality programme for the more able, first I had to establish methods of identifying pupils. One problem with introducing TQ initiatives is the lack of sound data on which to build them. Suitable techniques and procedures include:

- observation and nomination by teachers
- assessment by teachers
- observation of pupil performance
- observations and nominations by parents
- checklists of general and subject characteristics of high ability
- primary school profiles and assessment records
- standardised achievement and intellectual ability tests.

Then I specified a number of mechanisms, procedures and processes that would cover the key areas of curriculum provision, organisational strategies and teaching methodology:

- **Curriculum provision**. Incorporating extension and enrichment in schemes of work will help able pupils develop wider knowledge and use high-level skills or creative responses. Individual study programmes will cater for those with specific talents or deep interest in a topic. Enhancement should extend beyond subjects to a central programme of problem-solving, visits, courses, workshops, competitions, etc. There must be scope for 'fast-tracking' to GCSE, A-level and even first-year degree work, taking advantage of modular courses and distance-learning materials.

- **Organisational strategies**. Most able pupils benefit from interacting with each other, although other types of grouping should be employed, such as mixed age and specific interest. Operating withdrawal groups is a further option. Classrooms and resources should be organised to allow for group work and supported self-study.

- **Teaching methodology**. Teachers should use a broad repertoire of open-ended tasks, group and individual work, problem-solving activities and investigations, as well as more formal teaching. Differentiation of this kind will help them match tasks to the variety in pupils' preferred learning styles. Variety is important, too, in the means by which they record their work and the resources available. Tasks should be challenging and sometimes the cause of struggle. Repetition must be avoided, since bright children usually need the least reinforcement.

How is one to ensure that these characteristics of a quality programme actually appear? The ideal may be that everything is done right without checking (Crosby, 1979), but in reality it *is* necessary to employ quality assurance measures. It is here that I return to my earlier points about the part to be played by everyone, from senior staff to classroom teachers, in monitoring the translation of principle into practice. If anyone has the key role, arguably it is the latter. TQ is a means of improving personal effectiveness and aligning all individual effort throughout an organisation (Stott, 1994, p. 192). The active involvement and responsibility of everyone in agreeing a process, and then implementing it in a consistent manner so that they become managers of their own quality, is what marks a genuine 'democratising' of quality within the institution (Harvey and Green, 1993, p. 16). One practical way of reducing variation and working towards 'conformance to specification' would be to use procedural and documentary guidelines that 'shadow' the SEN Code of Practice.

Of course, quality assurance mechanisms may be indicative simply of the fact that there are bureaucratic processes in place. BS EN ISO 9000 (formerly BS 5750) is an example of this approach. How far do they guarantee the *spirit* of quality provision as well as its letter? The measurement of quality, its potential for incrementally improving and developing pupils' needs (similar to what Tom Peters describes as making him 'glow' and 'tingle'), are questions that go beyond a mechanistic preoccupation with prevention and processes. Consequently, there must be assessment and monitoring procedures in place to gauge each child's progress, the extent to which value is added and the continuing 'fitness for purpose' of the overall programme.

However, to be sure that the quality of provision is what it should be, quality assurance must be linked to the *moral basis* identified for the programme, viz. the creation of an appropriate learning environment for the most able. The implication is that teachers see their role in terms of raising questions, offering challenges, encouraging the use of divergent learning activities and providing a responsive environment that makes the act of learning an interactive process. Underpinning this must be the cultivation of a reflective understanding of the basic learning processes and how individuals differ in their capabilities to learn. By marrying prevention to vision, one should be more certain that pupils are benefiting from the enhancements offered and that these do indeed constitute challenging experiences. Also, one can more confidently claim to be working towards a state of 'zero defects' in terms of optimising the achievement of all the pupils involved in the programme.

Appropriately, this leads to a discussion of how far my programme for the most able represents quality to the 'customer'.

Customers

Who *are* 'customers' in schools? The philosophy of total quality points to those people 'who receive products or services from an organisation, including those within the organisation' (Smith, 1996, p. 21). Applied to a school setting, they are simple enough to identify. The internal customers are, first, the classroom teachers who look to their senior staff to 'supply' the programme for able pupils. In turn, they make the appropriate implementation for *their* customers, viz. the pupils who are in direct receipt of provision. The next link comprises the parents (Murgatroyd and Morgan, 1992, pp. 52–55). This notion of the internal/external customer chain is a key element of TQ. I referred earlier to the importance of an inclusive definition as far as the pupils are concerned, in view of the growing recognition that high ability can take various forms. Only a small minority of pupils are academic 'all-rounders', whereas 25 per cent or more of a school's population will excel in one or a few areas (Denton and Postlethwaite, 1985). It is a mirror image of the bottom end of the ability scale as identified in the 1978 Warnock Report and the 1994 SEN Code of Practice.

This focus on the customer can be problematic for a sector that traditionally has been supplier-led, particularly given the basic tenet of TQ that quality is defined by the customer (West-Burnham, 1997, p. 122). Are the pupils identified as having high ability actually customers? Is the term better applied to their parents, who expect appropriate educational provision for their children's needs in return for their taxes funding schools? It might be more accurate to refer to the children as 'consumers' or 'clients'. Do the pupils actually *know* their needs? Are they in a position to judge whether they are being met? Are their parents, given their sometimes over-optimistic opinions of their children's talents, in a position to judge?

Should we reject such product-based notions as inappropriate to the education service and think of teachers as having a transformative relationship with their 'customers' because they do something *to*, rather than *for*, them (Harvey and Green, 1993, p. 24)? These questions explain why education has long defined and interpreted quality in Platonic terms of what pupils are assumed to need. They also reveal the semantic and conceptual nature of attempting to define the 'customer' in a service that is not accustomed to such thinking (West-Burnham and Davies, 1994, p. 50).

I have found it difficult to identify a precise mechanism by which my programme can fit Juran's axiom: 'Quality is what the customer says it is' (Davies and West-Burnham, 1997, p. 10). However, in a more general sense, schools can show how responsive they are by the type of learning strategies extended to the most able. Offering pupils some ownership of the organisation and completion of their work, permitting a variety of means of recording work, promoting the use of creative and critical thinking skills, and employing internal rather than external methods of motivation are all means by which they can be transformed into critical, self-aware and autonomous individuals. It will better equip them to make informed choices and decisions. This particular focus in making them co-managers of the teaching and learning process requires their teachers to become more like enablers and guides and resource managers. There is likely to be no turning back. Once pupils have tasted the 'delight' of a quality learning experience, they will not accept something inferior (Tribus, 1994, p. 104). Again, it brings one back to the over-arching vision of what a school should be offering by way of a suitable learning environment.

Quality assurance must involve some kind of mediating influence from pupils and parents, based on assessments, tutorials, consultation evenings, etc., so that they can declare their levels of satisfaction regarding the fitness of provision. Customer requirements exert an influence, too, with the increasing 'market economy' in which schools exist: parents will pick and choose establishments that offer services for the most able matching their own specifications. The DfEE's Circular 9/94 recommends that every school should include in its prospectus details of its arrangements for bright children. The customers might not be sovereign, but the effect of their notional 'spending power' on the formula funding of schools cannot be ignored. It would be a foolish (and unfit for purpose) establishment that allowed its provision to be seriously at variance with their broad expectations of what should be available. The time has long passed when parents were prepared to be passive recipients of professional opinions, and it mirrors the expectation of customised quality and service in other 'markets' (Davies and West-Burnham, 1997, p. 5).

Self-reviewing quality provision

Awareness of the responsibility to review and enhance the quality of any educational programme has led me to some initial thoughts on a suitable model for reviewing the effectiveness of the strategy I have formulated for Walsall comprehensive schools. The four headings under which my programme has been discussed from a total quality perspective have a lot in common with the typology comprising the European Foundation for Quality Management (EFQM) model, which has been translated into a setting more suited for educational use with support from the Royal Mail and Sheffield LEA (Sisum, 1996, p. 4; West-Burnham, 1997, pp. 125–126).

Adapted to my programme, the components of the model could consist of:

Senior leadership

- proposing a vision and relating the programme to it
- prioritising provision via school development plan
- co-ordinating, monitoring and evaluating whole-school and department provision
- allocating appropriate and sufficient resources
- organising in-service training (Inset) for professional development of staff in this area
- recognition and celebration of pupil achievements in school and the wider community.

Staff management and involvement

- motivation, involvement and confidence of all staff in implementing provision arising from shared sense of purpose
- pursuit of professional development regarding provision for the most able through Inset
- development of identification procedures for departments
- employment of appropriate curriculum, organisational and teaching strategies
- use of school procedures for assessing and monitoring pupils' progress opportunities for regular review and reflection.

Policy and strategy

- development of a policy and strategy embodying total quality principles
- foundation of policy on knowledge of effective learning processes and awareness of good practice in similar initiatives elsewhere

- clear communication, a strong sense of purpose and identification of defined goals
- regular review and up-dating of policy.

Resources

- timetabling of central enhancement programme
- funding for appropriate departmental resources
- facilitation of alternative grouping arrangements and withdrawal classes
- GEST allocation for staff professional development.

Processes

- establishment of clearly defined procedures for identifying able pupils
- specification of processes for translating principles into practice in terms of curriculum provision, classroom organisation and teaching methodology
- active involvement of staff in implementation of policy on consistent basis
- use of common format for assessment and monitoring records
- effective liaison with partner primary schools to ensure systematic transfer of information
- continuous evaluation of provision to monitor its continuing 'fitness for purpose'.

Staff satisfaction

- researching, evaluating and responding to staff perceptions of, and satisfaction with, policy implementation.

Pupil and parent satisfaction

- researching, evaluating and responding to pupil and parent perceptions of, and satisfaction with, the variety of classroom learning experiences available
- extent of pupil involvement in voluntary and extra-curricular activities organised as part of the programme
- extent of parental involvement in providing a supportive home environment, and engaging in regular dialogue with the school.

Impact on stake-holders

- popularity with prospective parents of identifying arrangements for able pupils

- co-operation of partner primary schools in establishing effective liaison arrangements for transfer of information
- interest and involvement of governors in development of provision
- support from LEA in terms of resources, guidance and external auditing from inspection/advisory team
- interest and involvement by members of the wider community, e.g. business and industry, the media, higher education.

School outcomes

- creation of a school culture in which able pupils are positively encouraged to express their talents
- contribution to the creation of a high-quality teaching and learning environment for *all* pupils
- fulfilment of the comprehensive ideal of providing an appropriate education for children of all abilities and aptitudes.

This is not intended to be an authoritative or exhaustive list of components and I would not purport at this early stage to allocate to each grouping percentage values, as is the case with the European Quality Award (EQA). Definitions of what constitutes quality vary and reflect different perspectives and interests. It is easier to state one is working towards quality than to define what it actually means. A process of experiment, modification and adaptation, therefore, may be necessary until proven applications emerge. Strategies take time to establish and sustain themselves and mature only over time. All I would claim here is that the EFQM model seems to represent a useful framework to develop and customise when reviewing strategies for school improvement. In the situation I have written about, it offers scope for a holistic approach to evaluating a programme of provision for able pupils based on the principles and processes of total quality. I look forward to the day that it becomes an integral element of schemes for improving quality and performance in schools.

References

Barber, M. (1995) 'From characteristics to strategy', *The Times Educational Supplement*, 6 October 1995, p. ii.

Bleach, K. (1997) *Meeting the Challenge of the Most Able*, Walsall, Walsall Education Services.

Crosby, P.B. (1979) *Quality is Free*, Maidenhead, McGraw-Hill.

Davies, B. and West-Burnham, J. (1997) 'The nature of reengineering and quality management', in Davies, B. and West-Burnham, J. (eds) *Reengineering and Total Quality in Schools*, London, Pitman Publishing.

Deming, W. (1982) *Out of the Crisis – Quality Productivity and Competitive Position*, Cambridge, Cambridge University Press.

Denton, C. and Postlethwaite, K. (1985) *Able Children: Identifying Them in the Classroom*, London, NFER/Nelson.

Gardner, H. (ed) (1993) *Multiple Intelligences – The Theory in Practice: A Reader*, New York, Basic Books.

Hampton, G. (1994) 'The Buckpool experience of developing quality systems', in Doherty, G. (ed) *Developing Quality Systems in Education*, London, Routledge.

Harvey, L. and Green, D. (1993) 'Defining quality assessment and evaluation' in *Higher Education*, 18(1), pp. 9–34.

HMI/DEF (1992) *Education Observed: The Education of Very Able Children in Maintained Schools*, London, HMSO.

Juran, J. (1964) *Managerial Breakthrough: A New Concept of the Manager's Job*, New York, McGraw-Hill.

Murgatroyd, S. and Morgan, C. (1992) *Total Quality Management and the School*, Buckingham, Open University Press.

Perkins, D. (1995) *Outsmarting IQ: The Emerging Science of Learnable Intelligence*, New York, Free Press.

Pfeffer, N. and Coote, A. (1991) *Is Quality Good For You? A Critical Review of Quality Assurance in Welfare Services*, London, Institute of Public Policy Research.

Sammons, P., Hillman, J. and Mortimore, P. (1995) *Key Characteristics of Effective Schools: A Review of School Effectiveness Research*, London, OFSTED.

Sisum, C. (1996) 'The Scarman papers' in *Quality and Learning*, 2(1), pp. 2–5.

Smith, P. (1996) 'Tools for measuring quality improvement' in *Management in Education*, 10(2), pp. 21–23.

Stott, H. (1994) 'A foot in two camps: doing BS 5750/ISO 9001 in higher education and industry', in Doherty, G. (ed) *Developing Quality Systems in Education*, London, Routledge.

Tribus, M. (1994) 'Total quality management in education: the theory and how to put it to work', in Doherty, G. (ed) *Developing Quality Systems in Education*, London, Routledge.

Weller, D. (1997) 'TQM: Georgia's approach to educational reform and school restructuring', in Davies, B. and West-Burnham, J. (eds) *Reengineering and Total Quality in Schools*, London, Pitman Publishing.

West-Burnham, J. (1992) *Managing Quality in Schools*, London, Longman.

West-Burnham, J. (1996) 'The components of total quality', in lecture notes on Total Quality in Education issued for Ed.D. students at Lincoln University Campus, December 1996.

West-Burnham, J. (1997) 'Leading and managing for quality', in Davies, B. and Ellison, L. (eds) *School Leadership for the 21st Century – A Competency and Knowledge Approach*, London, Routledge.

West-Burnham, J. and Davies, B. (1994) 'Quality management as a response to educational changes', in *Studies in Educational Administration*, 60, pp. 47–52.

3
■ ■ ■

Learning and caring

GILLIAN BOYD

Imagine the following. A headteacher receives a telephone call from an angry parent berating him for providing pupils in the school with the National Curriculum when, he said, the whole world knew that all they needed was care and supervision; that lessons in such subjects as maths and geography were irrelevant; and the teaching of reading an impossible task. All the pupils should be under the Health Service and not part of the Education Service at all. Another telephone call to the same headteacher two months previously from a former pupil had requested his school records. He was 33 years old and married with two children. He had recently been diagnosed as dyslexic. This man, too, was angry – angry that he had not been given an education. He described himself as having been written off as not being able to learn. No one, he said, had been in the least interested in finding out what his learning difficulty was and as a result he had spent his school years feeling angry and resentful. He explained that he had found employment despite the stigma of having a special care school on his curriculum vitae and now attends adult literacy classes.

How could the same school receive two such conflicting views of its pupils? There was only 14 years age difference between the former pupil and the oldest pupils now in the school.

The following will tell the story of a school's progress from being primarily a provider of care for the 'mentally handicapped' to providing expert and specialist teaching and advice for a number of severe learning difficulties and access to mainstream curriculum in just ten years. The school was established under the Health Board in Northern Ireland. It grew from a two-class school in 1963 to having 80 pupils in 1996 when legislation on special education in Northern Ireland placed such schools under the direction of the Department of Education (DENI). As the school population grew in numbers over the years, it moved premises several times, finally transferring to an old hospital. The building had three floors and a basement. Offices and therapy rooms were on the ground floor, classrooms on the first and second floors, and there was a residential and day hospital for children for whom no teaching was provided. From 1985 the school was used for day pupils only and day hospital pupils received teaching input.

The school had no outside play areas for the children. It was an imposing building but probably quite forbidding for any prospective parents. Inside, however, the school had been painted bright colours and there was an extensive display of children's work throughout. The classrooms varied greatly in size. There was a small lift, woefully inadequate for the numbers of children in wheelchairs. The dining room and kitchens were in the basement of the building. Toilets and bathrooms had been fashioned from sluice rooms. One large ward had been turned into a softplay room. There was a gym on the second floor which also served as an assembly hall. The attics of the school had been converted into 'workshops' for boys who had finished their school careers – they simply moved upstairs when they became too old for school. There was no similar provision for girls. A purpose-built adult training centre for all young people leaving the school at the age of 19 was built in the eighties and the attics were not used again.

Special care was provided for the children but there was very little emphasis on education. Staff worked hard and genuinely cared for the children's well-being but there was little opportunity to access a wide curriculum and the world of the community outside school. This led to a narrow curriculum and, as a consequence, limited expectations as reflected by the views of the parent not pleased with the much broader curriculum now offered by the school.

The school staff were from both medical and educational disciplines. Teachers, care assistants and nursing staff were all employed by the health authority. There were seven teachers who had qualified as special care teachers after a two-year course with extensive placement as student teachers in special care schools; one had qualified in English with a Certificate in Education. The care assistants had no training. Physiotherapy, speech therapy and occupational therapy were provided by the Health Board.

The school was organised into classes where age differences could be as much as seven years and teaching was aimed at the needs of the group rather than at the individual needs of the pupils. Class sizes varied from nine to 16. There was very little planning or progress reports for classes recorded, and no overall planning for the school and its curriculum. There was no monitoring and evaluation. Teachers planned their own curriculum with little or no consideration of what the pupils had covered to that point. There was little evidence of information on pupil progress passing from class to class.

The school did not have separate departments and staff meetings were rare. Integration of pupils with mainstream schools or the local community was minimal. Transfers of pupils to different types of schools (mainstream or moderate learning difficulties, for example) were unknown. When children were sent to the school at the age of four it was expected that they would stay there for their entire school career and that most of them would need a care facility after that. Again, this led to certain parental expectations – that their child would receive state care provision for the rest of their lives. This is no longer the case in the present economic climate.

The Education Act of 1986 brought special care schools into the Northern Ireland Education System. They were now known as schools for severe learning difficulties (SLD). The school immediately recruited five extra teaching staff and classes were grouped by age, with the exception of a 'special needs' group who all had profound and multiple learning difficulties. A new principal was appointed and all Health Board staff were relocated. The considerable changes also involved amendments to the whole-school curriculum. All teachers were now required to produce a timetable which included all the subjects being offered in mainstream schools, but naturally these had to be taught so as to be relevant to the pupils. The local Education Board and DENI provided in-service training for staff on curriculum development. There were considerable differences in both opinion and practice in what was provided in the classroom.

Subject co-ordinators were established to study the Northern Ireland Curriculum (NIC) and to attempt to define its aims and strategies within the school. Each teacher took a subject with their individual interests being used as much as possible. Almost immediately after the NIC was introduced working parties were established for the core subjects, which led to the production of 'Stepping Stones'. These detailed the progression from early development to level one of the curriculum and cited good practice, giving many examples for teachers to follow. Stepping Stones have since been produced for all curriculum areas and have been further revised and refined. There is no doubt that they have been a major contributor to teachers producing a broad and balanced curriculum which is relevant to pupils in special education. There is now a structure which allows and encourages teachers to ensure continuity both within their classroom and from year to year. The Individual Educational Programme (IEP) is essential for each child and has made redundant the old idea of a whole-class approach. This should ensure that no pupil in the future will have the justifiable complaint that their needs were not addressed throughout their time in school.

Under education the school was given posts of responsibility which led to the development of a senior management team (SMT). There were three department heads – infant, junior and senior – a vice-principal and principal. SMT meetings were held every week, as were staff meetings, in order to plan whole-school strategies. A staff room was provided for the first time. Each department also held weekly meetings to plan together and to try to ensure continuity and progression.

Change did not come easily to all staff. Some did not see the NIC as relevant to SLD pupils and made no secret of their opposition to it. The majority, however, worked hard together and a General Inspection report in 1992 was very favourable and concluded that the school could move forward with confidence.

Pre-school provision was begun from the school, with a teacher going out to work with both child and parent as the child was identified as having special educational needs, thus giving valuable early access to education. Group activities for the children and parents were organised in school one morning each week. This gave the parents involvement from the earliest stage both in the school and in the teaching process. This has proved extremely valuable in raising parental awareness and expectations for their children.

A new school was purpose-built and opened in 1994 and I became school principal in the same year. The building is on one level with extensive playgrounds, gardens and a hydrotherapy pool. Each classroom is bright and airy with good heating and ventilation. There is great emphasis on displaying children's work in all areas of the school. The hall is large and can be used for football, badminton or tennis, and has a portable stage. Meals are cooked on the premises and eaten by the staff and children in a bright, cheerful 'social concourse area'.

The school staff made a decision to integrate the special needs group into classes with their peers in the new school. The children who were both blind and deaf are grouped together from the age of five until ten when they, too, are integrated with their peers. Pupil numbers have risen steadily, possibly due to the removal of the stigma of special care in some parents' eyes. As the pupil numbers have risen, so too have the numbers of pupils with autism. From three pupils with autism, the number has risen to 26 within eight years. Children are being diagnosed at the age of two, making it necessary to establish an assessment class solely for autism, with structured teaching provision in a continuous stream throughout the school for those who require it. In these classes there is a very structured, visually explicit environment which is vital to enable this group of children to learn.

A new VP and two department heads were appointed. The SMT was reorganised into departments for primary (3–11 years), secondary (12–16 years) and further education (16–19 years). This matched the NIC Key Stages for the first time and made the progression of age-related activities more easily planned within departments. Records of Achievement are presented at the end of the primary and secondary departments. The FE department curriculum requirements are outside the NIC and so involve a three-year cycle which is heavily orientated towards life and job skills and experience. Accredited courses at the local technical college are widely accessed.

Seven teachers on the staff took distance-learning courses in specialised areas including autism, sensory impairment, behaviour difficulties, learning difficulties, speech and language difficulties and profound and multiple learning difficulties (PMLD). Teams were then established to share the valuable expertise gained by these teachers and to produce quality teaching guidelines in these areas. The guidelines are very much 'user-friendly' and specific to the needs of the school, its pupils and staff. Team leaders are often asked to contribute to courses run by the local education board and are frequently asked for advice by other schools, near and far. The provision for autism is visited continually by groups from all over Ireland.

The primary department puts great emphasis on working with parents. Some mothers come in to help with their child's class, and there are regular coffee mornings and talks by speakers suggested by parents. The department felt that a good foundation built in this area in the early years would lead to a close partnership between school and home during the child's time in school. IEPs are written with parental participation and copies of everything planned and assessed are sent home. Videos of the child at school have been particularly useful in this area. The assessment classes are part of the Effective Early Learning project being run by the University of Leicester. This has been valuable in focusing staff objectively on the learning process of the children. The skills developed during this project will be disseminated throughout the school.

Perhaps the biggest change and challenge introduced into our new school has been the senior department timetable, which has established modules in the afternoons instead of classwork all day. The modules include art, drama, music, outdoor pursuits, gardening, recycling projects, cookery, massage and sensory stories. The classes are divided into ability groups so that, for example, those with PMLD have a member of staff each to help them access their sensory-based activities. The most able students are able to pursue Duke of Edinburgh awards and accredited courses. The change to modules from all-day classwork has meant that staff can incorporate their interests and talents into their teaching. Extra staff are available in the afternoons for this as the children under seven years old go home after lunch.

The FE department has two classes, L1 and L2. Their joint three-year curriculum has more emphasis on life skills and on the transition to post-school activities and training. Accredited courses at the local technical college are widely accessed. L1 and L2 eat by themselves, serving and helping one another. There is great emphasis on age-appropriate activities, thus promoting skills which are vital for socialising with others outside school and family. Pupils in the FE department also have a different uniform from the rest of the school – if a grey sweatshirt and dark-coloured track bottoms can be called a uniform. A look at any teenagers will confirm that this is what most teenagers wear when given a choice. Clothes chosen by parents do not always have the same 'street cred'. It is essential that our students blend in with the norm when out and about from school.

L1 is based in the home economics room, giving much scope for food preparation and home management. L2 is based in a newly built room which has its own kitchen and dining areas, pool table, relaxation area with TV, video, hi-fi and magazine/papers/book library. Its work area is based around a large island unit. The class has been very successful with its team enterprise industry of making greeting cards and has won numerous awards for the quality of the work. Close co-operation with employees on work experience has led to much greater awareness of the many excellent qualities our pupils can bring to the workplace and special education has become more of a recommendation than a stigma on our pupils' CVs.

There are many links between school and the community. Each class links with a mainstream school. Weekly classes are jointly planned and taught by both class teachers in usually art, music, P.E. or science. The youngest children in the assessment classes go two at a time to the local nursery school where they are exposed to their peers' communication and play skills. The mainstream schools often visit our school, too, and thoroughly enjoy our facilities.

Each class has a school bus for half day a week in order to access activities in the community. Visits from school include shopping centres, parks, the beach, farms, bowling alleys, libraries and museums. Swimming sessions are held in the local pool each week for the primary department, and for once a week for a term for the senior department as swimming alternates with other sporting activities. The school participates in as many mainstream activities as possible, including Duke of Edinburgh awards, cookery competitions, art competitions, drama activities and courses at the technical college.

The community is involved in school activities as much as possible through volunteers with expertise in areas such as gardening, golf, hillwalking, swimming, rugby, football, table tennis, bowling, canoeing, drama, story-telling and music.

The school works in multi-agency teams which can include health, psychology, psychiatry and voluntary agencies. Among these are the Prince's Trust, Downs Syndrome Association and Mencap. All staff took a three-day training course in Movement Opportunities Via Education (MOVE), which seeks to enable children with severe disabilities to sit, stand and walk. Parents are closely involved with the programmes and with fundraising for the equipment needed. Links with parents are seen as particularly valuable in working for the optimal development and education of their children. More is expected of parents than before. School can provide programmes and implementation of these for only part of the children's lives. Parents are encouraged and trained to work effectively with their children. With this in mind the school is beginning a parenting programme in partnership with a local voluntary agency. Other whole-school training has included courses on music therapy, child protection behaviours management, and a course run by SENSE, a charity advising on and giving information about sensory deprivation matters.

Planning, monitoring and evaluation of pupils' work are now all part of the teacher's role. These are co-ordinated and overseen by department heads, the vice-principal and the principal. All class paperwork is kept in a file which can be accessed by management or temporary teaching staff. Teachers have been working on a self-evaluation project, collectively identifying good classroom practice, and looking at ways of self-improvement. The principal monitors classroom teaching, subject by subject, through observation and talks with the class teacher. These visits are greeted with enthusiasm, and teachers want to demonstrate both their own work and that of their pupils. School development planning has become more specific, with targets set and met, and all staff are involved in its production and implementation.

Special education has changed almost beyond recognition in the past ten years. The school has been restructured and reorganised twice in this time due to the demands of educational reform and to the needs of its pupils. It continues to evolve, its changes now being more subtle and specific. The staff have risen to each challenge with energy and commitment. We are enabling parents and the community to become much more aware of our work and to join us in providing a well-rounded and balanced curriculum for our pupils. We can call ourselves an effective school only if all our pupils reach their full potential.

4
■ ■ ■

Putting learning first

ANN COCKERHAM

Introduction

A concern to provide the best teaching and learning is, quite obviously, the *raison d'être* of all schools. Yet take a close look at the roles of senior staff in many secondary schools and this would not always have been apparent. In some schools, roles have remained unchanged for generations, with posts of responsibility being awarded for discipline and control or for being concerned for the 'pastoral' well-being of groups of children. In others, the initial trauma of being faced with local management of schools saw a rise in senior teaching posts pre-occupied with administration.

We do not often take the opportunity to look afresh at the way in which we organise our work and to question how well such work supports student achievement. However, the advent of a new millennium can inspire even the most reluctant to participate in a spot of 'futures thinking'. This is the story of our school's attempt to rethink the way in which we work.

The context

> *A good past is positively dangerous if it makes us content with the present and so unprepared for the future.*
>
> (Eliot, vice-chancellor, Harvard University, 1900)

Many schools nationally could identify with the context of Ratton School, Eastbourne, which has built a sound reputation over the past ten years locally, is over-subscribed, enjoys reasonable examination results and was recently the subject of an excellent report from OFSTED. The danger for this school was that, unless it was prepared to change in order to successfully adapt to a future context, it would become what Dean Fink describes as a 'cruising' rather than a 'moving' school; a good school 'if this were 1965' (Fink, 1995).

The challenge, then, for this particular school was to shift the trend towards complacency to transcend the 'if it ain't broke, don't fix it' mindset, and to develop a new dynamic. It was important to recognise, as Davies (1997, pp. 18–19) suggests, that an already committed staff would not improve the quality of the school by simply working harder – they would need to work smarter. The smarter course involved not slicker ways of doing the same things, but fundamentally different ways of doing things.

Futures thinking: developing the vision

Ratton already had established reasonable systems for planning development (on a three-year cycle) that included input not only from staff and governors but also from parents and pupils. All stakeholders were involved in evaluating and reprioritising developments regularly during the planning cycle. While this inclusive approach was effective up to a point, it encouraged incremental development. What was required now was a more radical vision of what the future might hold. The senior managers and governors already had a realistic appreciation of the school's strengths and weaknesses, opportunities and threats. What would move the school forward would be some speculation. What would Ratton be like in an ideal world? What would excite people and create opportunities well into the new millennium?

Ratton's headteacher also believed that it would be important for the school to invest in the development of management skills and competencies, recognising that effective leadership of teams throughout the school would impact upon the quality of future development.

A weekend management conference was set up to which all the school's team leaders and governors were invited. The theme of the conference was 'What roles are required to lead our school successfully into a new millennium?'. Its purpose was to challenge current mindsets and build a vision of how Ratton might be organised in the future. It was important to establish a clear and collaborative notion of the overall direction in which to go; to re-establish the core purpose and overall aims of the school; and to speculate – what would Ratton be like if it were to be a leading school in 2020? The use of external facilitators to launch the debate helped to challenge current patterns of thinking and to provoke real discussion without any of the participants being able to establish their own agenda. The conference was successful and generated some informal discussion in the staff room. There had been a realisation of the need to rethink the traditional organisational structure, an important prerequisite for the desired change in culture. The challenge now would be to set in motion moves towards a reorganisation of the school's staffing structure so that teams could be best supported to achieve their goals and respond flexibly to the changing circumstances and challenges that the future would hold.

Managing the change process

There is nothing more difficult to execute nor more dubious of success, nor more dangerous to administer than to introduce a new order of things; for he who introduces it has all those who profit from the old order as his enemies, and he has only lukewarm allies in all those who might profit from the new.

(Machiavelli, 1513)

How to involve people in reviewing and changing systems which were perceived, for the most part, as satisfactory was a key challenge. A full staff meeting was held soon after the conference in order to present the key issues arising from it to all colleagues. The proposal was to review the school's staffing structure in order to establish roles that would be needed in order to best support teaching and learning into the new millennium. As part of this full staff meeting, all colleagues engaged in a SWOT analysis of the school's current structure.

A device was needed to keep up the momentum and continue creative discussion about the future. A volunteer task group was set up to work on possible models for a new organisational structure. The task group was to operate throughout a four-month period, informed by feedback from the conference, staff meetings and various formal and informal consultations with colleagues.

Our leaders must allow themselves – and us – to believe that followers are not passive reactive tools of charismatic power figures. They are, instead, the creators of energy. They are the architects of the open moments into which some people must be the first to step. As followers, they are the agents who show their leaders where to walk. They are the ones who validate their leaders stepping out in a direction that has meaning for all of us.

(Nicoll, 1986, p. 34)

Representing a wide cross-section of the school community, this task group was able to pick up and respond to all levels of concern in its planning and thoroughly debate the issues arising. There would, inevitably, be those at Ratton who would rather opt out of direct involvement with the voluntary task group set up to explore models for the new structure, and who would question why the headteacher simply did not decide the structure and tell the staff what it would be. There would be those, even among the task groups, who would suspect that decisions must have been made and that the game they had to play was to discover the blueprint. There would be those, too, who would be prepared to engage fully in the debate and contribute creatively to move thinking forward. It was through the participation of this latter group that models emerged which were far more radical than the headteacher had envisaged. It was refreshing to step into uncharted waters and explore collaboratively new ways of working.

The task group worked in a highly consultative way. Its inclusive approach gained support and it developed a creative energy in proposing new ways of doing things. Feedback from the task group and its subgroup meetings was given via full staff meetings, middle management meetings, governors' meetings, and summarised discussion papers circulated to all staff and governors at regular intervals. Colleagues were able to voice concerns or comment on issues raised via formal meetings or by talking directly with task group members or their school-based union representative. The Local Education Authority was kept informed and involved in the planning process, as were regional union representatives. The process of researching the change required, and planning the shape of such change, would seem to some colleagues to be prolonged and too exhaustive. Nonetheless, the process would impact positively on the implementation of the new structure. By its democratic nature, this process also set out a clear marker as to the culture that the headteacher wanted to achieve through the restructuring.

A new model emerges

The first thing that the task group did was to establish some basic principles on which any restructuring should be based:

- improving the quality of teaching and learning should be the clear focus of every management role
- any new structure should be simple and line management clear
- there was a need in this school to cut down on 'too many hats' being worn by a few, e.g. some staff had accrued responsibilities which were not often interrelated
- restructuring should provide an established staff with fresh challenges and opportunities to develop further their skills of leadership and management.

These were principles that made good sense to everyone. The new structure would be less hierarchical than the existing one and would place emphasis on team approaches to development. There would be three tiers of support for students' learning:

1 teams of teaching and associated staff
2 team leaders (curriculum managers)
3 school support team.

At points 2 and 3, there would be individuals paid at different rates to reflect their levels of accountability and the size of their teams, but this would not affect their status within the tier – all being of equal value and importance in meeting the needs of others. Within tiers 2 and 3, associate staff as well as teaching staff would feature as managers of teams.

The task group set about reforming the way in which job descriptions were to be drawn up for the new structure. The group worked with team leaders to establish a common (generic) format: a move away from the task-driven job description to the more flexible job profiling. The job profile would be explicit in stating why the role existed in relation to the school's core purpose and what were the key accountabilities of the post. The annual priorities for each team leader would be negotiated by his/her mentor (or coach) – a member of the School Support Team.

Three fundamental changes to the structure put forward were:

- the abolition of heads of year
- the establishment of Key Stage co-ordinators (to review the quality of experience of students across a key stage)
- the creation of a School Support Team to include the headteacher, deputies, three +4 postholders (the learning support co-ordinator, staff development co-ordinator and student development co-ordinator) and the finance officer.

The message conveyed by the structure would be that the quality of learning must be supported and developed and that there was to be no academic versus pastoral divide. As a learning organisation, the way in which our school demonstrates care for students is to provide them with the best learning experiences possible. Personal specifications for all new posts would highlight the need for individuals to keep abreast of national and international developments in education and to be committed to improving continuously their professional skills and competencies.

Managing resistance to change

I was to learn later in life that we tend to meet any new situation by reorganising and a wonderful method it can be for creating the illusion of progress while producing confusion, inefficiency and demoralisation.

(Gaius Petronius Arbiter, AD66)

There will always be those who are sceptical or resistant to change, no matter how inclusive or consultative the process devised for bringing about that change. The headteacher was very aware of this and of the need not to dismiss resistance or cynicism too readily. To do so would deny individual needs and affect the implementation of change itself. Furthermore, it would contradict all that she had declared previously about the type of culture she was keen to establish. As Fullan (1993) states, one lesson to be learned in managing change is that 'problems are our friends'.

There would be some tension to be managed as new associate staff roles developed to take on administrative responsibilities previously undertaken by teachers (e.g. monitoring student attendance and punctuality, student counselling, exams administration, perhaps, eventually, cover for absent teachers and timetabling?). The only way of successfully working with those who felt threatened by the impending changes was to deal with each individual's anxieties by listening to concerns, understanding the position and exploring the new role so that she/he could see the value and importance it had in achieving whole-school improvement. In designing roles, it was important to ensure that, within each one, there was a clear link to support for high-quality teaching and learning, professional challenge and opportunities for continuous professional development. The concept of every member of staff playing a valuable and important role in development as a team player, regardless of rank, was not easy for some to accept, and team members, as well as team leaders, questioned the lack of hierarchy within the new model.

Schools, it seems, are essentially hierarchical organisations, and breaking away from the culture of dependency endemic in such an organisation would take time. Once accomplished, though, perhaps Ratton would be in an even better position to attempt to create independent thinking learners among its students.

Conclusion

From inspiration through to initiation of the change to the school's staffing structure took two terms. By the end of the spring term, appointments had been made to the new roles, and the summer term was to be given to planning and training for implementation of the new structure from the start of the autumn term. It will be important to monitor the impact of the new structure on roles and relationships throughout the school and to employ rigorous methods of evaluation before any judgements can be made as to how successful the change has been. In employing such methods, it will be helpful if they can be embedded within everyday working practice. In this way, evaluation will not be an event in itself, but a continuous process of gathering information and acting to make the refinements needed to improve practice.

Feedback will be continuous, and responses which are quick and effective in meeting identified needs will promote confidence throughout the school in the principle of critical reflection as a means of achieving continuous improvement. This principle in itself is an essential component of the culture which the new structure seeks to promote.

References

Fink, D. (1995) 'Educational requirements of the post modern age', *Orbit*, Vol. 26, No. 1.

Davies, B. (1997) 'Rethinking the educational context', in *School Leadership for the 21st Century*, Brent Davies and Linda Ellison, London, Routledge.

Fullan, M. (1993) *Changing Forces: Probing the Depths of Educational Reform*, London, Falmer Press.

Fullan, M. (1985) 'Change processes and the strategies at the local level', *The Elementary School Journal*, 85(5), January.

Nicoll, D. (1986) *Leadership and Followship in Transforming Leadership: From Vision to Results*, Alexandria Va, Miles River Press.

5
■ ■ ■

The management of teaching and learning at Queen Elizabeth's Grammar School

GRAHAM HARRISON

Introduction

Improving schools has moved teaching and learning to the forefront. The former emphasis on management seems to be shifting back to the classroom. Obviously, how pupils learn and how teachers teach play a central role in this reorientation, and this realignment will have to be embraced by all schools if they are to improve to their maximum in the future. The traditional perceptions of school management, together with outdated structures, will similarly have to change drastically if education is to be adequately equipped to face the turbulent future. The following initiative attempts to bring about such a reorganisation of traditional ideas and practices.

Queen Elizabeth's Grammar School in Gainsborough, Lincolnshire is a well-respected selective grammar school with skilled staff and highly motivated pupils. Recognising this shift in emphasis, the school was quick to embrace any attempt at improving the areas of teaching and learning within the school. It was agreed that a working party should be set up to investigate both areas from a practical viewpoint, with reference to the relevant theories, and to use the findings to inform future improvement and planning strategies. This summary of the main points attempts to inform the reader of the framework employed at Queen Elizabeth's, and to provide a workable outline 'for reflection', as well as to suggest possible future initiatives and their implementation.

Pupils at the centre

The initial step was to set up a working party of volunteer staff and to create a workable action plan. This was broken down into summer, autumn, spring and summer terms and would culminate in a report submitted to the senior management team and to the staff of the group's findings. The summer term consisted of the organisation of the research programme, with related Inset courses being attended and the information shared. Related theories in the field of learning, such as Piaget and Rogers, were also discussed, and their future value to the investigations considered. The work in this first term provided a sound basis on which to build future operations. The autumn term saw the commencement of the pupil interviews and teacher observations. In this term, it was agreed that the work would be divided into pupil and teacher observations at Key Stage 3 and Key Stage 5. These key stages were considered to offer the most potential, in terms of diversity of teaching and learning.

For the pupil interviews, it was agreed that each member of the working party would be assigned three pupils, chosen at random, and a selection of questions would be asked informally. There was great emphasis at this stage on creating a non-threatening environment in which pupils could respond freely to the questions. The interviews were generally carried out at lunchtime and lasted approximately 15 minutes per pupil.

The sorts of questions asked included:

1 At school, what type of work do you enjoy/dislike? Why is this?
2 What type of lessons do you find the most rewarding? Why?
3 When do you work best?
4 How would you improve your learning?
5 What type of homework do you prefer? Why?
6 How much time do you spend studying at home?

7 Could you think of one special learning moment when you really felt that you had suddenly really understood something or that you became really interested by a subject? Why, in your opinion, was this so?

All findings from these interviews were then recorded, discussed and retained for future analysis by the group at specially convened meetings.

The second stage of the Key Stage 3 work was centred on the teaching at KS3. Members of the working party were invited by volunteer staff to observe the teaching methods at KS3 in their respective lessons and to record the findings. By this time, the popularity of the initiative had created a favourable climate of trust between teacher, pupil and group member, without which future success would be impossible.

The purpose of these observations was twofold: observers were keen to see lessons outside their subject area in order to gain further insight into the 'Queen Elizabeth's pupil experience'; and the working party was trying to document the variety of teaching strategies and styles at QEGS. Within the lessons, the observers were looking for the types of activities the pupils were engaged in and any positive or special feature observed, as well as individual pupil response to particular methods of teaching. Similarly, this information was recorded and discussed and good practice highlighted.

The spring term saw the Key Stage 5 interviews and observations take place. Although the format of the observations at this key stage was identical to KS3, the nature of the pupil interview questions was naturally different. Sample questions included:

- How did you find the transition from KS4 to KS5?
- Why did you choose this school to continue your studies?
- How successful an experience has it been?
- Do you have a clear view of your future career?
- How and when do you learn best?
- Do you enjoy learning?
- How might your learning be enhanced?
- Which teaching strategies do you find most/least effective? Why is this so?

The information from research at this key stage was similarly collated and added to the growing body of findings at the disposal of the working party. The next summer term would see all information collated and presented in the form of a full and summary report during May and June.

The findings

The publication of the report represented the culmination of all information, including related theory, that had been accessed throughout the operational life of the working party. The report was duly presented to the senior management team and the entire staff of the school in the form of a 'reader-friendly' summary report.

The report highlighted the variety of good teaching at the school and provided valuable information on pupils' preferred learning styles. A subsequent Inset day, arranged around the topic of teaching and learning, facilitated general feedback from the staff as well as enabling individual departments to discuss specific details of the report. Arising from the consultation with staff, certain areas of priority were identified:

- staff should become more aware of individual learning styles
- teachers should attempt to employ varied styles of teaching within individual lessons/over a subject course
- an increased emphasis on practical learning strategies should be encouraged
- a variety of support materials should be used
- there should be cross-curricular informed teaching styles to inform practice
- there should be differentiated activities according to learning styles and not just ability.

From the above, many areas have been identified for development or change, and consequent action is beginning.

A departmental approach to future implementation

Clearly, this sort of research will have important implications for Queen Elizabeth's, and for all schools embarking on such an initiative. One possible strategy of implementing the findings of research in this area, which I have successfully introduced into my department, involves the use by individual departments of a departmental audit. Here, pupil interviews, as given here, would be used but the questions would be subject-specific and would investigate the particular optimum learning styles for that subject. Some examples for modern foreign languages are given below:

- What do you find easy/difficult about learning a language?
- Which type of language work do you find most interesting, most effective? Why?
- What could make it easier for you to learn a language?
- Do you prefer lessons taught in French or German or in English? Why?
- Do you learn by seeing, hearing or doing?

The findings from this departmental audit would then be used to identify 'best practice' within departments as well as providing further valuable pupil information. Once identified, this 'best practice' would be employed through 'peer partnerships', a concept which runs in parallel with the departmental audit within my department and which the school is considering at the present time to monitor the teaching and learning within other departments. Here, department members choose another member with whom they work closely through mutual observation, reflection and experimentation. Through these peer or learning partnerships, teachers are given the opportunity to reflect on their preferred teaching styles, using the information from the audit. Later experimentation with alternative methods of teaching ensure that all staff have the opportunity to select their preferences and exploit their teaching strengths.

The partnerships are changed continually to take further advantage of the different pairings of department team members and to investigate other aspects of the departmental audit of teaching and learning styles. This gives staff the opportunity to consider areas where they would like to improve their practice. Such a framework also ensures pair and group reflection on further best practice or modified approaches.

Professional development and Inset are, then, based on the identification of, and findings from, the execution of best practice. In this way, professional development is seen to arise directly from personally- and group-identified needs, based on practice in the classroom.

The future as change: building on innovation

The school is now looking to exploit still further the findings of this teaching and learning styles initiative, both on a departmental and on a whole-school basis. One suggested application which I am introducing into my department is to further use the information from the analysis of the departmental audit in the construction of individual pupil (diagnostic) profiles. Here, information on individual pupils will be ultimately combined with other relevant details to compile a personal learning plan, initially on a departmental level but eventually on a whole-school basis. The introduction of questions aimed at investigating preferred teaching and learning styles has provided the necessary catalyst for this type of work.

As pupil profiling and personal learning plans are a relatively new concept at Queen Elizabeth's Grammar School, the suggestions given are intended to provide only a guide to future implementation. My first step was to select a small, mixed ability group of pupils and to explain the purpose of the work. Second, the questions from the departmental audit were used to ascertain the preferred learning styles of the individual members. The work of Gardner (1993) on the seven intelligences, and the theories of visual, auditory and kinesthetic methods of learning, were extensively used to improve the audit questions.

The results of the audit questions were then analysed and recorded. Although providing the backbone of learning information on individual students, the departmental audit formed a small part of the information to be included in the profiles. Additional to the details on preferred learning styles, the profile attempted to include further information on non-preferred teaching and learning styles, strengths and weaknesses, both on a subject and on a whole-school basis, and extra-curricular strengths and talents. Clearly, this information is in no way exhaustive, but represents a tentative start to this new concept.

Based on the above profile, an attempt was then made to match the individual learner to a specific learner type. It was later intended that this information would also provide valuable assistance in matching individual learners with similar teacher/teaching styles. This would be achieved by means of teacher questionnaires and profiling.

OFSTED's recommendation that 'schools should enquire whether all teachers have adequate understanding of how children learn', provides a valuable source of support in introducing the above process. Knowledge acquired from interpersonal contact with the pupils was the only way to ensure that all members of the department were aware of differing learning styles among departmental pupils. The next stage was to employ these diagnostic profiles with long-term development in mind. This would take the form of personal learning plans.

A collaborative learning partnership

In order to ensure that the most practical match between teaching and learning was achieved, I considered it necessary to investigate the other side of the equation as well. Although an extremely sensitive area, a closer analysis of teaching styles by individual teachers within the department was the only way to ensure a 'perfect learning partnership' between teacher and learner. This would be achieved by a similar method as that employed with the pupils – by means of a questionnaire. This form of research on teaching styles and strategies represents uncharted territory. The end result would be a better match between teaching styles and learning styles, as well as valuable information on the interaction between teaching strategies and individual learning. It would also offer opportunity for teachers to reflect on the way they teach and their selection of particular teaching strategies for any given class. Although introduced into my department initially, interest by other departments will, without doubt, give this initiative the whole-school profile it deserves. A small sample of questions in the teacher questionnaire is given below:

- What style of teaching do you like/dislike?
- Do you tend to employ one style more than others?
- Do you actively suit your teaching style to different classes?
- On what do you base your decision?
- Which pupil factors do you consider when choosing a teaching style/strategy?
- Do you consider individual pupils' learning styles when choosing teaching strategies?
- Do you always teach in the same way?
- Do you have a preferred teaching style?

This questionnaire was later supplemented by 'reflective' questions based on classroom strategies. These would facilitate later research and included the following:

- Why did I pick this strategy for this class for this subject/topic?
- Did I have any prior knowledge of individual pupils' learning styles?
- Did I adjust my teaching strategy in any way for this particular topic/class?
- How will I assess whether my chosen teaching strategy for any particular topic/class/pupil has been the most successful to use?
- How will I investigate whether other strategies would have worked better?

57

- How would additional knowledge of particular learning styles have changed my intended/planned teaching strategies for this class/topic?

This proactive and reflective approach to the consideration of teaching styles enabled a more concentrated focus on classroom practice and ensured that departmental staff were fully aware of the necessity to initially consider, and later to take active steps, to investigate the diverse learning styles within a subject class. Despite initial reluctance to analyse and discuss personal teaching styles, all department members have become extremely enthusiastic about the increased effectiveness engendered by a better understanding of the learning styles of our pupils. This ongoing interaction, firstly between staff through 'peer partnerships', and secondly between teacher and pupil, has made all concerned responsible for the effectiveness of learning in the classroom. Professional development within the department is thus heavily centred around this interaction and the issues of teaching and learning.

The next stage, firmly rooted in the present, is concerned with how to maximise and utilise the information from the preceding research.

Towards a learning organisation

A synthesis of the information obtained on how children learn and how teachers teach must form the basis of any future departmental or whole-school action. I am investigating the possible introduction of individual personal learning plans. Here, the information from pupil profiles would be matched with the information obtained from the teaching styles profile compiled as a result of the teacher questionnaires. These personal learning profiles would have as their emphasis the best teacher-learner partnership and would include future development targets to be negotiated within the learning partnerships created. In this way, both teacher and pupil would be engaged in a 'learning interaction', where both sides learn mutually from each other. The opportunities for flexible learning within this system are obvious.

Subject-specific learning difficulties would be approached from an informed position, and pupil and staff development targets would be greatly influenced by these collaborative learning partnerships. A further step would be the implementation of these initiatives on a whole-school basis. In this way, the total learning of each pupil would represent the centre of the school's operation, and management structures would have to be altered to accommodate this change of emphasis. It remains a challenge to most schools to establish future management structures that facilitate, not hinder, this shift in focus.

My work on learning profiles is in its initial stages, so research information is limited. However, there does seem to be general agreement that this focus will acquire increasing importance as the search for improved effective learning becomes *the* educational imperative. There is enormous potential in this area, and I therefore intend to continue my research into the interaction of teaching and learning strategies and the necessary management structures to facilitate this.

The author wishes to acknowledge with thanks the co-operation and hard work of all staff and pupils involved in the above initiatives.

Reference

Gardner, H. (1993) *The Unschooled Mind*, London, Fontana.

6

■ ■ ■

The learning academy

JULIA SHAHID

This summer we will celebrate the ACT Academy's fifth anniversary. The school, in Texas, started with a $5.5 million grant from the U.S. Department of Education to create a 21st-century school based on the concept of the one-room schoolhouse. The grant embodied many of the components of educational reform, including full integration of technology; year-round, multi-aged, alternative assessment; self-directed learners, teachers as facilitators and students as active learners; a constructivist approach; non-graded, project learning; and the school as a community of learners.

I was an administrator at the district office when we received the one-of-a-kind grant. My daughter, Shanna, was a junior at the local high school and decided that she would want to attend the ACT. I had became involved, supporting the training for the new school as curriculum director. I therefore had the opportunity to experience the change the ACT Academy brought from the vantage point of a central office administrator and as a parent.

I immediately became involved in parent orientation, recording my feelings and thoughts in a journal. After the first meeting I wrote: 'There is a real feeling of belonging, and I sense that the ACT is going to be a cohesive unit. Interesting ideas are offered from all people present, and it is exhilarating to see this level of participation. I have never been involved as a parent to this degree and I find it exciting.'

Shortly after the first meeting I met the facilitator, or teacher, who would be working with Shanna. We spent 45 minutes talking about Shanna's strengths and weakness while developing an individual educational plan.

'At this time I am nearly overwhelmed by the possibilities available and the wealth of support and technology the students will have access to. Quite simply, it is using the best we have and know to work more effectively with students.'

Approximately three months after the initial meeting with the facilitator, Shanna discussed some concerns about school. She mentioned that the vision of the school that had been shared with her was not a day-to-day reality and shared her disappointment. After visiting the campus as a parent and as a district administrator, I wrote: 'Is change possible? Where is the transition between theory and the reality of implementation with students? I hope that this chaos that the school is experiencing is just a transition. My hopes are still high, but I'm concerned that this may not be an academically rigorous programme challenging to all.' After observing a class at work on the writing process, where all learners were responding to a similar prompt in a manner matching a traditional school setting, I wondered: 'Whatever happened to the individual educational plan? Am I expecting too much too soon? Are my expectations unrealistic?'

As the year progressed I became involved with supporting curriculum through a collegial coaching approach. In this role, I asked facilitators guiding questions that led them to reflect on their instruction and planning. Learners were more focused on projects as they exercised choice on project work and provided input into evaluation criteria. The earlier feelings of doubt had abated. 'I get this feeling that this is going to be a wonderful school but most likely will take a development year to get there.' In November I had my first portfolio conference with Shanna and her facilitator. Shanna had put together two impressive projects relating to social science along with rubrics to access her work. She was pleased with her efforts. 'Shanna seems to be thriving in this environment. For the self-directed learner, this is an ideal environment.'

Towards the end of the school year I compared what was occurring at the ACT Academy to what was happening at the high school in similar courses, and I saw that Shanna was ahead in social science in terms of depth and complexity, but had lost ground in maths and Spanish. She had again voiced cynicism about the school learning environment, focusing on the reality of daily occurrences in the classroom versus what was promised in this 21st-century school. Taking initiative was critical in this new learning environment. 'Shanna will have to set her goals, timelines, extra-curricular activities, if things are to occur. I wonder if we have made the wrong choice. We have been so optimistic about the possibilities of the ACT environment and the proposed change which so closely matches school reform advocated by the "experts". Is it idealistic that people will just learn what they need?'

Shanna found out what it took to achieve mastery on her benchmarks in each of the content areas and graduated from school a semester early. Even though she had been a student at the ACT for only one and a half years, I could see the difference in her being a self-directed learner. She functioned successfully with open projects, knew where to get primary resources, was able to present the learning in a meaningful manner using technology, and developed her own timelines to make sure the work was completed. In the short time she attended the ACT she developed competencies in the ACT lifelong-learning standards.

The original director left shortly after Shanna's graduation to pursue a business opportunity and an interim director was appointed. The interim director, possessing years of experience as a school administrator, immediately addressed issues pertaining to the learners, facilitators and parents. She began to take the initial chaos that was part of the new school start-up and brought a sense of order through dialogue with stakeholders. Concerns were addressed through a shared decision-making model, ensuring that the third year of the school exemplified continuous improvement. This director left after one and a half years, and I became the director in January 1997. 'I'm full of anticipation as I think about the journey ahead. The directorship of the ACT is a match for the skills and educational experiences I have had over the past 20 years. The four and a half years at Central Office have been years of intense professional growth, and I look forward to the journey ahead.'

The first month as director I asked all staff to respond to questions about goals, strengths, areas of growth, vision for the ACT and concerns. This provided an opportunity for focused discussion and helped me gain a deeper understanding of each person's role and how I could support that person. 'I believe that this will be of great use as I set my own goals and clearly articulate a vision for the ACT.' Coming from a position at central office that was service orientated, I knew I was not responsible for the organisation but key in making sure the organisation was owned by the staff. The first several months were devoted to supporting the current status of the campus while developing an understanding and appreciation for the complex issues at work. Goal-setting was modelled for staff. The Boys Town model for teaching social skills was considered as behaviour concerns were voiced by the secondary facilitators, while visits to other schools were planned to help us all see how other schools in the district were involved in educational reform. In each of these endeavours, the staff voices were heard through shared decision making.

By March, after a staff meeting where the details for the off-site visits were shared, including examples of the types of things to look for with possible guiding questions: 'I am amazed at how each of the staff is openly vocal about concerns with absolutely no regard to my viewpoint. It is difficult not to feel defensive. I remain neutral but find it hard since I do have a vested interest. The staff question every decision and every approach. Frankly, I am growing a little weary of this.' All of these ideas brought me back to the issue of empowerment as I pondered such questions as; 'What are the boundaries? What is the director's role? What is the facilitator's role?' Later in the month I reflected on the March meeting: 'I think I felt threatened by the questions, and I was not clear in my mind about qualitative observations. Should I have paused, asked people to examine their assumptions, charted their concerns, or worked on restating and paraphrasing? I know a healthy climate encourages active questioning and I don't want to stifle this.'

In the summer we all participated in an off-site session focusing on community building. Evidence of dysfunction in a pseudo-community abounded, and I became the centre of attention as a catalyst of the current status. At that moment I was miserable and knew I had to make a choice. The dilemma was: 'Do I throw in the towel or stay and continue to support and push for change that I believe in?' My choice was to stay, knowing that the ride was not going to be an easy one. 'So what have I learned? My skills on dialogue have grown by leaps and bounds. I will work on restating and surfacing assumptions, and then providing direction. I also will evaluate decisions I make and determine why I am not communicating with the group. I will better follow the decision-making model already established. I will be resilient and committed to the work.' The off-site learning session served as a rite of passage, moving me into a deeper understanding of the directorship.

One year has passed since the last journal entry. Change abounds. The school, after five years of existence, is more secure than ever. Last year's staff are still on board, with few personnel changes planned for the coming school year. Internally, two facilitators have changed positions based on their need for a fresh challenge. A new commitment has emerged as groups have determined the professional development needs for the school for the additional 41 professional development days. An underlying understanding exists that if we are to survive as an alternative school, we must be united in our vision and mission. Our charge is to offer an exemplary academic programme to all our learners, resulting in superior performance as measured by determined benchmarks and life-long learning standards.

We are in the process of fine-tuning many procedures with which we have struggled over the past few years, including the use of portfolios along with rubrics, benchmarks and the transition process as learners move from various learning areas when mastery is shown. We are simultaneously taking on new learning, knowing that we must push the window of education as we know it. We continue to look for ways to communicate with the district as well as outside the district. Our existence depends on presenting a viable alternative to traditional schooling.

Meanwhile, we are planning the five-year anniversary to celebrate our many accomplishments. This year we have 13 learners graduating, learners have put in a record 2 000 hours of community service, parents participate regularly in learner-led portfolio conferences, graduates present graduation portfolios using multimedia to demonstrate mastery of the ACT lifelong learning standards, and the school is characterised by self-directed learners taking charge of their learning. The focus of all our decisions is learner-centred, and we all believe that we are truly making a difference for learners in this learning environment. The journey is challenging and requires persistence, commitment, a shared vision and a passion. We all believe that we can make a difference in the lives of young people. Perhaps Margaret Mead says it best: 'Never doubt that a small group of thoughtful, committed, determined people can change the world. Indeed, it is the only thing that ever has.'

7

■ ■ ■

Timetabling to enable change

GEORGE THOMAS

The Journey

I arrived at headship having travelled a fairly conventional journey. I had become second in English at my first school; head of English and subsequently senior teacher in my second; was promoted to assistant headteacher in my third school; and so arrived at the tail end of the mid-eighties' industrial action and just prior to Bakerisation of... well, just about everything.

I had had very good experiences in generally very well run, idealistic comprehensive schools. I had, and still have, a passion for English literature, and a belief, normally justified in practice, that children/students of all abilities could enjoy and appreciate great poetry, drama and prose. I belonged broadly to the tradition of seeing literature at the heart of the human endeavour to understand the world we live in, and to bring values and sensitivity to it. I had also had the advantage in my first school of being in a very well led team, and in my second of being, I hope, a good team leader. To work in a department where a commonly understood sense of values led to a unity of approach and purpose, far from stultifying individuals, actually liberated us and generated enthusiasm and direction. If a leader can provide vision and confidence, the performance of all is raised.

Nevertheless I had learned along the way that there were different ways of organising schools, their subjects, time resources, etc., and that some ways were better than others. In my first school I had learned how badly I could teach a 40-minute lesson – I remember once arriving late on purpose, throwing the class out because they were noisy, throwing them out again, then proceeding to hand back their homework, often sarcastically, then reading the next chapter, setting new homework, and finally waiting silently for the bell to go. To think that a class could endure six or seven lessons of this kind in a day.

In my last year as an assistant headteacher I had the responsibility for the school timetable, an interesting and incredibly powerful job. The school was 1 000-strong and had some link courses with the local college, both at Key Stage 4 and at sixth form level – just to make things simpler. It is not insignificant to note that just as I was getting down to this task, I was appointed as headteacher some 250 miles away. After I had success-fully timetabled first the sixth form, and then the Year 10s and 11s, I was down to the thoroughly devious and manipulative nitty-gritty of Years 7–9. When it got down to seeing if the caretaker was free to teach Year 8 science for a split double on a Friday afternoon, I knew that 250 miles was only just far enough and that I would be wise not to leave a for-warding address.

Arrival

And so I arrived in the summer of 1986 at Kesgrave High School in sunny Ipswich, Suffolk. This was a challenge and I was determined to take it. At the interview stage I had learned a lot, but the crucial things I established were first that there was a great deal about the school that I wanted to change, and second there was an acceptance that change had to come. Two things stood out: the school had three bands, A, B and C; and the timetable was a seven-period day run over a six-day week. I had never met 'banding' before and was prejudiced against it; and while I had taught six-, five- and four-period days, a six-day week was new to me. The deputy head girl who showed me round the school was eloquent about banding. She explained that when she came to the school she had been placed in the B band, but that she had worked very hard and had been promoted to the A band. She described the three bands lucidly – the A band were bright, but didn't have to work very hard as they knew they were bright; the B band were mediocre, but worked very hard to get better; and the C band were thick, and knew they were so didn't bother working. Even though she had been in the A band for four of her five years, she still saw herself as fundamentally a B-band person – hard-working, but dull. Some teachers in the school were C-band specialists and they saw the C band, affectionately enough, as the remedials.

Changing the ethos

My first act as head, in August, with the enthusiastic help of the two deputies, was to ensure that in September at least Years 7, 8 and 9 would be in mixed-ability tutor groups – teaching groups I conceded would take longer. The effect of this one change alone was to be very powerful on the all-important culture or ethos of the school. Implicit in the way the school had organised the pupils were attitudes that at best were paternalistic and patronising, and at worst were deeply divisive and damaging to self-esteem.

Apart from that decisive act, I had no clear or well worked out agenda. I thought the staff needed liberating; I thought banding was wrong; I thought the timetable was crazy, and probably took a year to construct; and having attended my first heads of department meeting, I thought 24 nodding heads around the large tables was about 14 too many. I decided to launch in to one term of brainstorming. In order to shake things up a bit, I put the staff into cross-curricular working groups. Typically, every-one thought I had a clear, but hidden, agenda – word had even reached the staff that in the authority that I came from, uniform had been abol-ished (worse, that in my previous school I had attempted to move things forward through the stodge of industrial action and had written a pam-phlet entitled 'Timetabling to enable change'. This had proposed a faculty structure, and suggested that longer periods of time would aid flexible approaches and stimulate teamwork).

To start the ball rolling I published a very short paper which included the following: 'The conception of the curriculum as the sum of many isolated parts is an unfortunate development, especially when it leads a teacher to limit his teaching to a narrow "subject" field. The curriculum should move away from restricted subject treatment and towards integration. It should be "of a piece", its parts related, its whole having pattern, meaning, and purpose. It is for this reason that we must consider the content of the cur-riculum in terms of areas of activity rather than in terms of separate subjects. Though we believe that a curriculum may be weakened by over-crowding or by the construction of artificial subject barriers, we desire that, within a simplified organisation of the curriculum, a pupil may sample as wide a range of different forms of activity as possible. In a new activity, he may find an interest, a talent, an unsuspected opportunity for self-fulfilment and success, an enthusiasm which may lead him into new fields of worthwhile endeavour.'

This was provocative enough, but when staff realised that I had pinched this from 'The curriculum of the secondary school', published by the NUT in 1952, there were some surprised looks. And what about this from the same publication: 'Whatever method may be appropriate in a particular situation, it should be "active" in the sense that it aims at stimulating spontaneous and purposeful activity on the part of the pupil and at releasing his creative energy. The curriculum should make use of different methods – formal class instruction, individualised teaching, and group work – all of which are appropriate to particular circumstances of learning.'

A further stimulus for surprise and energy was my finding of an old pamphlet in the depths of the cupboard: 'The new era in home and school.' This was a 'progressive' publication dating from April 1935, and the reason that it was still buried in a cupboard in the head's study in Kesgrave High School was that it featured an article by one Captain Harrison, who was the school's first head. Actually the title of the article is 'Kesgrave Area School', and Captain Harrison is referred to as 'principal'. In the article he explains his aims, which I still use in our school brochure: 'We endeavour to teach the children how to live so as to get the best out of life; we strive to get down to realities. To do this, three things were necessary:

1 to make a suitable environment and to create the right atmosphere;
2 to enable the children to learn through doing;
3 to teach the community spirit.'

In early December the working parties reported back, and not surprisingly there were many superb ideas; getting rid of bands; integrated humanities; block timetabling; work experience, to name but a few. I, too, had had time to think, talk, look, read and reflect. So using a lot of the staff's ideas, many pirated from experience and wide reading, plus some of my own, I decided to act.

Setting new directions

'Timetabling to enable change' became the watchword. If I can distil all that I have learned into a few ideas it would be to say that I attach a great deal of importance to teams, to real time, to coherence, and to organisation and management serving the core purpose of the school, rather than the complex, bureaucratic, and often deeply mysterious webs of planning, subverting and ossifying. So I went for simplicity:

● we would have five faculties
● there would be a three-session day
● a whole year group would be with a faculty at a given time.

The five faculties are:

- communications (modern languages/English)
- science/IT
- humanities (history/geography/RE and business studies at Key Stage 4)
- maths/technology
- creative physical (PE, art, music, drama).

Each faculty would have 20 per cent of time, cater for a whole year group at once, and have a large enough session of time to be flexible, responsive and dynamic. I had toyed with a four-period day, but rejected it in favour of three as three allowed for a stronger emphasis on the morning, and gave sessions which were long enough to really satisfy the needs of very practical subjects. A tremendous advantage of this is that each faculty has a Period 1, a Period 2 and a Period 3 with each age group.

I had never really understood why it seemed perfectly rational to organise a primary school day in large blocks of time, and to accept that in the sixth form that was also desirable, but that magically between the ages of 11 and 16 we had to chop time, curriculum areas, year groups, etc. into as many fragments as possible. Was it a divide and rule mentality? Are timetablers good at their jobs because they're control freaks? Having made the big decision, it was clear that current Year 10 would be the problem. Their three quite different timetables had to be fitted in to the new organisation for next September. The task was eventually completed, but not without having recourse to the dubious benefits of private study for the C band. For the other four year groups the key word was 'enable'. The new timetable did not force change, it enabled it. One change, however, that everyone seemed keen on was that the new Year 7 should at least start their life with us in mixed-ability groups. As time went on, individual faculties could determine their approach to groupings in the light of their professional judgement – not mine.

Three major curriculum changes were needed, however. Suffolk had at that time been piloting the 'Suffolk Science' course. This was a co-ordinated course leading to two GCSEs and requiring 20 per cent of time. It was essentially a very active course – teaching people to be scientists, rather than just 'learning' science. As luck would have it, one of the leading lights in the development, a science advisor, was also the school's 'link' or 'pastoral' advisor. (He had, in fact, been involved in my interview.) This therefore fitted my plans to perfection.

The second initiative was to introduce business studies to Key Stage 4, and budget for the school's first computer network. Key staff were enthusiastic, the LEA was helpful, and so come September we were ready. The course proved immensely popular, and although its content has changed many times, it is still a major player in our delivery of IT at Key Stage 4, and has led successfully into our developments with ICT. The third was to introduce an integrated arts course. In a school where music was not a success, and drama did not exist on the curriculum, the adoption of this course was either foolhardy or adventurous. Yet there have been many rich dividends, and the final confirmation – a purpose-built arts/PE block – will open next summer.

Chance conversations in December had led me to challenging a bright and enthusiastic member of staff to find as many work-experience placements for Year 10 students for two weeks in June/July. From a base of zero she managed to place the whole year group. While Year 10 were out I planned to have an activities fortnight for the remaining years, 7, 8 and 9. This would force a change in the culture – we would mix up year groups, have residential trips, mix up staff, even have no uniform. Out of this culture have arisen many excellent developments, much increased extra-curricular work, a strong tradition of residential experiences, and an ever-burgeoning Duke of Edinburgh Award scheme. This last, along with the Young Enterprise scheme, has proved very successful in motivating pupils, providing opportunities for teamwork, and bringing different staff into co-operative units.

I was able, by September, to bring much greater coherence to where the various subjects were placed around the school. Sometimes specialist accommodation would inhibit our ambitions in this respect. As the school has grown we have been able to gradually improve in this area, so much so that by next June, each faculty will be united. A huge advantage of this plan had to be that there would be genuine teams of teachers; each team would be dealing with one age group at a time; and preparation and planning at maximum had to be for only three sessions in a given day.

The next major focus was to prepare the whole staff. We hit upon the idea of what we called then a 'management' course: for six or seven twilight sessions over the next months we had a go at looking at all sorts of issues – time-management, pupil records of achievement, a content-free curriculum, and so on. At the time Suffolk was putting on some good courses, and I was able to persuade many other staff to contribute and to lead sessions.

The results

Over the next few years it all began to work. Real teams now exist in the school, and they do have significant autonomy when it comes to timetabling, resourcing and accommodation. In particular the timetable presents us with no problems – my job is simply to make sure that each faculty has enough staffing, and that where there is a surplus or deficit, staffing can be swapped. In terms of outcomes, everything began to work, too. The school's examination results have improved dramatically over the past ten years, from the mid-30s to the mid-50s (5+ A–Cs). Apart from many other contributory reasons I am convinced that the disappearance of 'banding' has been a major cause.

Obviously over the past ten years there have been huge changes in the powers which schools have to manage themselves, and equally big changes to the organisation of the curriculum. We have always tried to take opportunities to increase coherence and respond creatively to new ideas. It is perhaps worth mentioning two areas that ten years ago would not have been thought of, and they both have relevance to the modern jargon of 'para-professionals'.

Gradually at Kesgrave we have built a situation whereby each faculty area has its own 'curriculum support'. That sounds simple, but the energy it can release, the sense of liberation it can bring, are hugely significant and beneficial. It has increased the sense of self-respect in the teams, led to greater efficiency, and as a consequence is hugely cost-effective. Along a similar track we have moved to a situation where all extra hours used for statemented hours or for any 'special' need are delivered by a growing group of 'learning support assistants'. Our equivalent of a Senco (Special educational needs co-ordinator) is a head of learning and assessment. Again this has been liberating, effective and efficient. We have been able to seize on the latest advances in interactive learning programmes, and encourage an atmosphere of target-setting and daylong learning. The move to a three-period day and a simplified division of time, and the change from departments into faculties, has stood us in good stead over the years of change – we have been able to field each update, alteration, etc. of the national curriculum with considerable ease. We have been flexible enough to take account of new opportunities, and to absorb each innovation with relative cheerfulness.

One clear proof of the efficiency of the system is that over the past ten years, and even with incredibly difficult budget settlements, no one at

Kesgrave has taught a timetable of more than 80 per cent. I believe that providing the right conditions for learning to take place goes hand in hand with providing the right conditions for teaching to take place.

8

■ ■ ■

Bias towards action

ERIC TOPE

This is a case study of a school written by an experienced practitioner who has been privileged to be its leader over the past 15 years. The St. Thomas the Apostle College is a boys-only, Roman Catholic, GM comprehensive school in a deprived part of inner South London. As a close-knit community it has battled to survive through reorganisation, falling rolls, fierce competition and the ill-founded parental fear of urban boys' culture manufactured by the media through the eighties and early nineties.

The opportunity to write this study presented itself during the weekend break of the 1998 Principals' Institute held in Philadelphia. While others cavorted around the hot spots of New York and Washington D.C., the author quietly went to church and then put pen to paper, encouraged in no small measure by an injured knee. The study is based on a presentation on the recent story of St. Thomas the Apostle to a group of American principals attending the Institute. The theme of the Institute was entitled 'Bias towards Action' and thus this piece is about reality and written by one of the practitioners at the centre of the action. I trust it will be of use to the reader to follow a few of the signposts through this story and these are provided by strategy, professional development and crucially action-based aspirations.

To set the scene, this school opened in 1965 to serve the sons of working-class Roman Catholic families in the borough of Southwark. The initial intake was predominantly white with Irish, Italian and other assorted European ethnic backgrounds. The majority of boys with academic aspirations attended one of the four Roman Catholic boys' grammar schools in the neighbouring boroughs. After initial rapid expansion from four to six forms of entry, the dwindling urban population of the late seventies started to bite, forcing closures and exposing the vulnerability of inner city boys' schools. Popular opinion was formed that girls thrived in girls only schools and boys in mixed establishments. Consequently, Roman Catholic schools were reorganised in the mid-eighties and we once again became a four-form entry, 11–16 comprehensive with an intake of 90 boys, of whom 40 per cent were from Afro-Caribbean backgrounds.

We had done well to survive the process of reorganisation, others had not. One grammar had gone and the others, fed on a diet rich in complacency, were weakening. We survived, not weak but lean, with battle-hardened staff and fiercely loyal parents and friends. In retrospect, the reorganisation provided our high-octave fuel for accelerated improvement and other events provided the direction which we were all to follow. Our new faculty and pastoral systems were installed and developed by a teaching body of 50 per cent new members and the very best of the old. We were optimistic and forward looking and shared a sense of facing the future with confidence. This community of boys, parents, governors and staff shared a culture of survival, street wisdom, urban nerve, celebration and Christian Catholic care.

Our story for this study will cover 1993 to 1998, a five-year period of outstanding achievement sandwiched between OFSTED inspections and garnished by self-governing status. Our '93 Report tagged us as 'satisfactory', which was viewed with disappointment in the early days of evaluation. Our initial period of sulking was tempered by the mechanics of operating our self-governing status, and by the end of the inspection year we were ready to 'move ahead'.

Townsend (1995) presents research that indicates that truly effective schools have clear goals centred on learning and achievement, with a positive climate of pride. The newly introduced league tables of GCSE examination results presented the opportunity to be united in improving our effectiveness and performance. Improving schools need to set their own criteria for success (Stoll and Fink, 1996) and we unashamedly saw league-table improvement as the key criterion. Once our post-inspection goals for each subject area had been set, and staff had reflected on their use of energy, we discovered a more enlightened collegiate atmosphere where we worked a lot smarter if not harder.

1994 – quality management

Aligning theory and practice is not easy, but an acknowledgement that good theory and good practice are interwoven is necessary for effective action. Much has been written by researchers and academics on quality management, effective schools and school improvement. Worryingly, it is common to hear practitioners bemoaning their situations where the daily routine leaves little or no time for study, reflection and discussion. Increasingly, as a more experienced practitioner, I grow convinced that such 'luxury' activities are at the heart of effective leadership. The reality is that much time and energy is misused in the world of the daily administration routines which are at the periphery of successful moving schools. With this conviction I, as the senior leader and practitioner at our school, embarked on my MBA studies in 1994 to both 'sharpen the saw' and acquire the theoretical skills to enhance our practice.

An early area of my studies which seemed to provide an opportunity for combining theory and practice was quality management. The work of Myer and Zucher (1989) names five features of so-called quality organisations. These sat quite naturally on our existing culture, and communicating vision, teamwork, addressing customer needs, setting challenging goals and the systematic recording of performance did not prove to be difficult. As with all successful change, processes and cultures, a readiness existed, commitment was there in abundance, and eagerness lubricated our channels of communication.

Our staff training in 1994 allowed adoption of the five features:

- whatever aspects of quality examined, they must relate to our *shared vision* and reflect our shared commitment
- the generation of an awareness of individual pupil journeys through our school, and their current and future needs, would supply *customer driven provision*
- focusing on the work of our individual *faculty teams* would encourage shared values, provide creative conflict and accelerate performance
- provision of *challenging goals* would ensure a determined commitment to regular, significant improvement
- the *systematic recording* of performance and feedback would keep us all on track.

We agreed as a staff to concentrate our energies on just two whole-school areas to make sure that action really did take place. Faculties reserved the right to nominate a third area, but in reality the two proved to be enough to contend with:

- percentage of five A/C grades
- levels of literacy.

Our work of 1993/4 had involved individual action-planning with border-line pupils and moved five A/C results from 22 per cent to 29 per cent. Building on the success was a natural step towards ambitious department team targets. Not one member of staff dissented from the view that an urgent need was for a literacy improvement programme in Year 7 to address the low mean reading age of 9.6 years across the entry cohort, and all the consequent learning problems. Clearly staff recognised the need to improve the quality of this aspect in order to improve the quality of the former. *Action* on levels of literacy meant:

- systematic collection and distribution of reading 'ages' on entry and through Year 7
- subject-based 'Key Words' scheme
- whole-school support with daily use of Key Word pupil books
- successful support from the Basic Skills Agency.

Additionally, the need to address levels of numeracy was suggested by many staff early in the initiations. Action on improving GCSE A/C grades meant:

- identifying weak departments
- ambitious department goals
- increasing range of potential A/C pupils
- increased external action planning.

During the 1994 year all subject areas developed Key Word lists and a high-quality booklet was produced. Subsequently pupils were regularly tested on pronunciation, spelling, meaning and context use. To date every pupil is experiencing a culture of basic skills improvement. The norm enables him to acknowledge gaps in his learning and he expects to be sup-ported to remedy these weaknesses. The percentage of boys with five or more GCSE A, B, C grades moved from 29 per cent to 41 per cent during our quality management year. Success of course breeds further success and as a faculty body we were happy to reflect on our change of approach and the related improvement.

1995 – the way forward

Our next move forward was prompted partly by my studies and partly by a need to re-examine the annual production of our development plan. It is important for a moving school to maintain its momentum (Stoll and Fink, 1996). Like the majority of schools we had become very efficient at this cycle of audit, plan, implement and evaluate. It was also clear that many schools with impressive plans were not really 'on the move' – many were happy with average or above average results and strolling seemed to describe their progress best. Like many others, our cycle of planning was becoming detached from ambitious goals. One year's 'progress' was dictating the next, incremented progress in some departments was falling short of the exponentially increasing steps of others. The 'real world' pace of change was outstripping our progress and the danger of incremental drift creating a gap between our planning and our needs was looming. Strategically our solution was to focus on five years ahead, to the year 2000. Our training programme asked the faculty, the departments, the individual teachers:

- 'Where do we want to be in AD2000?'
- 'How will we get there?'

Our training day provided an opportunity to stimulate reflection, discussion and to look into the future. Possible changes were suggested in three key areas: environment, curriculum and technology. Suggested possibilities at the time stand up well in 1998.

Environment

1 Change of status for GM schools.
2 Removal of the assisted places scheme.
3 Population increase in Southwark.
4 Rising demand for church school places.
5 Closer ties between Anglican and Roman Catholic clergy and laity.
6 Demise of local authority housing and growth of local housing associations.
7 Strengthening of local, national and international pressure groups.
8 Rising demand for one-stop 11–19 schools.
9 Introduction of voucher schemes into mainstream schooling.
10 Decreasing powers of local and national governments.

Curriculum

1 Increasing emphasis on currency values of public examination results.

2 Stronger links between Key Stages of the National Curriculum.

3 Emergence of *academic* portfolio of achievements from 4–19 years.

4 Increasing use of curriculum trainers both in schools and as part of outside agencies.

5 Parents becoming increasingly informed on all curriculum matters and pressurising schools (departments) to perform well.

6 Further development of the 16–19 curriculum involving mix and match courses based on GNVQs and modular A–levels.

7 Possible emergence of 'core' subjects through to 19 years – literacy, numeracy, modern language, IT and science.

8 Creation of diploma qualification (similar to matriculation) based on attainment levels in core and 'other' subjects.

9 Individual schools *marketing* their own curriculum offer(s).

10 Moves towards 'self-monitoring' of quality of learning in schools involving pupil and parent surveys.

11 Progress towards a global curriculum based on pastoral, economic, environmental needs and rapid access to existing and new information.

Learning technology

1 Revolution in manufacturing techniques with dramatic reduction of cost and ease of availability.

2 Expansion of global networks and easy access to knowledge base.

3 Miniaturisation of hardware to accelerate, providing easy transport (and security problems).

4 Rapid expansion of school networks and CD-ROM technology with external links.

5 Change of learning styles for teachers and pupils and *parents* with home/school link-ups.

6 Regular (frequent) training for *all* teaching and support staff.

7 Creation of teacher-assistant and other forms of education support staff.

8 Moves towards 'third age' students linking with schools (with vouchers?).

9 Schools creating and selling materials and expertise.

10 Enhanced status of 'informed' teacher profession with creation of possible 'elite' based in and marketed by individual schools.

Questions

1 In what direction is your subject moving? What will it be in five years' time?

2 Do you see your area of the curriculum playing a part at 16+?

3 How is the 'new' technology changing the nature of your subject?

4 How will you use technology to change your teaching style(s)?

5 What additional (updated) resources will you need by the year 2000?

6 Will you be able to build these resource needs into your next development plan?

7 Can you identify a teaching assistant role in your faculty/department?

The outcomes of the training day were requested in three parts:

• a description of each department in the year 2000

• a look back from 2000 and a production of a five-step plan to reach the 2000 position successfully.

• an outline plan for 1995/6 as a first step towards the department's 2000 position.

The new development plans resulted in our slower moving areas setting improvement targets far more in line with our high performing departments.

1996 – towards 2000: teaching quality and pupil performance

Of course, high targets on their own do not produce high performance. Setting ambitious goals without the accompanying action does not result in improvement. By 1996 it was clear that a more prescriptive approach would be necessary to force our slowest moving departments to 'get in line' with the rest of the college. Basically there are four ways of dealing with the future:

• ignore

• predict

• control

• respond.

We realised from 1995 that prediction does not produce results – what was needed was action-driven *control*. In any organisation there are always dangers that some teams plan in isolation and ignore the creative thoughts of other areas. It was decided that our long-term shared aspirations needed to be supported by short-term goals with structures to enable us to form action strategies towards their achievement.

1996 college areas for development

- continuous professional development.
- research, development and teacher training
- recording and assessment
- special educational needs (SEN)
- pastoral curriculum
- 16–19 curriculum
- basic skills
- quality of teaching and learning
- support centre
- primary liaison.

Each of the ten areas had an action outcome for 1996/7 and a named member of staff responsible for that area. The action spreadsheet included staff involved, a monitor, required Inset and costs for each area. A parallel spreadsheet was provided for each department to complete and a monitor assigned to review department progress through the year. The presence of a monitor to discuss progress in individual departments was to prove to be the action which moved even our slowest areas towards a cycle of real improvement.

The central theme of our 1996 development was teaching quality and pupil performance, thus one of the key target areas was that of the quality of teaching and learning. The associated action was to introduce classroom observation and agree on the essential elements of quality teaching and learning offered in the classroom. During the year every teacher was observed formally on at least one occasion and an in-house observation form was completed. Our driving force for the future was to be continuous professional development. To facilitate this, the college established a centre for professional development and appointed a high-profile head of centre to establish this venture. During the year both the head of centre and myself trained as OFSTED inspectors, thus closely linking classroom observation and professional development.

1997 – every teacher a learner and every child an achiever

In the summer term of 1996/7 a training day was dedicated to classroom observation. During the year a planning group had been formed involving two senior teachers, the head of research, development and training, and myself. Our group discussed, reflected and shared ideas for future quality improvement action and found increasingly that the focus was classroom performance. The observation training day was carefully prepared by the planning group and provided activities designed to measure 'teacher-feelings' towards formal observations. The information provided by questionnaire, interview task and discussion groups played a significant part in our planning for 1997. The nature of, resistance to and readiness for change had all been explored and helped clarify ways forward. The data generated showed overwhelmingly a readiness for observation and a need for constructive feedback. How the process would proceed clearly needed careful, reflective thinking and sharing linked to clear, sensitive planning.

An additional factor to influence planning for 1997/8 was an even more spectacular improvement in GCSE performance. Our target of 45 per cent five A/C passes had been exceeded with a 53 per cent performance. Once more our inner-city boys had shown what enormous potential they possessed. All groups had performed well regardless of ethnic background, initial literacy levels or social-economic status, which contrasts sharply with national performance data. The scale of what had been achieved by planned quality action had surprised us all and in particular the longer-serving members of faculty. Even allowing for highs and lows in a particular year, the line of 'best fit' moved steadily upwards. 'Just how much higher could we go?' was a question on everyone's lips.

Our planning day for 1997 was designed to answer these fundamental questions:

- Just where are we?
- How did we get here?
- Where are we going next?

Our roll was growing, our staff numbers increasing. New and often inexperienced teachers were unaware of the events of the past few years, old and new needed the consolidation exercise of answering our three fundamental questions:

1 We started our corporate planning day with the often misunderstood concept of shared vision. There was no attempt to articulate but rather to share our feelings by examining and reflecting on Senge's (1990) concept of vision:

Shared vision *is not an idea. It is not even an important idea such as freedom. It is, rather, a force in people's hearts, a force of impressive power. It may be inspired by an idea, but once it goes further – if it is compelling enough to acquire the support of one person – then it is no longer an abstraction. It is palpable. People begin to see it as though it exists. Few, if any, forces in human affairs are as powerful as shared vision.*

2   We revisited the sigmoid curve of Handy (1994), which seemed to clarify our position in the past.

3   We extended Handy's concept into a series of curves which I believe is necessary to maintain momentum and continue our improvement.

Fundamentally what we were doing was mapping our own way forward, making our choices based on past performance, present reality and whatever academic advice suited us best. In short, our consolidation exercise was about fresh choices and fresh action to maintain our unique improvement in performance. Our planning outcomes for 1997/8 were condensed into five features:

- 1996 development areas to remain
- monitoring to be improved and sharpened
- observation to be developed
- initial teacher training to be expanded
- Continuing professional development to further expand and move towards personal portfolios.

1998 – where we are

We have now reached the end of our 1997/8 academic year and return in the autumn to our second OFSTED inspection, a good time to take stock. We are at last beginning to share good classroom practice, and our formal system of observations is slowly taking shape with time allocated on the 1998/9 timetable. In order to improve further we need to share skills and thoughts and critically support one another in teaching and learning situations.

Our results to date have attracted local and national media attention, with tenth place in the *Observer* newspaper Top 100 Schools and 11th place in the DfEE Improved GCSE table. The Uden Centre, attached to the school, is establishing its reputation for practitioner-led consultancy and associated courses. A close link with the University of Greenwich has resulted in our centre-based MA, which has a first cohort of 14 teachers and a second cohort involving neighbouring schools is planned for next year with present staff as tutors. The head of the centre has been involved in National Professional Qualification for Headteachers (NPQH) training, OFSTED inspections, a highly successful Timetabling Made Easy course and related consultancies. The recent OFSTED publication 'Improving Schools', a report for the first five years of inspections, highly praises our performance, and associated research projects are under way as part of our post-graduate programme. During the year an ambitious initial teacher training (ITT) programme was planned for and implemented involving 12 students on their first practice over seven weeks full time. Over half of our staff were involved as mentors and four as senior mentors/tutors.

It appears from the above non-exhaustive list that change and success provide their own enthusiasm and energy, provided of course that they go together. This, then, is a snapshot of where we are now and hopefully prepares us well for the unknown challenges of the future.

Where next?

As I mentioned earlier we are not in the business of prediction, but hopefully we will maintain control of our actions and continue to improve. Systematic self-development will take us towards our individual and corporate self-mastery (Senge, 1990). We as teachers have learned that our personal development and our school's development go hand in hand. Hopefully what we have in place will enable all of us to become part of a true learning community where we reflect on our learning and share our ideas.

Our minds are focusing on our autumn inspection and we look for a report that will guide us towards our future. We will lose our grant-maintained status during the next year but hopefully our culture of self-governing will remain and be shared by others.

We have gathered much wisdom over the past five years, including the fact that we still have much to learn and indeed to share with others. Our Uden Centre will provide the facility for our own reflective practice and will be a beacon for our consultant-practitioners.

Whatever action we initiate and implement in the years ahead it will always involve our special ingredient of real care for one another. Stoll and Fink (1996) refer to this care as the magic ingredient for successful change. We will care for one another as students, parents, friends, governors and staff in all aspects of our pastoral and spiritual welfare, but also in all aspects of the quality of learning enjoyed by every member of our community. Our actions will be guided by our aspirations and be planned for our unique needs.

References

Myer, M. and Zucher, L.G. (1989) *Permanently Failing Organisations*, Beverly Hills, CA, Sage.

Senge, P. (1990) *The Fifth Discipline: The Art and Practice of the Learning Organisation*, New York, Doubleday.

Stoll, L. and Fink. D. (1996) *Changing Our Schools*, Buckingham, Open University Press.

Townsend. T. (1995) 'Community perceptions of what makes schools effective: implications for leaders of tomorrow's schools', *Leading and Managing*, 1(2), pp. 111–136.

9
■ ■ ■

Raising standards in school

JOHN VERSEY

The previous position

Goffs School, in Essex, had a high reputation for many years and had reasonably good academic results. Popular with parents, it was well known for its language teaching, the previous head having been a language specialist. I was looking forward to leading it.

The OFSTED Report in November 1993 had, however, highlighted a number of serious weaknesses that had been largely ignored by the governors. More able pupils were not being stretched sufficiently and the pass rate, particularly at A-level, could also be improved. My first observations of the school suggested that this might be true. As I began to delve below the surface, I found a surprising degree of complacency. When I interviewed all the staff with responsibilities, I found that they did not feel there was any need for significant improvement since Goffs, and the rival school three miles away, were not seriously challenged. Its management was based on a sixties' grammar school model with the emphasis on high academic achievement. The pinnacle was seen as the sixth form and this was the only area that was given significant responsibility. It was the classic case described by David Hopkins (1994) as the 'promenading school'. This type of school is notoriously difficult to change because the recipients feel that there is no need, they are successful already, and thus there tends to be a great deal of resistance.

Fortunately, I had a very good management team, largely in tune with what I wanted to do, respected and able to implement change. I was appointed in December 1993 and took up my appointment at Goffs School in September 1994. We used the intervening time to plan what we could reasonably achieve. I had initially intended to come in slowly and take my time about implementing change. It was clear, however, that this would not do. The inherent resistance would stop any change, so I had to jolt the school quickly so that I could generate some creative tension and start the process of change. Michael Fullan (1993) warns of the difficulties and pitfalls associated with change and I was mindful of the need to monitor carefully the attitudes of the staff, the parents and the pupils as we began to make changes which inevitably could be painful to some. However, there was hope. The staff was very committed to the school and its success. They were fairly adaptable people and many actually thought there was a need for change.

Identified weaknesses

The OFSTED Report of November 1993 had highlighted the following key points for action that we needed to address:

- Build on the school development and strategic plans, supported by subject development plans, so that these become a more effective means of planning the school's future.
- Examine the reasons why the school, in the context of good overall results at GCSE, is not achieving the highest standards for its ablest pupils in the core and some other subjects at GCSE; why the A-level results were not as good in 1993 as the intake of pupils to the school suggests they should have been; and take appropriate action.
- Fundamentally review the system of reporting to pupils and parents on pupil achievement in Years 7–9, so that the grades for achievement do record achievement rather than broad rank order in the class, and so that the system accords with National Curriculum requirements and recommendations on reporting to parents.
- Consider whether all procedures and teaching methods give all pupils equality of access to learning and a full involvement in the school.

All the structures in the school were designed to maintain the status quo. The emphasis was on academic achievement and going to Oxbridge. Even the admissions policy, based heavily on past attendance by parents and siblings, kept the current position and organisation as a grammar school. However, the comprehensive intake of the school and its current status belied these facts. The school has a full range of pupil ability. The management structure was designed to ensure that an autocratic style prevailed. It was not consultative, having 26 heads of department, who met occasionally to discuss matters of policy, although there were no minutes taken. The method of assessing pupil performance was norm-referenced so that no real diagnostic measure could be taken. Although there was a semblance of sharing information about pupil achievement, it was of limited value. Parents felt that it did not tell them anything and, in the eyes of the staff, it was largely discredited. This was endorsed, as can be seen from the above, by the OFSTED inspection. Teaching was good and committed but was far too directed in nature. I knew this would be difficult to change.

One of the most serious aspects that needed addressing was that there was no culture of self-evaluation in place and no attempt particularly to address real problems associated with school improvement. There were no mentoring systems and no proper target-setting arrangements.

Planned changes

I felt that I had initially to make some major changes to the ethos of the school, but I had to be careful – I did not want to damage what had essentially been a good school. I had to retain much of the tradition and good practice while, at the same time changing the mindset of the staff and the pupils. I decided that it was going to be important to bring in a proper quality management model along the lines described by West-Burnham (1997). I would want to flatten the decision-making structures, limit major responsibilities to a manageable few, and create a full team structure. Responsibility was going to be delegated for as many items as possible – finance, monitoring, Inset, strategic planning linked to the school development plan. It was going to be important to ensure that everyone understood the necessity of an emphasis on good planning and evaluating everything that we did. We needed to make sure that this more consultative style of management was open and that meant significantly improving our communications.

We began the process by holding a full staff conference in October 1994. We collected data from parents and pupils using a GRIDS questionnaire. From this, we were able to identify the strengths and weaknesses of the school and could start to draw up a list of priorities. A working group rewrote the school aims, emphasising the needs of all pupils and also those of adults, and presented it to the staff in April. The mission statement made clear that the learning process should be seen as enjoyable and lifelong and should be based on celebrated achievement at all levels:

> *Goffs School aims to be a caring community in which all individuals are able to learn, grow and develop, with as much enjoyment as possible. We aim to prepare our pupils to contribute to and cope with the demands of our rapidly changing and demanding world.*

Once the major priorities had been identified, I laid out a strategic plan outlining the developments that would be needed over the next five years, their rationale and careful costing. I ensured that the developments were manageable by identifying when in the cycle each should occur. The timescale demanded a cracking pace, but I felt the school would cope with it. The OFSTED Report had identified several serious weaknesses and these could not be put right quickly; neither could we afford to ignore them. Our first cycle of development planning was rushed. The process required the generation and acceptance of a major new strategic plan and the consequent annual development plan, fully linked to departments and fully budgeted. All this had to be achieved in two terms. With hindsight, it might well have been better to delay slightly, and our subsequent planning has occurred in two phases: the generation of the whole-school priorities linked to the budget, and then the departmental targets and budgets linked to this.

Initial plans were only partially effective. The school had never done development planning before. To satisfy me, the managers produced reasonable sounding targets linked to the plan but quite separate from their own agendas, which were not published. The result, of course, was that they had, in the end, to deliver not only my targets but their own hidden ones as well. I am glad to say that the school learned by this mistake and has not repeated it. The senior management team roles reflected the old ethos of the school. They would need to be changed to give the deputies far more responsibility for pupil learning and to take day-to-day responsibility for a section of the school. I decided to split the school into lower and upper sections rather than the traditional boy/girl split that had been prevalent before. The senior teachers would eventually have oversight of specific areas, the curriculum and assessment. This, unfortunately, could not be managed straightaway – it took more than two years to complete the process. We were finally able to separate most of the day-to-day administrative tasks from the teachers and appoint both a finance and resources manager and an administrative manager to the management team. We also made sure that our regular communications with teachers, through a published weekly bulletin and staff briefing, were effective and clear.

The new management structure relied heavily on the creation of teams, based on curriculum areas. A curriculum area leader, who took responsibility for several departments, led each team. These area leaders were themselves meant to act as a team of advisers to the senior management team and to take on a whole-school monitoring role. There were two other important strands to the strategy. It was really important to try to raise additional funds from a variety of sources so that the facilities could be improved which, in turn, would enhance learning. Finally, the esteem of the school would need to be raised after such soul-searching by using well-known quality audits, the 'Charter Mark' and 'Investors in People'.

Improving the quality of teaching

If the standards of the school were to improve, it was clearly essential to improve the quality of teaching. The school already had committed teachers who gave their all. This was not the problem. I needed a more professional approach – reviewing their practice, observing each other's lessons, and making sure that the emphasis really was on learning objectives. If we were to improve the performance, particularly of the more able pupils, we would need to have in place an effective means of assessment. I wanted to make sure that there would be a real measure of pupil performance which was properly understood by everybody and which could easily be used for diagnostic judgements. The tutors' role would need to be emphasised, so that they could act as mentors to their pupils, and to help them to improve by setting targets with them. They would need accurate information. It would mean a change to more formative assessment and monitoring and an emphasis on learning.

The other major plank that would be required would be to raise the profile of special needs, which would help to address the problem of equality of access to the curriculum and increase overall performance. We moved the department into much better facilities and placed it in the centre of the school. We enhanced its provision of staffing and resources and ensured that more support could be obtained for everybody. The department was renamed to reflect its new role – learning support. Only by doing this would there be any chance that the weaker pupils and departments could be given a chance to succeed. Weaker departments were also strengthened by improving their staffing and facilities and by providing them with clearly defined areas in the school.

The introduction of a co-ordinated transparent assessment scheme

The main task was to overhaul the assessment scheme. The previous scheme was rigidly norm-referenced. There were five streams of ability in the school and pupils had to be grouped according to a normal distribution in which grades A to E were awarded. Those with 'A' were praised, those with 'E' placed on report. It took no regard for actual performance, in effect rewarding only effort. The scheme was intensely disliked by parents and little understood by anybody. Its only real virtue lay in its open nature – the full details of the pupil performance were available to all the teachers in the staff room.

We started in the upper school, introducing a system of predicted grades based on expected GCSE or A-level performance to Years 10–13. All teachers initially were required to predict reasonable expected performance at the end of Year 10 (after the summer examinations), half-way through the autumn term in Year 11, and then after the mock examinations in January. A similar pattern was repeated for the sixth form. The results were collated on to an Excel spreadsheet and published to all staff. The pupils' results showed the expected performance in each subject, and were placed in order of the number of GCSE higher grade passes expected. The data revealed much more information; it indicated the average point count per entry, and also the performance of the departments, and this information was released to everybody. It was interesting watching the effect in the staff room. The staff would look closely at the results and, of course, match the performance of the pupils they taught with similar performance by other teachers or other subjects. They would not say anything, but the increased competition that this raised has definitely contributed to increased pupil performance. After all, if you teach pupils whom you think are capable on a good day of getting only a 'D' grade, yet others think they are capable of at least 'B' in other subjects, then maybe you have been setting your expectations of them too low.

Now a meeting is held of our consultative committee, made up of representatives of all staff in the school. The results are discussed and pupils identified who are considered to be performing particularly well, or who are under-performing, for a variety of reasons. The deputy head, upper school and the head of Year 11 interview these and other identified pupils to provide counselling help, target setting and occasionally to give them a 'rocket'. In all cases, this discussion is meant to be positive. It is intended this year to include the tutors in these discussions so that more time can be devoted to each individual.

At first, the results were rather erratic, but the teachers have become far more adept at judging performance and are normally pretty close to the final result as the process develops. Understanding and knowing actual performance has helped to raised standards and is now fully embedded in the school's culture. This change in ethos, focusing far more on pupil performance, enabled us to move to the second phase of this development. We introduced a series of interim reports at four intervals throughout the year. The first interim report occurs after approximately seven weeks and reports simply progress and effort. It is intended merely to find out how the pupils are settling into the new course and year group, and to identify any cause for concern. It is expected that the tutor will discuss these grades first with the pupil and later with the parents. This year, for the first time, we introduced an academic review day to give quality time for the tutors to discuss these grades with each pupils and then to set simple targets to gain improvement. It was followed up a few days later with a parents' evening. Parents have been very pleased with this innovation.

Later in the year, attainment grades are added, loosely based on National Curriculum levels. A subject evening occurs in the middle of the year to give parents the chance to discuss the progress of their children and to discuss how well they are meeting their targets. At the end, a summative report is issued and a second academic review day takes place to review progress to meeting targets and to help set targets for the following year. In this way, there is a constant dialogue between teacher and pupil and also between teacher and parent. One essential feature of such a system is the need for constant performance monitoring. Tutors are encouraged to withdraw one or two pupils each week to discuss individual progress throughout the year. They should record progress themselves and also in the pupils' homework planner. This document forms an essential part of the dialogue with parents and is comprehensive, containing much information. It is very successful and will be expanded next year. In a highly motivated school like ours, these methods are extremely successful. Parents appreciate knowing and understanding the performance of their children and the part they can play in trying to help them to succeed. I cannot, of course, say whether such a system would work in other schools. However, I have heard comments to suggest that it is applicable.

This newer system allowed us to adapt our predicted grade system so that forms of predicted grade are released from early in the GCSE course, becoming more refined as pupils progress through the course. We use the CAT system in the Year 9 to indicate to pupils the minimum target grade they should be working for in GCSE, and repeat the process in the sixth form using the ALIS system to identify potential A-level grades in each subject. Tutor work in the sixth form is more refined because the group size is smaller and there is more time available for tutors to discuss performance. Negotiated reporting is used three times a year on an internal basis and then sent home. Students are expected to assess their performance and discuss this with their teachers and jointly draw up suitable targets. The two heads of year can target specific individuals and in this way are aware of the problems students may be encountering. A far more adult attitude is taken and this was remarked upon by the OFSTED team. So far, this system has been a great success and has been identified by the students as contributing to their improved point score.

The results of these changes

The main obvious consequence of these changes has been a dramatic improvement in performance in examination results. GCSE grades have improved across the board. No pupil has left the school in the past two years without some success at GCSE, and most have at least five passes, probably due to marked intervention by our special needs department. GCSE higher-grade passes have improved considerably. Our pass rate for five higher-grade passes has improved from a steady figure of around 58 per cent to 70 per cent in three years and nearly half of the entries were at grade 'B' or higher in 1997. In addition, the number of grades 'A' or 'A*' reached nearly 20 per cent, good enough to get the school into all the national papers' league tables of good schools. We have regularly appeared at A-level but the lists favour selective 'comprehensive' schools and grammar schools. At A level, our average point score per candidate increased steadily from 15.0 to 18.1 and nearly 20 per cent of the candidates achieved 30 points or more.   ·

Performance increases are seen not just at GCSE and A-level. Pupils taking the SAT examinations now regularly perform well above the national average, particularly in science and mathematics. This is all the more significant when it is realised that this performance has been achieved for pupils who were already performing at a high level at Key Stage 2, even though their general ability measured in CAT tests showed a national average performance. These results were highly commended by OFSTED.

It is not just in academic performance that these policies have paid dividends. Not surprisingly, perhaps, the number of applicants has doubled and the number of pupils admitted to the school has had to be increased. We have increased the opportunities that pupils have to take responsibility. We have introduced a school council to give pupils a voice and they take their duties very seriously – the level of debate is high and sometimes we find their conclusions rather unpalatable. Year 8 pupils are used as receptionists in the foyer and visitors to the school never fail to remark on their courteousness.

Finally, tremendous efforts have been made by the team to raise the profile of the school and to generate more funds. We work in partnership with several companies and institutions on a variety of projects. We gained Language College Status two years ago and acquired a new Astroturf pitch in conjunction with Broxbourne Council. The total now stands at nearly £2 million raised to provide more buildings and facilities over a six-year period. The key is to ensure that sight is firmly maintained of the purpose of these efforts, which is to increase the opportunities for our pupils to love learning. I was pleased when the 1997 OFSTED inspectors highly praised the school and the achievements we have made in the past three years.

Still to be done

There is still much to be done. Our tutors recognise their importance in the system and carry out their mentoring duties diligently. Our pupils value the time the tutors spend with them and the help they give. The assembly withdrawal time is still new and is variable in its effectiveness. Where it is applied properly, it is valued by the pupils but, as with all change, it takes time to be absorbed properly.

All change goes through a cycle. There will always be initial resistance and anger, followed by depression before letting go and starting to rationalise and accept the change, and the length of this cycle will vary from person to person. As Michael Fullan (1993) puts it:

> Change is ubiquitous and relentless, forcing itself upon us at every turn. At the same time, the secret of growth and development is learning how to contend with the forces of change – turning positive forces to our advantage, while blunting negative ones.

This process of change has not been easy. It has demanded much time and effort and a degree of tolerance from us all. There have been many times when the level of resistance has appeared too high, mostly because the demands of the timescale we were operating, was too short. You have to retain the vision and make sure you keep on track. So much of what we were planning was interdependent and, until it was fully in place and embedded, its effectiveness could not be judged or appreciated. We have made mistakes because some of our innovations have been brought in too quickly without thinking through the implications fully enough. However, I do believe that you have to force change; that it cannot wait and that a reengineering approach was really needed if we were to effect the sort of change that we wanted, as was shown in several articles by Davies and West-Burnham (1997). The 1997 OFSTED inspection team has evaluated the processes we have gone through and the results we have obtained. They were greatly impressed with the improvements we had made.

The A-level results are not yet as good as the GCSE results would predict. Evidence from the recent inspection shows that we are adding considerable value up to GCSE but this drops off in the sixth form, where performance is at the national average in most subjects. It is clear from the analysis done by OFSTED that the teaching still remains too teacher-directed, and there are not yet enough opportunities for independent learning to develop.

We have significantly raised pupil performance, but it is probably at a price at the moment. Pupils are achieving higher results and teachers are more aware of their performance and how to help pupils. The pressure placed on teachers to get results, both nationally through league tables and in the high levels of focus placed in the school, may have led them to concentrate too much on the 'syllabus' and the need to deliver the 'correct' answer. There may not be sufficient time for teachers to explore new ideas, and the pressure on them to perform may, of itself, militate against experimentation. The hardest part will be to change teachers' attitudes to their teaching. To effect fundamental change in the way people act takes much longer than mere structural change. We will continue to develop our model of peer observation of good practice and increase the focus on learning objectives and developing skills. We need to focus our attention on more research-based and exploratory learning, in which there is more discussion and group work. We will retain our major focus on learning and moving towards a learning organisation, and we will be working with the Cambridge Institute on the IQEA project (to improve the quality of education for all), focusing on developing these independent learning skills. We will need to relax our drive for ever-higher performance at GCSE in favour of developing more thinking skills in the lower school. In the long run, our pupils will be better able to cope and to apply their knowledge to new situations. This is a higher-order skill and, ultimately, should be reflected in much better performance at A-level. At any rate, the resultant skills they will acquire will better serve them in the 21st century and, ultimately, that is what it is all supposed to be about.

References

Davies, B. and West-Burnham, J. (1997) *Reengineering and Total Quality in Schools.* London, Pitman Publishing.

Fullan, M. (1993) *Changing Forces: Probing the Depths of Educational Reform*, London, The Falmer Press.

Hopkins, D. (1994) *The Yellow Brick Road*, Cambridge Institute of Education Reports 3, 6, pp. 14–17.

West-Burnham, J. (1997) *Managing Quality in Schools*, London, Pitman Publishing.

Part 2 – Reflection and review

■ ■ ■

1 How aware are you of the social, economic and technological trends challenging our notion of what constitutes an educated person?

2 How much review, analysis, monitoring, is actually taking place in school?

3 Do you have appropriate policies covering the central issues of learning, achievement and teaching strategies?

4 What is your strategic view of the changes that will be needed in learning, the curriculum, methods of assessment and the nature of educational outcomes?

5 Is your school designed (i.e. time, space and resources) to facilitate learning?

6 What is the key rationale for the organisational structure of your school?

7 Are the school's vision, values, aims, mission, known and understood by every member of the school community?

8 Are you leading for improvement or managing for stability?

9 How do you define achievement?

10 How do you celebrate achievement?

PART 3

■ ■ ■

Learning and teaching strategies

This section focuses on our understanding of what we mean by learning. The case studies present often highly personal accounts of changes in understanding and, importantly, the actions that followed. In a number of vital ways the strategies and processes that are described represent radical departures from a range of norms. Yet in every case they are shown to be practical and possible, given belief, energy and commitment.

10
■ ■ ■

Reengineering the classroom

DR STEVEN DAVIS

Abstract

In considering strategies to introduce the concepts of reengineering into the classroom, I first look at a definition of the term. I feel that the word reengineering is too closely associated with the management of businesses to sit comfortably in the educational world. I therefore attempt a definition of reengineering which retains its essence and spirit, but which is more conducive to an educational milieu. This definition is then augmented by reference to the reengineering project – the Pride (professionalism results in demonstrable excellence) Project – at Sydney Smith School in Hull.

The body of the paper is divided into three parts, which deal principally with the ways the Pride Project impinges on the classroom. The first part examines the reengineering of the classroom within the broader, school-wide reengineering context. I argue that it is impossible to reengineer the classroom without reengineering other aspects of the school which are associated with the classroom. In fact, reengineering the classroom is possible only as part of a broader reengineering activity. The second section of the paper looks at aspects of the classroom that can be reengineered. Although some of this discussion is theoretical, much rests on either practical example or the direct implications of practical example. The aim here is to show how reengineering principles can be used to add value. Finally, I look at the issue of empowerment, which needs to be considered if the practical reengineering of the classroom is to take place.

Although the paper aims to make some firm recommendations about reengineering the classroom, it is to be remembered that it is still an interim effort. The work of reengineering, by its nature, goes on, and to this end no closing statements can ever truly be made.

Reengineering as an educational concept

Reengineering can be conveniently defined as the fundamental and radical redesign of processes to achieve dramatic improvement in critical measures of importance. This definition leans heavily on the work of Champy and Hammer (1993), as do many of reengineering's fundamental concepts and approaches. It is to be remembered, however, that this seminal text was written for particular application to business and manufacturing processes. It is, consequently, more difficult to apply concepts found in these areas, such as 'selling' and 'customers', to an educational environment. It seems to me that if we are to apply reengineering successfully to education, we need at first to give it a broader basis, which allows education to more easily interpret and inculcate its concepts. The process of reengineering at Sydney Smith School has, in its early stages, involved thinking about the theoretical aspects of reengineering as much as actually applying it in practice. To this end, I found post-modern thought, captured in the works of someone like Jacques Derrida, as particularly useful. Certain tenets of post-modernism clearly relate to reengineering; in fact, I feel it would not be stretching a point too far to say that reengineering is post-modernism applied to management. This idea was discussed generally by Bowring-Carr and West-Burnham (1997, p. 41), but I wish to be more specific here since my interpretation of reengineering is critical to its acceptance by teachers, pupils and parents. There follows, therefore, an attempt to derive an educational paradigm which is both comfortable and relevant:

- Both post-modernism and reengineering assume a holistic rather than a reductionist view of the world. Both quite clearly see that it is impossible to break down items into a series of discrete pieces or blocks. Instead, borders between the constituents of a system are vague. The concept of task orientation, which sees processes as a neat set of repetitive jobs, is not valid either in post-modernism or reengineering. To take this issue further, the distinction and boundaries between activities *must* be blurred if they are not already. Champy and Hammer (1993), see this as the fundamental process of reengineering, in that the blurring of boundaries leads to a process rather than task orientation. In post-modernism, the move to blur distinctions and dualities can be thought of as the basis of deconstruction. See, for example, Derrida, J. (1993):

To put old names to work ... involves some risk: the risk of setting down, or regressing into a system that has been, or is in the process of being, deconstructred. (p. 5)

Inscribed within dissemination is precisely the impossibility of reducing a text as such to the effects of meaning, content, thesis or theme. (p. 7)

Two texts are transformed, deform each other, contaminate each other's content, tend at times to reject each other, or pass elliptically one into the other and become regenerated in repetition, along the edges of an overcast seam. (p. 355)

The trace that implies both its mark and its erasure. (p. 5)

- The activity of deliberately obscuring boundaries tends to make systems more ambiguous, an ambiguity which needs to be fostered, especially by the acceptance that opposites can co-exist. This is only accepting the inevitable: that some measure of ambiguity and paradox is endemic to all groups and group decision-making. (Davis, 1995, pp. 225–6). This creativity also expresses itself in the recombination of ideas and activities into new structures and processes.

- Within post-modern thought, participants both interpret and are affected by the things that happen around them. See, for example, Derrida, J. (1978, p. 11):

Meaning must await being said or written in order to inhabit itself, and in order to become, by differing from itself, what it is: meaning.

These interpretations are essentially local and personal, having validity only within individuals and the groups they comprise. This leads to the development by individuals and groups of specific solutions to specific problems, an approach particularly appropriate to education which, of all the professions, is the most influenced by localism – the teacher alone with a class in a classroom for a given period of time. Grand theories and structures can tend to founder on this simple truth, the essentially isolated nature of education, a truth which educationalists tend to forget. The emphasis on individual empowerment – to solve local problems in a specific way, and to react to the environment subjectively – is a keynote of both post-modernism and reengineering. They both, in this sense, emphasise the need for interpretative cultures (Bowring-Carr and West-Burnham,1997, p. 42). By these, I mean groups where individuals explore the environment subjectively, then share and define the outcome of this exploration with others in the group, and in ways relevant to the group. It is necessary, consequently, for each school to define what it means by education, assessment, value-added, acceptable behaviour, and so on; to question the hidden or tacitly accepted assumptions which underpin educational debate. In this way, concepts which survive scrutiny gain validity: in a post-modern sense they become *legitimised.*

My approach to reengineering the classroom is essentially, therefore, to deconstruct it in post-modern terms. The result is an approach which is bullet-pointed here, and which I shall explain more fully in the rest of this paper:

103

- the classroom must be part of a holistic school environment and its processes, not a separate entity
- the classroom must become an ambiguous, creative environment where pupils and teachers are encouraged to ask questions and put ideas together in new ways
- there must be a blurring of distinctions and boundaries
- classroom reengineering must be an interpretative activity, where concepts are defined and legitimised, and the processes of education clearly understood by all
- all participants must be changed by their experiences in the classroom – they must have value added to them.

It is equally important to understand that post-modernism and reengineering do not imply wishy-washiness. Indeed, the above will not be achieved by some vague commitment to try harder, talk more or let it all hang out. The attempts to achieve the above at Sydney Smith School rest on practical reform, based on the manipulation of familiar school items – timetable, resource provision, information and communication technology) (ICT) packages and so on. Within the realms of these concrete, practical items lies true success, their application and importance being enhanced when they are given justification and coherence within a framework of engineering.

The classroom in context

Reengineering processes should either directly add value, or contribute to a process that directly adds value. In the case of schools, we have one direct process, the educational one. The others should terminate their outcomes in this main process, and may be called administrative processes, in that they support the direct process. Teachers are principally responsible for the educational process, managers and administrators for the administrational processes. In order to make this situation apparent, it is essential that an analysis of the school's processes be undertaken.

Such an analysis quickly makes it clear whether a particular process adds value by supporting the educational process within the classroom. Any process which does not terminate in the classroom should either be discarded, or reengineered so that it does. Any proposed 'improvements' can be evaluated in these terms. For example, several thousand pounds can be spent on computer equipment, which might improve certain people's working conditions or increase their output. If, however, this improvement or increase does not contribute to added value in the classroom, then the money is wasted. Without some kind of systems analysis, it becomes very difficult to decide how improvement can be brought to bear on the classroom, or even if it is justified. Without a process diagram, therefore, plentiful change can be introduced without in any way ensuring that the classroom has adequate support or resources. Change, in this case, easily becomes tinkering, not reengineering.

A process analysis also gives a positive embodiment to the spirit of re-engineering. The processes should be thought of as giving our ideals, feelings and desires a concrete shape. If we cannot demonstrate that our wants are represented by actual processes, then these wants become mere platitudes. If, for example, we say that 'our first concern is for the chil-dren', our processes should reflect and enable that statement. Further, a well-constructed and meaningful process diagram can provide a positive manifesto for reform, by emphasising the centrality of the classroom and value-addedness, and showing how change takes place within the context of a few major processes, rather than within the ambit of a large number of bewildering, disparate and often contradictory tasks.

Once the process analysis has been constructed, it is important to publish it. Methods of achieving this may vary, but I opted for a formal input within a training day. Not only did I publicise the analysis, I also used the opportunity to clearly indicate the vision and mission of reengineering, the Pride Project. I cannot emphasise enough the importance of sharing these sorts of ideas with both teaching and non-teaching staff. Everyone must see the point of reengineering before the reengineering of specifics, such as the classroom, can be undertaken. I also produced papers for those who wished to know more: 'Reengineering explained'; 'Reengineering and the role of management;' 'Reengineering at Sydney Smith'. The thrust of these papers, and the training day input generally, was to show that all aspects of the school's purpose and organisation were available for consideration and reform. My particular concern was to emphasise the need for the removal of as many administrative tasks from teachers as possible, in order for them to be free to work to the best of their ability in the classroom; to allow them to promote ambiguous, testing, creative environments. Again, the central-ity of the classroom, and the teacher's role as the adder of value, was emphasised. Likewise, the *raison d'être* of administration was seen to be its support of the classroom: administration had no independent life of its own. A clear-cut route to reengineering and adding value was, therefore, indicated by the process diagram and my preparatory talk – that is, teach-ing goes to teachers, administration goes to administrators.

Reengineering classroom processes

I shall consider several aspects of classroom reengineering. These relate to the items I discussed in the introduction. The aspects are:

- the overt commitment to value-addedness by the use of target setting and monitoring based on clearly identified items of data
- the deliberate blurring of boundaries
- the removal of unnecessary administration by the 'fire and forget' principle
- the conscious decision to create opportunities for communication, interpretation and sharing
- the importance of ICT and the development of the information-rich environment.

The overt commitment to value-addedness by the use of target setting and monitoring based on clearly identified items of data. Once one becomes involved in reengineering in an educational milieu, it soon becomes obvious that its principal tenet – that everything is up for grabs and open for discussion – is not actually viable. Schools and teachers have to operate within a series of givens that circumscribe change. An example of this is in the proposed statutory provision of targets for schools and authorities. Whether we agree with target-setting or not, we will have to do (or perhaps 'undergo') it. I feel, however, that legal requirement or authority policy is not an item to derail reengineering, but to challenge it. We should want to reengineer the things we are forced to do into items that will benefit us: into things that we want to do. Target setting is a good example. Although we are obliged to set targets, I feel we should also welcome this obligation. The thrust of the target-setting initiative is to base targets on objective data, such as cognitive ability tests or standard national test scores (*see* SCAA, 1997). An examination of these scores can tend to indicate future attainment at GCSE (SCAA, 1997). Further, these scores tend to subsume into them factors such as attendance and socio-economic background, so that a pupil's future attainment, as time goes on, becomes more closely indicated by their prior attainment (SCAA, 1997). I accept that this issue is open to debate, and many teachers will claim that the indefinables and subjectives (such as the pupil's background and attitudes, their attentiveness and presentation) all affect outcome. This may be so, but work I have been involved in within my own authority shows a strong correlation, across the authority, between prior attainment and future attainment. Further, the project at Durham University, which has resulted in the YELLIS test, and work of NFER with its QUASE information, again supports the view that attainment can be largely predicted by prior attainment alone. To this end, we are instituting a procedure at Sydney Smith where all classroom teachers are provided with prior attainment scores for their pupils. As algorithms for prediction become more refined, these will be converted into targets for each pupil in each subject.

The point of this activity might not be obvious, but I see it as a key issue in classroom reengineering – a sort of *sine qua non*. First, prior attainment scores (for example, CATs or SNTs) with their associated targets provide a basis for grouping or setting. I am aware, again, that I am entering a controversial area. After debating the issue at Sydney Smith, however, we came to the conclusion that no one – teacher or pupil – was best served by teaching or being taught in a class of 30 that might contain a CAT spread from, say, 75 to 125 (which some classes did before we began to group). Further, by introducing more tightly banded groups, it became possible to set realistic targets for the group. In this way, it is gradually becoming possible to make a teacher of a class accountable for that class's success. This attribution of accountability is an issue I have discussed above (and will discuss in more detail later) and is a fundamental tenet of reengineering, in that it makes people question their activities and to be more creative in achieving their goals – it *empowers* them. The derivation of targets based on hard data become a way of challenging and empowering the teacher in the same way. More importantly, and to my mind crucially, target setting by prior attainment data also challenges and empowers the pupil. Too often, I feel, pupil achievement becomes a self-fulfilling prophecy. Once we began, at Sydney Smith, to consider Year 7 CAT data as a basis for grouping (in Year 9), it became obvious that several pupils with ability had begun to languish during Key Stage 3. Their lack of effort or self-esteem, which resulted in poor classwork and achievement, had tended to result in them finding themselves in lower groups. This tended to reaffirm their lack of self-esteem, so their achievement deteriorated more. The issue became even more prominent in Year 11, where several pupils underachieved in their GCSEs in relation to their prior attainment in SNTs and CATs. I realise, of course, that with that statement I leave myself open to the rejoinder that perhaps prior attainment scores are not a good basis for prediction. I would turn that argument on its head and reply that if, conversely, prior attainment is a good basis for prediction, what is happening in the classroom to prevent pupils achieving their potential? *That* is the reengineering question, a question I prefer to a resigned belief in our inability to predict future scores. And even if prior attainment isn't a good predictor but its consideration makes teachers think about their responsibilities, makes pupils think about theirs, and opens a general educational debate, then it serves a purpose.

Within a week or two of writing this paper I will be asking curriculum leaders to explain why certain of their pupils did not achieve the GCSE grade indicated by their scores in CATs and SNTs. In some cases, the answer might genuinely be that the pupil did not do what was required of him or her. I hope, as well, that the answer will be that, in some cases, the teacher did not enable the pupil's learning thoroughly or explicitly enough. From this kind of honest debate we can begin to reform the class-room – the teaching and learning that goes on there – to better allow the pupils to achieve their potential. I would argue, therefore, that in the first instance target setting, the review of targets met, and a clear accountability on the part of teachers to meet targets are an integral part of the process of classroom improvement. From this, there will naturally and expediently evolve a debate on issues germane to raising achievement – homework and marking policy, the nature of setting and grouping, ways of creating the appropriate learning environment, and so on.

The deliberate blurring of boundaries. It is not enough to begin to make teachers accountable and then assume that a whole raft of reforms will be introduced into the classroom. I believe it is also the responsibility of man-agers to proactively reengineer aspects of the classroom. In particular, managers should try to make a process out of education rather than the set of discrete tasks – subject specialisms – it can tend to be now. This is achieved by blurring the distinctions between subjects in three ways: the introduction of classrooms where the common factor is the teacher and pupils, not the subject; the reduction of the divide between subject and subject, teacher and parent, and pupil and parent in terms of the setting and completion of homework; the introduction of pupil mentoring.

At Sydney Smith we introduced in the (academic year 1997/8) the Year 7 Programme, a change in the way we teach and manage our new-intake pupils. Its principal aim is to break down the distinctions between subjects by placing pupils in a single tutor/teaching group which will be taught by the same teacher for much of the week. In other words, the programme continues what the pupils have experienced throughout their primary school years. The reasons for introducing this system – for reengineering our approach to teaching Year 7 – are worthy of consideration in that they show the benefits that reengineering can potentially bestow. First, we wanted to introduce this system quite candidly to copy what had gone on in primary schools. Like many urban schools, we have to attract pupils and are in competition with many nearby comprehensives. Discussion with parents revealed that the move to the 'big' school (1150+ pupils) from a primary school of perhaps 200 pupils was intimidating for both children and parents. This seemed to outweigh a potential concern that we had as teachers that pupils and parents might want, by Key Stage 3, the provision of an education which would bring specialist teaching to bear. This concern was unwarranted, since pupils and parents voted with their feet. From a predicted entry of 214 we achieved 248, necessitating the employment of a member of staff and an increase to nine forms on entry instead of eight. All requests for transfer by those parents/pupils who were allocated Sydney Smith School but wanted to go elsewhere have since been dropped as the pupils have experienced the new situation.

It would be unfair to attribute the introduction of the Year 7 Programme in any great way to the need to increase pupil numbers. In fact, this was a secondary concern. Our greater interest was to consider the education of pupils in reengineering terms. At stake was one of the sacred cows of secondary education and secondary teaching: the supposed self-evident benefit of teaching one's specialism and being taught by a specialist. We believed this self-evident truth was a chimera, and in fact prevented the introduction into the classroom of educationally more desirable factors to do with pastoral care, continuity, resourcing, behaviour modification, accountability and access to the pupils. We considered that the welfare of pupils was better catered for by a teacher who sees them for most of the week, rather than by a selection of subject teachers and a personal tutor, all of whom see their pupils for only a comparatively short time at periodic intervals. This teacher can provide continuity in support, teaching styles and classroom expectation, obviating the need for pupils to accommodate to several different personalities and approaches. Within this continuity, the single teacher can see, emphasise and articulate the skills which connect different subject disciplines, and enable these connections with cross-subject project work. A wide range of resources can be centred on the classroom, rather than being dispersed between individual curriculum areas. In this way, pupils always have access to pens, pencil, paper, glue, scissors, and so on. Each base room also contains a small library and, in some cases, a computer. Where possible, a furnished area is given over for quiet reading. Most importantly, pupils have a place to leave their bags, possessions and books. It has been of great sadness for me to see, over the years, the decline in secondary schools of personal space for pupils, even if it was only a locker. It seems now that the personal space has been reduced to a bag, which the pupil works out of all day. This, I suspect, is a result of the fact that all rooms have become specialist rooms, and pupils move to them. Also, the need to secure personal space for pupils in what are otherwise public areas – cloakrooms, corridors, and so on – has become prohibitively high. The baseroom, which can be locked when not in use and is not used by others, has reasserted the pupils' right to unassailed personal space.

The most useful outcome of the Year 7 Programme has been the removal of the problem of access to pupils. Whereas pupils in the departmental structure can be anywhere on the school site, Year 7 pupils are now mostly to be found in one place. Further, one person is responsible for them, and sees them enough to make that accountability a practical item: too often we make a personal or form tutor responsible for a group of children when they might never actually teach the group, and see them for such a small portion of the school day that they are really not able to distribute praise, follow up problems and ameliorate behaviour. Further, the Year 7 teacher has to worry about only 30 pupils. At the other extreme, a single-lesson subject teacher, such as an RE teacher, might teach more than 700 pupils within a week.

The issue of specialisms, as we expected, has largely resolved itself. We deliberately decided to start the present year's timetable during the summer term, thus allowing the putative Year 7 teachers to be off the timetable for six weeks. This gave them plenty of opportunity to prepare work. We also ensured that every subject specialism was represented by at least one teacher in the group, so that the right kind of input and leadership was given for each area of the curriculum represented. In the end, it was decided to include in the Year 7 core every subject taught in Key Stage 3 with the exception of technology and PE, which were excluded for reasons of health and safety, and modern languages, art and music, which were excluded because they were too specialist for the teachers in the programme. Once the course has worked itself through for one year, its teachers will be much more proficient in a number of subjects. They can, consequently, either rejoin the Year 7 Programme next year, or move with their pupils into a proposed Year 8 Programme. This will begin in the next academic year for the present Year 7s, and will be almost the same, although some subjects will be removed, for example, science. Gradually the need for Year 7 and Year 8 teachers to imbibe new subject specialisms will decline as they teach through the programmes. The school has also introduced a policy of appointing, where appropriate, teachers of general subjects rather than subject specialists.

The blurring of boundaries is to be further promulgated by the proposed reengineering of homework. Homework is to be set with the objective of involving parents by providing them with a half-term's list of homework activities in advance. In this way, parents are encouraged to enquire whether the work is completed or, more proactively, to set it from their list. Some homework tasks include, for their completion, help from parents. This approach obviously renders inadequate the present approach to homework which tends to be set by teachers piecemeal, and may often consist of completing work begun in the lesson. The new approach implies homework tasks which have a life of their own, lasting for several weeks at a time. Once this type of homework, planned well in advance, is accepted, there is no reason for it to be related to, or set by, individual teachers. This approach enables cross-curricular homework involving a number of subjects, again blurring the boundaries between areas of the curriculum. Perhaps the clinching argument for the development of such a strategy is that it also blurs the divide – the generation gap – between child and parent. Parents have indicated that they would be thankful for any opportunities to be able to talk productively to, and work productively with, their children at a time when adolescence continually drives them apart. In some senses the parent becomes the teacher, which is again a blurring of distinctions.

For several years, Sydney Smith School has, with varying degrees of success, used a mentoring scheme for Year 11. This has taken the form of senior managers and pastoral heads working with four to eight pupils each: to discuss their progress, to work with them on action planning and revision, and to nag them about attendance and completion of coursework. The target pupils have tended to be conscientious ones to ensure they stay on task, and pupils who are capable of achievement but are not aspiring to it. The success of this system has varied according to the ability of mentors to create quality time with their charges, a problem when managing several. Our concerns over inconsistent examination success in relation to prior attainment, which has now become evident with our work on the relevant data, has driven us to a more radical solution. The target group of pupils will remain the same – pupils who are doing well but must not be allowed to slip and pupils who should be doing better. This generally generates a group of about 60. The intention this year is that quality mentoring in time and attention will be enabled by each individual member of staff (again about 60) becoming a mentor to a single pupil. As with our general policy in reengineering, this personal mentor will acquire some measure of accountability for their pupil's success.

Obviously, the single teacher cannot hope to cover all the specialisms which a pupil undertakes during a GCSE course, and it is important for me to emphasise that our commitment to blurring subject boundaries peters out in Key Stage 3. By Key Stage 4, all pupils are taught by specialists in the conventional way. However, the teacher will provide a cross-subject component to a pupil's study, and allow him or her to discuss their progress in general, rather than in particular. In this way, it is hoped that the mentor can provide balance to study, encouraging pupils to prioritise, concentrating in their turn on the subjects which have upcoming coursework or revision deadlines. Likewise, the personal mentor can ensure that a balanced and far-reaching revision programme takes place, which emphasises the centrality of systematic learning and practice in an examination system still dominated by the examination paper. Finally, the mentor has the authority with his or her colleagues to clear up problems arising in lessons during the course of the year, and to nag colleagues about the need to provide practice examination papers and regular homework.

The removal of unnecessary administration by the 'fire and forget' principle. A few years ago we reengineered (although we did not think of it in those terms) the registration system in school, replacing the old blue handwritten registers with an optical mark system. The benefits of this system became quickly apparent, as teachers completed their registers, returned them to the school office, then forgot about them. They did not return for counting, checking, cross-checking against other attendance information, and so on. Any information required about attendance was stored on the computer network and available to all staff. I christened this the 'fire and forget' principle: a piece of administration was quickly and easily completed, then did not keep returning to haunt the teacher.

Unfortunately, educational administration can easily turn into an elaborate game of pass the parcel, as items are copied, passed, checked, duplicated, rechecked, mailed, and so on. A classic case of such administration in schools is the reporting system, where there is an elaborate procedure for teachers to handwrite comments, which are then collated for each pupil, usually by the personal tutor who then adds another comment. The whole set is checked with further comments added by the pastoral head or deputy. Worse, all this often happens independently of the school's assessment procedure, which collects National Curriculum grades, GCSE predicted grades and other curriculum material, usually by another complex procedure. We tinkered with the procedure by introducing computer-based comment banks a couple of years ago. This relieved some of the strain of reporting by removing the physical task of writing, but left the process problems untouched.

It is our intention this year again to apply the 'fire and forget' principle. Assessment data, which will provide the basis of the school assessment database and the parental report will be captured by optical mark reader sheets. Having handed these in, the teacher forgets them. The sheets are read centrally, being collated by a computer assessment package which makes every pupil's scores available on the network. The scores will also be attached to a comment bank, which will evoke comments that can be compiled into a parental report, putting our data into a readable and easily digestible form. In this way, we can provide three or four reports a year, rather than the one we provide at present. The 'fire and forget' principle, which can be applied in several areas, removes the burden of administration from the teacher and places it on to ICT. The teacher is freed to teach, the administration goes to administration.

The conscious decision to create opportunites for communication, interpretation and sharing. The key to the success of classroom reengineering is the ability to produce a continuous succession of new approaches to teaching and learning. It is tempting to look outside of school for these ideas, bringing in consultants or trainers, or sending staff on Inset. I would not belittle these devices, but it struck me several years ago that the best source of new ideas in any particular school is the teaching staff. The relationship to post-modernism here is in the belief in the essentially local nature of structure and decision making, and the need to develop an interpretative culture. Since, therefore, the teaching and non-teaching staff of Sydney Smith School probably possess between them all the strategies, skills and knowledge necessary to allow Sydney Smith pupils to succeed, the challenge for the school is to enable these pieces of individual skill and knowledge to be made freely available to all. To this end, we instigated three-weekly staff meetings which were both training sessions and sharings, and whose input came from the staff themselves.

It is fair to say that the success of these gatherings has been patchy. On the whole, formal input or presentation has been well received, and has made some impact. For instance, the rewriting of the school classroom code in affirmation rather than imperative style was implemented and greeted with enthusiasm. Attempts at sharing, however, where individual teachers would talk for up to five minutes on a particular classroom strategy that worked well for them, has not had a great impact, even though a compilation of suggestions was given to all. As we have embarked on reengineering, however, the need for such meetings is becoming increasingly apparent. Although we persist in the sorts of normal cycles of meetings which most schools use – pastoral, faculty, SEN, IT, and so on – I feel that the need for a much looser structure is indicated, and particularly to call the whole staff together regularly. I also envisage the nature of these meetings changing, becoming more polarised as individual empowerment increases.

This last aspect of reengineering – its dialectic and argumentativeness – is emphasised by research in the USA on schools that have gained increasing control of their management (*see* Rinehart *et al*, 1997, p. 80). If reengineering has this concomitant combativeness, then the need for regular meetings becomes even more necessary. Only by open discussion and dialogue can polarities be eventually resolved. I see the issue of forums and meetings as a vital area for development and consideration, and a key to the successful reengineering of the classroom by the eventual production of a continuous stream of new ideas, acting upon each other and resolving into further change. To this end, it is my intention to do away with the present meetings pattern next term by placing the scheduling of meetings in the hands of an administrator who will book rooms, distribute agendas, distribute papers and so on, at the request of anyone wishing to call a meeting. Instead of a fixed yearly rota, there will be a flexible meetings calendar operating about a fortnight in advance, and scheduled to avoid calling and pressurising individual staff too often.

The importance of ICT and the development of the information-rich environment. It is impossible to overestimate the application of ICT to reengineering activity. Not only does the use of ICT allow the construction of administrational systems which free teachers from much of the paperwork that presently dogs them, but it also allows the development of the curriculum in the direction of what Bowring-Carr and West-Burnham (1997, pp. 61–66) call the 'information-rich' environment. The assumption that underpins traditional classroom practice is that information is severely restricted, contained in a few expensive textbooks or, more fundamentally, in the head of the teacher. Much classroom activity is centred on transferring this information, by copying, into an exercise book which the pupil can then take away and study or memorise. This approach leaves little time for discussion, or the development of skills which allow the acquisition of information independently by pupils. As information becomes increasingly available – the classroom environment becomes information-rich – the traditional approach becomes increasingly inappropriate. The emphasis in classrooms inevitably changes from the provision of knowledge to the development within pupils of the skills necessary to acquire and assimilate knowledge for themselves.

Two examples from Sydney Smith, from opposite ends of the information milieu, illustrate what I mean. Our head of science recently purchased a full-colour revision textbook for chemistry which costs £2. It covers all the work needed to cover the chemistry component of the GCSE Double Award science syllabus. He observed that it was as cheap as an exercise book and its provision to each child would allow his staff to concentrate on reviewing and demonstrating the information and ideas behind it, rather than getting the pupils to copy it. Reengineering here consists of questioning, in a fundamental way, present classroom practice. We have also been approached by a company which provides a 'video on demand' service to act as a pilot school. This will allow pupils and teachers to browse through any amount of educational material, stored on a large network processor and brought to the school on ordinary telephone landlines. Further, by the use of a cheap digital video camera, we can manufacture our own material – videoed lessons, records of field-trips, and so on – which both pupils and staff can call up and review at any time. Although this service will at present be restricted to our school site, the prospect of the company extending the service to the local area opens up the possibility of a consortium of schools providing for their pupils a sort of 'open school', where lesson materials would be videoed and available to all. In this sense, the classroom could be reengineered to extend right into the homes of pupils, and their parents.

Legitimising educational reform

It is tempting to argue that the sorts of reforms outlined in this paper will not be countenanced; that legislation, LEA *diktat* or media pressure will prevent them actually taking place. My first, simplistic answer to this objection is that most of the items mentioned here have actually been introduced at Sydney Smith, as well as, presumably, at many other schools. My second answer to the objection raises the more fundamental question of legitimisation: of what makes something acceptable and capable of actual introduction. Again, this is an issue that concerns post-modern thought. The answer to the question of legitimisation lies at the heart of the basic tenet of reengineering – that anything is acceptable providing it achieves the required outcome, and is acceptable to the people who have to manage it. In other words, legitimisation lies at the level of the workforce in its place of work, not at some remote centre of bureaucratic activity or in a structured, *ex officio* stratum of management. In a very real sense, schools decide what is appropriate for them to do in order to develop their pupils in the classroom, and what is successful here is also legitimate.

Of course, this legitimisation is easier said than done, since it implies a conscious effort on the part of staff, parents, pupils and governors to interpret the school's putative culture and reach a consensus on it, an issue for communication and forum organisation I have discussed above. As important is the necessity for schools to make it clear that legitimisation in this local sense is not an excuse for 'please yourself'. In fact, I would argue strongly that quite the reverse is appropriate; that schools need to be meticulous in laying down clear expectations and outcomes, and making staff accountable for them. The area for personal creativity, development and job satisfaction lies in ways of achieving these. I think of empowerment (often a nebulous and ill-defined concept in education) as precisely this process of creating a free space within tightly prescribed boundaries. Since I think this type of empowerment is crucial to reengineering the classroom, I will explain more precisely what I mean.

At Sydney Smith, we refer to the non-negotiables – the boundaries – as 'bottom lines'. These are expectations, targets, outcomes and responses. They serve two purposes:

- They help the organisation or a particular group within it to move in a particular direction, by laying down statements about expectations and goals. Without these, a school would drift in any direction it chose, and might end up neither discharging its legal obligations nor growing and developing into a successful institution.
- They provide a constraint which enhances ambiguity, creativity and dissonance reduction within individuals. In other words, they pressurise individuals into action, without so controlling their lives that they lose creative independence and simply do as they are told.

Bottom lines are therefore vital to an empowering approach to management, in that they drive the school in both its motion and direction – the two meanings of the word 'drive'. Empowerment is enabled by this drive. Its ethos is one of muscularity and clear-headedness, not wishy-washiness. It is a 'tough love' system, aiming to improve the school by making individuals manifest the best of themselves, and thus to develop their self-esteem and independence of thought. It teaches the school and its member to stand on their own two feet. And it relies ultimately on this paradoxical truism: true freedom lies in restraint. It encourages what Bowring-Carr and West-Burnham (1997, p. 28) refer to as deep learning:

A change in behaviour, a change in the way the learner sees the world, a change in the reality which that learner is continuously creating.

The key to designing an empowered system is for managers, at any level of the school hierarchy, to design bottom lines which drive the system without stifling it. The successful construction of bottom lines is a key to the successful implementation of empowerment. For them to be successful they must, above all else, be easy to assert. We must, consequently, ensure the following:

- bottom lines should be written so that they are clearly understood
- bottom lines should be easily assessable, for example, within a few minutes of entering a classroom

- they should be common to many different locations and situations, so that comparisons can be drawn between different times and places, and with notions of good practice
- they should, if possible, be quantifiable, again to facilitate comparison
- they should penetrate, and pressurise, many areas. In this way, individuals are forced into action, and the school is moved forward.

This emphasis on quantitative measurement and accessibility can be criticised on the basis that we will therefore tend to set bottom lines which deal with what is easily found or observed rather than with what is meaningful and appropriate but more difficult to apprehend or measure. I would argue that we have no choice but to measure what is available and measurable, not what is hidden or esoteric. Too often, in education, we try to capture the wordy, high-flown or philosophical in goals or objectives which are themselves wordy, high-flown or philosophical – laudable but impossible to perceive or judge in a practical way. The net result is that we have high ideals but no monitoring. Please note that I am not denying the place of the high-flown or the ideal. What I am saying is that the ideal must be translated into a set of concrete outcomes which can actually be observed and measured; in fact, the art of management, as I see, is to take the ideal and render it tangible. When we demand to see evidence of these concrete outcomes, then we are setting bottom lines by my definition. For instance, suppose we wanted to encourage classrooms where progress is the norm. Two bottom lines might be:

- individuals are valued;
- work is valued by being displayed.

I would argue that the second is a bottom line in that it is easily assessed during even the briefest of visits to the classroom; it is a characteristic of a classroom which can be compared with other classrooms or with the same classroom over time; it is measurable in its quality and extent; it pressurises pupils to produce quality work and teachers to assess it and display it. It makes a demand on individuals, since it is obvious that it is relatively easy for any visitor to see that it is being pursued. This bottom line contains within itself, therefore, both a challenge and the means to enforce that challenge. The first bottom line, on the other hand, is of a much more common sort, but is not so easy to assess, measure or compare in a short time. Individuals perceiving it can quickly assume that it cannot be easily enforced because the ways of judging its being adhered to are, by their very nature, subjective and nebulous. Except in the most obvious and acute areas of interpersonal breakdown, it would be very difficult for a manager to marshal enough incontrovertible evidence to show that individuals were not valued. I am not arguing against this as a classroom aim, since it is obviously laudable and worthwhile, but I would place this, at my philosophical, not at my bottom line, level.

What we need to do with a statement like this is to ask the question: 'How would this ideal, if it were being achieved, manifest itself in the classroom in a way that I can see, measure and compare?' Of course, the answer in this case is complex and many-layered, and there may be many manifestations of the ideal. One manifestation might be that 'work is valued by being displayed'. The job of creating bottom lines is therefore the delicate one of breaking down what we want into tangible, assessable outcomes. These form a web which gently but firmly circumscribes individuals, driving them towards the desired outcome. If we want our house painted, we don't go to a painter and say 'paint our house please.' Instead, we specify colours for doors, windows, and so on. The word 'house' need never be mentioned, but the result will be a painted house, not painted doors, windows, and so on. Likewise, in my system of bottom lines, we don't make demands like 'value your pupils.' What we say is 'display their work', 'mark their books', 'phone their parents', 'give them merits'. By these signs of esteem the pupils know they are valued, and managers can observe this valuing, or lack of it, expressed in concrete form.

Quality assurance follows from bottom lines, and is indeed defined by them. If bottom lines are to be rigorously enforced, then the job of quality assurance is to ensure this rigour. All members of the organisation must be monitored to ensure they are maintaining the bottom lines. This is not a difficult job, in that the bottom lines, by necessity, are few and, if well designed, easy to monitor. I say by necessity because it is to be remembered that the bulk of the space an individual occupies must be free for the individual to develop. Bottom lines are not applied in this space because they stifle creativity. Managers are not, therefore, spending their time enforcing large numbers of petty rules – this approach is more redolent of a task-orientated model, where workers are controlled, not empowered. Instead they enforce comparatively few, yet fundamental, bottom lines.

Conclusion

A conclusion to a paper on reengineering would appear to be a contradiction in terms, since reengineering, by its nature, has no conclusion. It is posited instead upon the need to respond to post-modern society by continual change. It might be appropriate, however, to bullet-point the main issues, as I see them, when the classroom is reengineered:

- Reengineering the classroom can take place only within the context of a broader commitment to reengineer the school. It is particularly important that this broader reengineering aims to move administration from teachers to administrators, and that administrative processes, in turn, can be shown to support classroom activity.

- An information-rich environment should be developed, particularly by the application of ICT. This information should consist of both assessment data, of use by the school for target setting and monitoring, and curriculum information, for use by pupils in their studies. An emphasis should be placed on teaching and acquiring information-handling skills, rather than on providing knowledge.

- It is vital to blur boundaries, and to provide a more continuous diet for pupils. This might take the form of a class being taught by a single teacher, by homework which encourages the support of parents, or a mentoring system which allows one teacher to advise a pupil in his or her work across a range of subjects.

- It is essential that teachers are able to talk to each other on a professional level in order to share good practice, and to develop the interpretative culture that legitimises their activities.

- Managers have to ensure that teachers are accountable for the outcomes of their work in the classroom by setting realistic but demanding bottom lines which are regularly monitored.

References

Bowring-Carr, C. and West-Burnham, J. (1997) *Effective Learning in Schools*, London, Pitman Publishing.

Champy, J. and Hammer, M. (1993) *Reengineering the Corporation*, London, Nicholas Brearley.

Davis, S. (1995) *Paradoxes in Decision Making and Their Relevance to Education*, unpublished PhD thesis, Hull

Derrida, J. (trans. Johnson, B.) (1993) *Dissemination*, London, Athlone Press.

Derrida, J. (trans. Bass, A.) (1978) *Writing and Difference*, London, Routledge and Kegan Paul.

Rinehart, J., Short, P. and Johnson, P. (1997) 'Empowerment and conflict at school-based and non-school-based sites in the United States', *International Studies in Educational Administration*, 25(1).

SCAA (1997) 'Value added indicators for schools, consultative paper: secondary', Hayes, SCAA.

11

■　■　■

The students' view

ROBERT GWYNNE

Background

In common with all schools, Longsands is determined to improve as an educational organisation. It has always been regarded as a successful community college serving the needs of a mixed urban and rural area several miles to the west of Cambridge. The town of St Neots is reasonably prosperous and, by national standards, is above average on a range of social and economic indicators. The college is large, with 1500 school-age students and several hundred adult users. Examination results are good (about ten per cent above the norm) but the pressure for continuing improvement is relentless. Parents who are well informed about the political drive for higher educational standards fuel competition between schools. The college is well placed to shake off complacency and to 'deliver the goods'. We can attract and develop good staff and the climate is conducive to good teaching and learning.

Seven years ago the college embarked on a journey of reform and restructuring. The purpose was to move from comfortable complacency towards educational excellence. OFSTED was then a mere twinkle in the Secretary of State's eye, but there was a feeling that the college could do better for its learners. Intuitive perceptions suggested a degree of under-performance and the climate was ripe for change and development. A new mission statement, fuelled by significant reorganisation and enabled by a talented and newly motivated teaching staff, spearheaded the developments. The drive was for quality, increased effectiveness and performance improvement.

Structural change in itself brought about considerable improvement on a wide range of fronts. However, the law of diminishing returns applied and, after the initial phase of reengineering, with its subsequent bonuses, a new impetus was needed to lift standards of teaching and learning further. OFSTED, and the arrival of the full-blown performance culture, helped to shift the focus from structural developments towards an emphasis on classroom learning. Despite one quarter of all teachers receiving C1 status in the inspection (an exceptional proportion), the leadership team felt that more could be done to improve the quality of learning and teaching. Along with this, a view emerged that we needed benchmarks so that classroom performance could be assessed and monitored. The subsequent story is outlined below in the hope that it may inspire other schools to stand on our shoulders and see a bit further. In so doing, no particular originality or panacea is claimed. We merely, and perhaps with some tardiness, found that we ought to listen more attentively to our students.

The college councils

A key development in the early days of change was the formation of student councils. Their purpose and constitution were not particularly clear but there was an underlying desire to involve students in the workings of the college. Their creation was an early move by me, as the new principal, to be regarded as a listening ear, less remote and less formal than my predecessor. The student councils were greeted positively by students, staff and parents alike. Organised on a year basis, two representatives were elected from each tutor group and each year council met with me once a term for an hour. Initially meetings were an opportunity for representatives to air their concerns on a range of usually mundane issues. This was helpful and informative because, as head of a very large organisation, it was all too easy to overlook the things that are critical to students and their daily lives.

The agendas rapidly became crammed with concerns about such matters as the position of the payphone and the state of the toilet door locks. This was all good stuff and it helped to sort out some important problems. However, as time went on the termly round of meetings became tedious, with me rationalising why the students' seemingly endless shopping lists could not be achieved. Occasionally we hit upon a good theme and there were some splendid meetings. In particular, the series at which we debated and researched the content of the youth activity programme was very valuable and formative.

In search of new ideas and the need to achieve a tangible outcome for the students' effort we hit upon the idea of giving each council a small sum of money with which to bring about an environmental improvement to the campus. This got under way with enthusiasm but got log-jammed alongside a large capital refurbishment programme; the estate manager's office simply could not cope with the extra burden of six more, albeit small, projects. Then, as so often happens, out of the blue came an opportunity that resulted in some of the best, most frank and incisive work I have ever seen from a group of school-age students.

The Longsands standard

Some 66 new policies and procedures later, and with OFSTED behind us, it was timely for the staff to look in greater depth at teaching and learning. It could be argued that our reforms should have begun at that point and not culminated there. Perhaps it's a question of style, but this particular leader works on the basis of developing the infrastructure first. It's a bit like ensuring that the ship's hull is sound and that the vessel is heading in the right direction before looking to the quality of the passengers' voyage.

One of the college management forums working groups set about establishing a 'Longsands standard' for classroom practice. This statement would become the benchmark that every teacher should strive for in lesson conduct. It would be used in the annual monitoring exercise for all teachers and for the assessment of our newly qualified staff. It aims set out the ingredients (observable over a period of time) that should be evident in each teacher's work. The emphasis was clearly placed on teaching skills, but it was soon clear from the development work that there were other significant contributory factors. For instance, evidence of student progress, contribution to the college corporate goals and target setting/achievement all have links back to the standard. The main headings of the standard are:

- relationships with students
- subject knowledge
- planning
- class management
- communication
- assessment
- reflecting on practice
- professionalism
- personal qualities.

Clearly, and without recognising it, we were for the first time getting close to a policy on learning. Coincidentally, and while the standard was at a formative stage, it was time for another round of student council meetings. For want of a fresh topic and to avoid the repetitive themes of old, I decided to pose each year council with the question: 'What makes a good lesson and how do students learn best?' Tutor groups were asked to discuss the topic and send their representatives to the council meetings with useful contributions.

The investigation and the findings

The year councils met for one hour each with their year co-ordinator and me. Realising the potential sensitivity of the issue and that the outcome was to be shared with the whole staff, ground rules were established. Specific references to particular teachers or lessons were not allowed; the students were encouraged to generalise their observations. I kept notes as the discussion proceeded and between us, the year co-ordinator and myself kept the discussion moving. As it turned out, the groups did not need much prompting and the discussion was free flowing. Care was taken to create a relaxed and secure atmosphere. The students warmed to this and enjoyed the sense of importance – all the more because we were in my room. Some representatives came with prepared material that had been generated through vigorous tutor group discussion. Other members responded spontaneously but with considerable perception and articulation. Points were aired, expanded upon and analysed. When a particular feature was identified, I often probed harder to gain a deeper understanding or clarification. This led to consensus, or in some cases, denial by the majority. At the end of each session the students were congratulated on their conduct and maturity. Such comments were heartfelt and genuine; I believed the students to have taken the task seriously and to have been thoughtful.

Reams of rough notes were accumulated and I was left with the task of analysing them and producing a single statement. Separate statements for each year group were not produced, as there was remarkable accord in all the meetings. The resulting memorandum to all teachers is reproduced below:

MEMORANDUM

TO: ALL TEACHERS

FROM: RLG

STUDENT COUNCILS, SPRING TERM 1998

Student councils this term considered the question: 'What makes a good lesson and how do students learn best?' The discussions were excellent. The students came up with very thoughtful ideas and points. The debate was not personalised (students were not allowed to talk about particular teachers or incidents) and the students' contribution is well worth including in our continuing discussions on school improvement.

What follows is a list of key points which emerged consistently from all the many issues which were raised and discussed. The points are not expressed in any particular order or framework. Similarly, this is not a prescription, but evidence worthy of professional reflection.

- Students have clear views on teacher discipline. They like and expect firm control but they do not like it when teachers become easily angered.
- Students like teachers who have a good sense of humour and who show respect for the students as individuals with feelings of their own.
- Students can sense when things are not well with a teacher and this does have an impact on their work and the lesson.
- Students are sensible to what teachers wear and believe that this has some impact on their attitude to learning.
- Students prefer to sit and work in groups rather than in straight rows.
- Students do not enjoy working in silence. They find silence inhibiting and it causes them to become embarrassed if they need to seek help or additional support.
- Students prefer lessons where there is a variety of activity. This preferably includes activities where there is a high level of involvement and a range of different tasks. Students judge that one-to-one encounters are very important. They prefer a quiet room but not silence.
- Students feel that they benefit from working with other students on research-type assignments.
- Students rapidly lose respect for teachers who do not mark or assess their work regularly.
- Students are sensitive and aware of bias among teachers; particularly it was noted that some teachers focus on asking girls to answer questions in classes.
- Students do not like being rushed in their work; they prefer deadlines which allow them time to explore topics thoroughly.
- Students do not like it when deadlines are set and not adhered to.
- Students are very sensitive to the extent to which teachers explain things in a differentiated way and/or are able to repeat an explanation in a different way.

- Students watch with interest how disruptive students are managed. They believe that a disruptive student who is not firmly and effectively handled gives other students licence to misbehave.

- Students find least value in copying, dictation and note-taking, but recognise the need for the sparing use of these methods. This was raised more than any other single issue.

- Students do not like untidy or muddled classrooms. They respect the teacher all the more if the room is well organised, tidy and well presented.

- Students thirst for more involvement with ICT and are ready for further developments in this respect.

Validity, reliability and generalisation

The investigation did not start life as a properly conducted piece of educational research. The methodology was spontaneous and opportunist. With hindsight I wish it had been conducted more rigorously as the topic is clearly worthy of thorough investigation. Perhaps this experience will inspire someone to do a 'proper job' on a similar theme some time in the future. Nevertheless, some analysis of the methods used will help illuminate the extent to which the results are useful in a wider discussion on teaching and learning.

First, the question of reliability must be explored. That is, to what extent would similar results have been achieved from the same groups on different occasions? A whole host of factors come into play here. Inevitably a key ingredient is the standing of the researcher. In this case the questioner and recorder was involved in the debate. The method therefore errs towards an action-research paradigm. Perhaps I steered the group unintentionally towards areas of personal interest or prejudice? Perhaps I wanted the group to express some of my own concerns about teaching and learning to give me evidence with which to confront teachers about whose performance I was concerned? Perhaps my role as recorder and analyst created a bias all of its own? These are legitimate concerns that could be overcome only by a more rigorous approach to the methods of the investigation. They therefore present real limitations on the use to which the evidence can be put. After all, if the group had different prior experiences of schooling and if I was not a prisoner of my own expectations and prejudices, the same topic discussed in the same room with the same group might have had a completely different outcome. For instance, if the students' main experience of lessons was active group work, they might have expressed a preference for didactic teaching, a change being regarded as good as a rest.

Second, the question of validity must be explored. That is, to what extent would different samples of students in different circumstances produce similar results? A qualitative approach such as this does not lend itself to a statistical analysis of validity. What can be argued, although evidence is not provided here, is that I was surprised at the commonality of thought that emerged from more than 50 tutor groups. An easy consensus appeared and this spanned the age range throughout Years 7–13. However, we must look carefully at the sample of students involved in the discussions. They were not picked randomly and, by definition, they comprise an articulate, outgoing and (possibly) highly intelligent sample from each of the tutor groups. To balance this, they were chosen by their peers because they are good advocates on their behalf. The validity of the results depends, therefore, on the extent to which a minority has successfully articulated the preferences of the majority. My intuition and years of professional experience of working with young people leads me to be confident in this respect on this occasion.

From this analysis, generalised comments can be made on the findings. For our college, with the current set of students and at this time, the results certainly provide some generalised information that can be used to fuel a debate about how to improve teaching and learning. This is the extent of the generalisation that can be confidently asserted. Other research in other contexts seems to produce similar findings, especially the need to match teaching styles more closely to learning styles. If educators are serious about the need to equip students with appropriate learning habits for the next millennium, it is timely to take note of the general message emerging from studies such as this.

Improving the research

Given the importance of this provisional study and its outcome, what improvements can be suggested for further investigations on the same research question? One approach could be to use the statements (*see* the memorandum) as the basis of an attitude survey administered to a large sample. The statements would need to be simplified to remove ambiguity and reduced to one clause per statement. The survey could then be administered to students from different schools, different backgrounds and different age groups. The amassed data could be used to produce a comprehensive picture of learning preferences. The research would be quantitative in nature with a quasi-scientific flavour. It would be based on provisional hypotheses (the statements themselves) which would be tested and validated using statistical techniques. Such methods, while useful in themselves, do not always fully illuminate the picture for the practitioner wishing to improve teaching and learning in classrooms. Alternatively, a method similar to the original one could be used, whereby small groups are interviewed under tightly controlled (i.e. a structured interview) conditions by external 'researchers' and a formal analysis of the outcome undertaken. This would provide a more rounded picture, but one in which the researcher is detached from the situation. This could provide consultancy-type data for the school, but little real advice or insight on how to improve.

For schools wishing to use students as part of the improvement process, an action-research approach is suggested. This would involve discussions like the ones undertaken by the student councils, but with an acceptance that researcher and student are involving themselves in a process of change. The findings would be used to bring about changes to classroom techniques. Subsequently those changes would be evaluated and the cycle repeated. This approach requires an honest commitment to change and the recognition that the interviewer (the principal, in our case) becomes central to that change process. As the picture unfolds, other players (the teachers and the parents) enter the game and it widens in an unpredictable way. How many schools are ready for such a scenario? We were certainly not.

Schools wishing to undertake studies like ours are advised, on the basis of experience, to give some serious thought to their methods and the use to which the results will be put. Only then will they truly stand on our shoulders and see a bit further.

Commentary on the findings

Returning to our findings, several interesting and generic points stand out. These may appear obvious, but I think it is worth drawing attention to them. As I see it, three key points emerge:

- Matters that adults (teachers) often regard as trivial or as of no consequence are important to students. This includes such things as dress, tidiness, quality of organisation, teacher mood and gender issues.
- Group work and active learning is strongly preferred to didactic teaching methods. I venture (possibly controversially) to suggest that this view emerged because of the predominant use of these methods at the important formative primary phase.

● Our students are well versed in the quality culture. They have a clear view on what standard of lesson they feel they should expect. They can also very effectively analyse shortcomings. While the origin of this is most likely enlightened self-interest, I think the students are perfectly capable of generalisation and advocating quality issues on behalf of whole classes.

What next?

This case study was written shortly after the basic work was undertaken. At the time of writing very little has been done with the accrued evidence other than circulate it (in the format shown) to all teachers. As in so many cases where important findings come to light, this poses the biggest challenge of all. I can think of many situations in school life where valuable ideas or evidence come to light and, for a short period of time, everyone is inspired to bring about change. After a while, however, the daily pressures of life (lost bus passes, shirts being worn outside trousers) get in the way and we lose sight of the big idea. Perhaps seven days is a long time in the school life of a big idea? Maybe I should convene the dreaded working party to look into the application of the findings. That would activate the time-tested technique of obfuscation beloved of true bureaucrats. With this one, I certainly do not intend to go down that road. One saving grace is that this work was done concurrently with the work on establishing the Longsands standard and it has thus become absorbed, albeit subliminally, into teachers' consciousness along with the other aspects of that work and its centrality to our next phase of development.

I think the real answer to 'what next?' lies in the subtle and often undramatic process of cultural change. The best kind of change happens incrementally, insidiously, and quietly. Ideas become absorbed and reflected in best practice and this itself leads to adoption by others. There is no going back once this happens, change is secure and not transient. This will happen if change is rooted in a fundamental and explicit set of values designed to improving our learners' lot.

Thus, we finish where we started. All schools are trying to improve; that is in the nature of educators and the organisations in which they operate. Here is an example of how one school is trying to become better at the core purpose – teaching and learning. In the jargon of reengineering, this is about improving quality. In this case it is our students who have become the teachers. Do we know how to listen to them effectively?

129

12

■ ■ ■

The never-ending story

HOWARD KENNEDY

Introduction

If you think you're good, you're dead.

(Hammer, 1997, p. 104)

If I knew then what I know now, it would have been a difficult journey. This is the story of where we are now but is the result of a school growing up from the excitement of birth through childhood, to adolescence and now, hopefully, to maturity. This is not the place for detail, but suffice to say we have had, and still have, all the trauma, jubilation, dynamism, emotion, success and failure associated with every family/community. The journey has been truly rewarding, although at times incredibly tough, and the feeling grows that the more we know, the less we know. Questioning, constant reflection and an in-built vocation to give all people the opportunity to succeed are the fuel for the journey, with the occasional success to keep us all together.

On my arrival, 14 years ago, Holy Family was a tiny 8–12 middle school of 128 pupils. It went through a combination on two separate sites (5–12), moved to one side (5–12), gained a purpose-built nursery to become 3–12, underwent local re-organisation to 5–11 and, four years ago, became self-governing. Change has been and is a constant. From the initial 4.6 staff, we now have 21 teachers, 15 teaching assistants and 450 children. Situated on the outskirts of Slough, the school is surrounded by motorways, while overhead, Heathrow's aeroplanes throb. It lies somewhere between inner city and leafy suburbs but I like to think of the pupils as the same as all other children, with the full spectrum of family backgrounds.

Background

Those who refuse to learn from the past are doomed to relive it.

(Porter, 1993, p. 103)

On my appointment to headship some 14 years ago, I set off with the intention of implementing a philosophy based on the belief that this was going to be 'our' school rather than 'my' school, that there was no such thing as a person who was below average, and a belief in the potential of all pupils to be achievers. The unravelling of this story is an account of a search for *alignment* in every aspect of the organisation. It has been a journey of discovery. It took a long time to understand that 'our' had to be systemic and built into every structure. It was often a lonely journey but, more recently, one which has been enabled through the help of 'critical friends'. It has never been stationary and exciting, and it has arrived at a most exhilarating moment as we explore 'alignment' with the most recent discoveries relating to the physiology of the brain, how it works and how learning takes place.

It is strange to discover the work of Purkey and Novak on invitational leadership (1990), for they write about everything we have been trying to implement and put our efforts into a detailed theoretical framework. It is also fascinating to watch the democratisation of the workplace, written about with great accord by all the major management philosophers (Hesselbein *et al.*, 1996; Gibson, 1977), for that has been our major challenge. It is also of interest to see the same process evolving in theology (Smith, A., 1996). And thank God for Michael Fullan. I'll come back to him later.

In the beginning ...

Tomorrow's successful leaders will value principles more than they value their companies.

(Covey, 1997, p. 34)

The very first activity we worked on as a staff, 14 years ago, was our statement of *aims*, *beliefs* and *values*. It is this statement above all else which has delivered the culture of our school and remains, to this day, the best thing we've ever done. Although initially the development of the statement required informed and strong leadership, it has been the subject of constant and thorough review, but throughout the wording has hardly changed. It is the most significant aspect of the school, underpinning every action and interaction, and is a constant living guide for all we do. It is this statement alone which has determined our culture, our relationships and our life together. It is tough because, 'lived out', the principles are demanding, but they have stood the test of time and are internalised, especially by the central core of staff. It is the environment created in putting them into practice which makes our school so attractive to parents and new staff but, equally, it is the reason for a few to depart.

We never quite believed in or were excited by the demands for mission statements, despite the pressure to conform. It was only recently that such a statement surfaced as a consequence of our work and it reads simply: 'Trying to make the world a better place.' An ennobling ideal and daunting responsibility, but a true reflection of our vocation.

One of the great challenges of a statement of beliefs and values is the capacity of the headteacher to 'lead the life' espoused in the words. If the head and their actions are not in alignment with the statement, then the whole fabric will be diseased from the core and will never wholly achieve. It is my experience that the person of the head cannot, in isolation, be the judge in this matter for it is only when the opinion of others is contributed that a true, comprehensive and accurate picture emerges. As a consequence of growing in understanding, and especially learning from the past, it became essential that there should be a system in the school which allowed the whole community to evaluate whether these principles were reflected in the actions of the head.

Chapter two

Tomorrow's successful leaders will be what Warren Bennis described as the 'leader of leaders'. They will decentralise power and democratise strategy involving a rich mixture of different people from inside and outside the organisation in the process of inventing the future.

(Gibson, 1997, p. 152)

When we became self-governing in 1993, we had the wisdom to purchase an external inspection which proved to be a daunting experience and, along with the new workload of being grant maintained, created a small crisis in myself. At this point I was lucky to be able to turn to Neville Stewart, a friend and educational consultant, who rode to our rescue. We now have a network of 'critical friend' consultants who work regularly with us to aid our development. We have learned that the best consultants don't tell us what to do but help us to see clearly what we are doing and enable us to make our own decisions. It is, after all, our journey, but one in which there are passengers.

Neville supported me through the self-doubt and helped me understand where a few fatal flaws lay in our structures. This prompted us back to the drawing board and a full review of basic principles which resulted, four years ago, in all our staff having a great weekend away working on a statement which would be the guiding principles for all *decision making*.

I had always thought I had been trying to implement democratic processes but had never had the wisdom to work this through with staff and write it down. This was the vital and missing ingredient. We had a great weekend and did some memorable work on Tell, Sell, Negotiate, Consult and Consensus. We now have a policy document which illustrates and underpins our belief in participative leadership, where all individuals in the school have the right to be involved in any decision which has an effect upon them. It also enshrines that our two deputies have the right of access to all information. Like all things, this took time to be embedded in all our actions, but now it is 'lived out' with great effect. It is manifested in the school council and in the voluntary executive meetings which have become our decision-making forum. The latter is chaired by one of the staff and I have only voting rights. Such procedures may be time-consuming, but they can be immensely beneficial to all as they continually promote the power of argument, intellect and knowledge through the power of speech and, in so doing, promote the leadership skills and knowledge requirements essential in any successful school of the future. They also make people feel good about themselves as they increase self-worth and generate a much greater commitment to the decisions taken.

They do not take power and authority away from the headteacher, rather the reverse, but only where the head has the intellectual capacity to understand the many issues in education and be able to communicate, verbalise, and provide meaning for others. It is the power of argument which encourages and convinces others to follow. Decisions are agreed by consensus and if they choose as a whole group not to consent, then perhaps it wasn't a wise place to be going in the first place. The system works for us, but I have witnessed enough violent response from others in education to realise that it does not suit everybody. There will be many different solutions in education, and this system rests easily in an 'aligned' position with all our other practices. There has only ever been one major issue with the process, and that is how you get a 'group' to embrace 'pioneering leadership', *hoshin* (a Japanese concept of 'outlandish thinking') or in being creative. This has been and is a challenge for the leadership of the school. We are making progress.

Flat organisations

What effective leaders are going to have to do is to create not just a vision, but a vision with meaning ... This vision has to be shared.

(Bennis, 1997, p. 156)

I once showed an interest in applying for a post as a school inspector, and the application form asked you to draw a picture of the organisational chart of your school. I couldn't do it and it became an irritating problem fleetingly returned to over a number of years. I couldn't quite illustrate what we were trying to do until one evening, four staff and myself attended a lecture by Meredith Belbin, and he drew it on the screen for us. There was our school, the 'Progression Helix', depicting the flat organisation, reflecting our corporate headship, roles and responsibilities, task forces and cross-functional teams (Belbin, 1996). He had done it all for us and, as the book illustrates, the 'Progressive Helix' is the culmination of his thinking after a lifetime examining effective and efficient structures for organisations. The theoretical framework he constructs provides a great basis for democratising the workplace.

In working with our external management consultant on organisational structure, we were attracted by the concept of a 'corporate headship' which, in effect, meant that each deputy was 'head' in their own kingdom, with full responsibility and accountability. This was a long process to see through, but it had undoubted benefits for the deputies and was as good a 'succession training' as we have seen. It meant they dealt with all agencies and relevant people with regards to their agreed role. This principle was accepted by all in the industry, but not by a group of colleague headteachers who found our deputy attending headteacher meetings as something akin to women going into the Long Room at Lords ... that's changing, too. The process has not been without difficulties and it is regularly refined, but it has been tremendously beneficial. One practical consequence of interest is that we all shared the same room and that probably is one of the best imaginable monitoring systems overseeing the activities of the head.

At the same time as this new development was being implemented, we set about the removal of hierarchical structures in the school which saw the disappearance of the senior management team, area co-ordinators and senior teachers, to be replaced with roles and responsibilities, teams and task forces. This was a tough period, initially resented by a few but with a dramatic and positive effect overall, especially on younger and newer members of the profession. As we worked through these changes, we arrived quite naturally at our present position where we perceive the

135

immediate future to be a new phase where the head and two deputies are seen as senior partners, core staff as partners, and new staff employed as junior partners. Within these structures the core staff would all be involved in determining whether a junior partner should be offered partner status.

As yet, we have not been brave enough to jettison the nationally agreed pay structure, but this looks to be an attractive option with people's pay reflecting the quality of contribution made rather than years of service. It is recognised that this is a particularly sensitive area, but the feeling is that it will happen.

One important consequence for career advancement is that staff applying to other schools have an interesting time in that their job titles are not of the norm and their experience in being involved in every aspect of the school is sometimes met with uncertainty. We have to work hard at providing a comprehensive portfolio for staff to secure their future.

Appraisal

Our experience with hundreds of organisations, over a period of 30 years, has led to the conclusion that organisations and nations don't change – only individuals change.

(Fullan, 1993, p. 142)

My own appraisal system has been a major change agent for the school, not just in improving my own performance, but equally as living exemplification of our beliefs in action: an illustration of aligning principles in systems and actions. The process has evolved over the years, but it is now led by the external consultant who interviews all interested parties: full governing body, administrative staff, maintenance staff, PTA members, representative children from every age group and all teaching staff. The consultant writes an interim report and presents it to me with all teaching staff present. We discuss his findings in front of staff, with them contributing for clarification. It would be fair to say, and probably easier to see, that the potential for a negative experience is great, so the skills of the consultant have to be considerable. It was one of the most difficult things I have done, but the rewards for the staff and myself have been huge and the benefits for the school enormous. All parties received a copy of the final report and it was available for parents. It had one memorable comment: 'We all have to die but there's no point in rushing there!' This should give

the reader some indication of human frailty and weakness in my performance, brought on by frantic and never-ending activity, the steady
correction of which has been a great education.

As I write, we are moving towards a similar but much simpler system for
all staff. Our appraisal system has been rewarding but it has not resulted
in enough impact on the learning of children. Although we have had
pupils involved in our most recent appraisals, we now intend to extend
this through the involvement of parents.

Training and development

*Creativity can solve any problem. The creative act, the defeat of habit by origi-
nality, overcomes everything.*

(Porter, 1993, p. 147)

We feel that we will need to be good at all things if we are to be fully effective and competitive in the future. Competition lies in yet undiscovered
places, e.g. the growing movement towards educating children at home
and the unknown implications of technology on how children will learn in
the future. As a response, one of our main roles is to ensure schools are
places of expertise in how children learn and, as such, see themselves as
ideally placed to be creative and innovative in extending the boundaries of
present practices. If we want schools to succeed, they must become places
where all students succeed. We have embarked on a search for new and
better ways to educate and, as a consequence, one of the main challenges
is to create a culture which embraces change but accepts failure as a necessary part of improvement. Schools must be places of innovation where
working practices illustrate how they have learned from the past and are
committed to finding new and better ways of educating children. This
predicates the fact that successful schools must therefore be learning
schools and, as this is essential, then they must become places of 'high
challenge and low stress'. This is stated as a consequence of all the recent
discoveries about our brains and how they work best. Ninety per cent of
what is known about the brain has been discovered in the past 15 years,
and most of these discoveries are yet to make it into schools. One thing on
which neuro-physiologists are agreed is that humans do not function at
optimum level when continually under stress. It is only too easy to be
sucked unwittingly into the pursuit of more and more, faster and faster.
We must all learn to do less better.

... most of the organisations that are trying to do things faster are going to fail dismally. They will get a little faster. But as Deming used to say. 'Sure you'll accomplish results, but you'll destroy the organisation to do it. And you'll destroy the people in it'.

(Senge, 1997, p. 139)

Unfortunately, like the majority of schools, we were hooked into 'more faster' as a seductive mirage of improved efficiency. It doesn't work, but it does increase stress. Stress is apparent in all our lives and we took some time out to 'systemise' our own antidote. We spend the large proportion of our lives 'doing', so we built in a time to 'be'. This developed into fort-nightly meetings which we termed 'triads', for they were in groups of three, and which initially quite strange for everyone, developed into an essential part of our lives. We are unused to spending time 'being', so we had to learn to cope with silence and stillness. I constructed the stimulus for the meetings. Each session began by listening to a piece of reflective and peaceful music followed by discussions on a variety of topics includ-ing 'big issues' like the meaning of life, death, stress, personal histories, memories, disease, why we work. As the meetings were completely confi-dential, I have little idea about how they are conducted, but the staff regularly vote for their retention and some people have become intimate friends through the process. The benefit for the school is enormous as the potential and importance of similar experiences for children has become apparent and begins to enter working practices. Some people's response may be, how can you find time to do that, and my response would be, how can you afford not to? (*see* Figure 12.1).

Everyone has his own specific vocation or mission in life ... therein he cannot be replaced. Nor can life be repeated. Thus everyone's task is as unique as is his specific opportunity to implement it.

(Kranckl, 1946)

An interesting aside and a comment on our westernised lifestyles was the experience of the very first session. Listening to a piece of music with two other colleagues was exceedingly difficult and silence and stillness was a real challenge. We even found it difficult to shake hands with each other. We suddenly discovered that we spend the majority of our lives together, but did we really know each other? This seems to have real implications for the purpose of our job and the purpose of education reflected in many management philosophers (Hesselbein *et al.*, 1996; Toffler, 1996), recently arriving at the big question: 'What is it all for?' Spending time 'being' could provide a few answers.

TRIADS

Lifestyles meeting 2 1996/7. Thursday, 10th October

Music: The Mission.

> *"Sometimes when I consider what tremendous consequences come from little things ... I am tempted to think there are no little things."*

Remember you are with a new group and much of what you discussed last year is unheard.

Two battleships assigned to the training squadron had been at sea on manoeuvres in heavy weather for several days. I was serving on the lead battleship and was on watch on the bridge as night fell. The visibility was poor with patchy fog, so the captain remained on the bridge keeping an eye on all activities. Shortly after dark, the lookout on the wing of the bridge reported: 'Light bearing on the starboard bow.'

'Is it steady or moving astern?' the captain called out.

Lookout replied: 'Steady, captain,' which meant we were on a dangerous collision course with that ship.

The captain then called to the signalman; 'Signal that ship: We are on a collision course, recommend you change your course 20 degrees.'

Back came a signal: 'Advisable for you to change course 20 degrees.'

'I'm a seaman second class,' came the reply. 'You had better change course 20 degrees.'

By that time the captain was furious. He spat out: 'Send, I'm a battleship. Change course 20 degrees!'

Back came the flashing light: 'I'm a lighthouse!'

We changed course.

Do we enjoy change?

Spend the first few moments discussing the first few weeks of term and describe all you have achieved – you are not allowed to say one negative.

Last time we talked about ourselves; can we take this a step further and describe the way the world has developed in your lifetime. Begin from earliest memories and come up to present day.

Now spend a few moments discussing the future ... what will the world be like in five years ... ten years ... 25 years?

Do we need to change with the times? Are we good at change or are we creatures of habit? Constant change can affect our health ... how do we stay healthy during the process?

Fig. 12.1 A triad session

The triads had an interesting impact on our attitude towards our health and our working environment. Out of confidential discussions arose a sharper focus on some of the non-aligned issues in school, like the effect of ever increasing workloads and manic activity on our health and lifestyles. Many are the times teachers have been heard to say that during term time they 'stop living'. Our children need energetic, enthused people to teach them, who have an active and stimulating social life. A recent training day concluded that our number one target for adults over the next three years is to create an environment which is 'health-giving' and not 'dis-ease' ridden. If we want efficient schools, we must invest in keeping people healthy. This is as applicable to children as to adults. Although we have had corporate membership of a leisure facility, we intend to extend this to incorporate opportunities for staff to participate in preventative therapies such as meditation, reflexology and massage. We are also in the process of building a small relaxation/thinking room, but have not been brave enough to incorporate the hammock recommended by Rosabeth Moss-Kanter (1989).

One other item which is quite revolutionary in education is the concept of providing time for teachers to read, which is a sad reflection on a profession involved in 'learning'. It is critical to the successful school of the future that all staff are committed to their own learning. If teachers as 'learners' and children as 'learners' are not in alignment, then somewhere in the process you have built in failure. One of the main and most simple opportunities for learning lies in reading. Teachers need time to read and it should be part of their working life, not an add-on. Although many might argue that every educated person should find their own time to do this, most teachers of my acquaintance are so shattered during term time that they meet any extra demands with a negative response. It is a vicious circle which needs attention, for it is only in reading that professionals will suddenly find better ways and, as a consequence, improve their performance and lifestyle.

One more aspect of our training and development came through my own reading, and is an illustration of how such an investment can influence development. If we stand still, we're going backwards, sounds like somebody should have said it, for it's true. We need to guard against complacency in every aspect of life. Take thinking as an example. Most of our profession probably believe they can 'think'. Think again! Michael J. Gelb's book, *Thinking for a Change* (1995), is a classic and should be an essential resource for all leaders. His concept of synvergent (the coming together of things that are normally apart, e.g. left-hand side of the brain working with right-hand side) thinking points the way to the future and is an illustration of the need to continually improve – we embrace change or die. His book also proved a source of inspiration which is helping to radically change the education of our children. I have long been an admirer of the ability of our public school system in enabling all their students to 'talk'. It is my experience that the majority of their pupils have a confident grasp of the English language, which provides them with an excellent platform for life. The antithesis of this is often evident in state schools.

Inspection is part of our in-house attempts to improve effectiveness, and recently our two deputies and myself observed every member of staff teaching and saw an interesting phenomenon throughout the school. It became evident that even in the most benign question and answer sessions between teacher and the whole class, lay the foundation for educational failure. From a five-year-old's earliest moments at school, it was obvious that even in the most capable hands, these sessions caused some children to 'opt-out' and throughout the school we could see these same children gradually becoming disenfranchised and losing the gift of speech. Michael Gelb (1995) illustrates the damage these sessions can do to children and adults. We are trying to make all question and answer sessions inclusive, so that organisational structures are in place which encourage all children to participate. Class sessions are regularly operating in which questions are asked and children talk with their 'paired partner' to help increase language skills.

Chapter 5 and onwards

As can be perceived from the above, we haven't exactly been inactive over the years and the school does have a certain pace and dynamism, but there has always been the nagging question of how successful all our activity has been in improving the quality of teaching and the standards of children's learning. We had outstanding SATS results and 11+ success (we live in a grammar school area), had transformed the school and were massively oversubscribed, but we were a long way from 'total success'. It was uplifting to read Michael Fullan's book, *Change Forces*, and realise that so many school improvement initiatives weren't working, and the scaffolding of activity so eagerly embraced in countless schools across the globe often camouflaged the lack of impact on the chalkface. This fact, and the illustration that change and effect takes years, not months, was a great source of comfort and support. His thoughts coincided with our experiences and gave me a personal boost to search for a better way. We needed to re-invent ourselves again – quite what into we were not sure – but we were certain the energy would be there, for the sole focus was to be on children's learning, the classroom, the teaching and teachers as learners.

Through reading, we discovered accelerated learning and enlisted the assistance of an educational consultant and amateur neuro-physiologist for one of the most exciting training days imaginable. We were introduced to the brain, how it works and all the wonderful developments in explaining how learning takes place. Neuro-physiologists know so much that it makes some of the work we do in schools seem positively barbaric. So we embarked on a journey of exploration in 'aligning' our learning practices with how the brain functions. Suddenly, our school leapt into being the 'learning school', with a new staff library full of exciting tomes (mainly American), and we became a place of innovation, exploring the value of neuro-linguistic programming, Brain Gym, the impact of music on learning, high-challenge–low-stress environments, accelerated learning, visual, auditory and physical learning, brain breaks, music therapy, integrated learning systems, alpha, beta, delta, theta brain waves and levels of activity, our memory and how it works, mind maps, mind stories. We began to embrace new learning technologies with some unbelievable results. Literally.

The change process was a novel experience, for it was written up as part of an MBA and a lot more reflection was accorded the process than had been done previously. Due to the fact that these discoveries were being generated by my evolution into the original 'frantic learner' (Stoll and Fink, 1996), I was fired with enthusiasm to 'have a go' myself, and began to undertake a series of new learning experiences with children with hitherto unforeseen potential. The results were quite astonishing – literally – which in someone who had been teaching successfully for 20 or so years was a revelation. The conversion was in the effect. We now find ourselves at the dawn of a new era where the potential suddenly surfaces to 'align' the way children learn with the way their brain functions and their individual preferred learning styles. Teaching becomes a science. We have only just begun, but already our school is a hive of innovation and teachers, including myself, have changed their attitudes and perspectives and suddenly the answer to enabling all the children to be 'average and above' has come into view.

It is worth illustrating one experience. I used neuro-linguistic programming (Alder, 1994) and new knowledge about the brain, stress-free zones, 'changing heads' and relaxation with, at first, an individual child and subsequently with larger groups. The first child was a revelation, and the revelation continues. All the children had problems with spelling and after five or so years could describe themselves as failures and were on the spiral of continual failure in this aspect of their lives. It showed. With a 100 per cent success rate, we moved the children, in one session, from failure to outstanding success and, in so doing, transformed their lives. Spelling was a side issue. Transforming children from failures to success is a gift for life. Once you learn the process, the skills are transferable. Initially, most staff were a little sceptical and demanded demonstrations to see if it worked, was a 'trick', or was really the 'magic wand' I was so excited about. So we did it again and again and they kept offering their 'very worst' child because: 'If you can do it with them, then I'll really take notice!' So the children came with a remedial list of words similar to 'where', 'were', 'when', and left with ability to spell *PYRRHULOXIA, MIS-CELLANEOUS, KANGCHENJUNGA*, with the meanings firmly embedded in their visual memories. So now we have great fun with parents and visitors as our 'remedial' group challenges them to a winner-takes-all spelling test. So far, they have beaten two inspectors, one headteacher and nearly all our staff. If kids can do that, they can do anything (Porter, 1993).

We are also moving into our own action-research programme exploring the impact and effects of Brain Gym, a series of exercises developed by Dr Paul Dennison to improve the performance of the brain and the capacity to learn. This is based on the importance of physical movement in learning and 'joining' the right and left sides of the brain in activities. Now this might all sound a little like science fiction or, at best, a little suspicious, until one hears that Brain Gym has been accepted by the National Learning Foundation of America as one of the top technologies for the 21st Century Learning Society.

Our interest in accelerated learning is leading to an exciting experience as we plan to introduce the learning of Spanish and French into our primary school, the operative word being learning, for we do not plan to teach these languages, we plan for our staff to learn them with the children. A brave experiment for the teachers involved, but the concept of learning a language using accelerated learning methods has already produced one convert, so we start from a positive basis.

We have quite a few visitors around the school, and inspectors and external examiners leave having seen a hive of innovation and new learning technologies being tried in the classroom. They invariably take a book list with them and spread the message to others. The reader can peruse the reading list and follow their own journey in much greater detail than this article provides.

After a thorough process of review, our number one priority for the future is 'total success' (centred on reading). We are convinced that yesterday's remedies will never provide the total success essential if all our pupils are to participate in society. The solution, we feel, lies in new ways and it is this voyage of discovery on which we have embarked. This is not about a calm lake, more a ruffled sea. The feeling remains that the solution has always been with us – our brain and how it functions.

My reading about the brain gave me a great personal enthusiasm for believing that all people can be geniuses and that the only thing that gets in the way is ourselves. I decided, where better to start than myself, so I put into practice a little bit of neuro-physiology and trained my brain into believing what was important to me for, as Frank Lloyd Wright states: 'The thing always happens that you really believe in: and belief is the thing that makes it happen.' (Porter, 1993, p. 100). We are on the verge of constructing the first purpose-built 'Brain Centre', sponsored by industry, which is enthralled by what we are trying to achieve and the potential it has for it. The centre aims to bring university department, research association, industry and the world of education together, with the intention of exploring the validity of new learning technologies. In the process we hope it makes our school a place of expertise and enlightenment in how people learn, which is what schools should have been all along. In doing so, it should provide achievement for all children, most notably in a 100 per cent literate and numerate population in our school. But it will also provide somewhere for the community of parents and industry to come to us as a place of expertise able to assist them in their learning.

Our never-ending story is literally one without end, for it is a living process of gradual enlightenment which frequently re-invents itself. While the journey is full of questions and uncertainty, there are periods of exciting developments, none of which, I believe, match our immediate future. The drive to change, to get better, comes from the commitment to improve children's lives, for it is the impact of our actions on one life that recharges the batteries. The more I read, and the more time I spend with children, the more I become convinced that it is not children who fail but headteachers and teachers who fail children. This is not a criticism of the teaching profession but a recognition of the massive task and a call for leadership. For we are living in an age which will demand and expect success for all, and we will be driven to finding solutions. It is a much better place to be in the driving seat. As Lewis Grizzard said:

Life is like a dogsled team.
If you ain't the lead dog,
The scenery never changes. (Porter, 1993, p. 206)

References

Alder, H. (1994) *Neuro-Linguistic Programming*, London, Piatkus.

Belbin, R. (1996) *The Coming Shape of Organisation*, Oxford, Butterworth-Heinemann.

Bennis, W. (1997) in Gibson, R. (1997) *op. cit.*

Covey, S. (1997) 'Putting principles first' in Gibson, R. (ed) *op. cit.*

Fullan, M. (1993) *Change Forces*, London, The Falmer Press.

Gelb, M.J. (1995) *Thinking for a Change*, London, Autumn Press Ltd.

Gibson, R. (ed.), (1997) *Rethinking the Future*, Nicholas Brealey Publishing.

Grizzard, L. (1993) in Porter, P., *Awaken the Genius*, Phoenix, Purelight Publishing.

Hammer, M. (1997) 'Beyond the end of management' in Gibson, R. (ed), *Rethinking the Future*, Nicholas Brealey Publishing.

Hesselbein, F., Goldsmith, M. and Beckhard, R. (eds), (1996) *The Leader of the Future*, San Francisco, Jossey-Bass.

Kranckl. V.F. (1946) *Man's Search for Meaning*, Washington Square Press.

Lloyd Wright, F. (1993) in Porter, P., *Awaken the Genius*, Phoenix, Purelight Publishing.

Moss-Kanter, R. (1989). *When Giants Learn to Dance*, London, Routledge.

Porter, P. (1993) *Awaken the Genius*, Phoenix, Purelight Publishing.

Purkey, W.W. and Novak. J. (1990) *Inviting School Success*, Belmont, CA, Wadsworth.

Senge, P. (1997) in Gibson, R. (ed), *op. cit.*

Smith, A. (1996) *The God Shift*, London, New Millennium.

Stoll, L. and Fink, D. (1996) *Changing Our Schools*, Open University Press.

Toffler, A. (1996) in Hesselbein *et al.*, *op. cit.*

13
■ ■ ■

Integrating the curriculum: the team small group model

IAN MCKENZIE AND SUZANNE NEXHIP

Introduction

Eumemmerring Secondary College is a large multi-campus school formed in 1993 with the amalgamation of Endeavour Hills Technical School, Hallam High School and two newly built campuses – Fountain Gate and Gleneagles. The total population is almost 3000 students and over 200 staff. It is the largest government secondary college in Victoria. The Endeavour Hills campus has a mixed socio-economic background, with a large number of ethnicities. There are 42 teachers, of whom 8 are part-time, and 500 students. The Endeavour Hills Campus is a Year 7 to Year 10 site (Year 7 being the first year of secondary education), feeding into the senior, Year 11 and Year 12, campus at Hallam.

The TSG (Team Small Group) Model is currently in place at Year 7 and Year 8 with approximately 100 students in each year level and 15 teachers in total. There have been attempts in the past to address the issues of:

- transition from Year 6 to Year 7.
- alienation of young people from their school life
- engagement of students in their educational experiences
- students' perceived lack of success in knowledge of how to succeed
- student ownership of decisions about learning
- peer pressures

- what it is about the way we organise our work that gets in the way of learning.

The TSG Model originated in Germany about ten years ago, after changes to their education structure in response to changes in world markets. Up to that point, the German education system had classified students in their early primary years, into three broad streams: those who went on to university, those who went to Trade schools, and those who left school and entered the workforce at Year 10. This meant that many potentially capable students were not given the opportunity to realise their abilities.

Some schools underwent restructure, many of them becoming much larger to cater for the increasing range of subjects being offered. In response to this, a group of teachers from the Saarland decided there were some critical issues to address, especially:

- *the isolation that students traditionally feel in a large school*
- *the development of an institution which could enable students of different abilities and backgrounds to reach their potential.*

(Ratzki, 1988)

The Technical school model in Victoria, before the 1990s, was highly traditional in that it consisted of three broad curriculum streams – Maths/Science, Humanities and Technology. This has fostered habits of individual subject learning, with little or no attempt to integrate the work in any way. Teachers from the Technical system have developed expertise in their own subject areas, much of it passed on by predecessors; this has led to stagnation and rigid curriculum.

The staff at Endeavour Hills have managed to make profound and long-reaching changes despite the rigid structures that existed. The curriculum in Victoria is also highly centralised, with Curriculum Standards Framework (CSF) documentation describing clearly the educational outcomes at each year level for each subject. The teaching teams have managed to cater for the mandated curriculum and still have an integrated, dynamic curriculum with tangible, relevant outcomes for the students.

Focus questions

The teaching teams at Year 7 and Year 8 have attempted to analyse their work practices critically and create situations for students which have meaning and relevance for them. The means by which this was achieved included asking some focal questions:

- Who decides on what the curriculum should look like?
- What sort of learning do we want?
- What is an integrated curriculum?
- What does it look like?
- What are the outcomes from an integrated curriculum?
- How do we assess an integrated curriculum?
- How do we effectively report on an integrated curriculum?
- Where are we now?
- Where do we go from here?

The model in action at Endeavour Hills

The Model has been operating in various ways:

- It began in a small way after a two-day inservice was run at Endeavour Hills, from which about five staff decided to run with the Model, which meant that the first days were challenging.
- The Model continued on a small scale for about two and a half years, after which teaching teams were provided with time to meet, using money from the National Schools Network. This meeting time in mid-1996 provided the structure and vision for the next twelve months.
- Up to that point, there was a teaching team of six people at Year 7 only.
- At the end of 1996, staff were asked for a commitment to the TSG Model. It was decided that most of the original team at Year 7 would go on to Year 8, while two would remain with Year 7.
- Eight new staff became involved in the teams and now there are teaching teams at Year 7 and Year 8, each made up of about eight staff, and student teams within those year levels.

Some rooms in the school are set up in team formation, with a 'herringbone structure' to allow the students in the teams to be the focus, not the teacher at the front of the class.

The students

The students are placed in teams of four or five in a variety of ways at the beginning of the year. Generally it is random. However, some teaching teams use other methods such as teacher selection and/or student selection. The students are not simply placed in their teams and expected to 'perform'. There is a great deal of emphasis placed on developing team skills. All teams go through a number of stages and are helped to develop skills in working together through the phases of:

- *Forming*
- *Norming*
- *Storming*
- *Performing*
- *Celebrating*
- *Reforming*.

(Taylor and McKenzie, 1997)

There are specific skills required at each stage and teachers need to be aware that the students need practice and 'real' situations in which to develop those skills. The students are required to work as a team and to contribute equally.

The teams are gender-balanced where possible. However, as the Model tends to attract more females (the school population has changed from about 70 per cent males five years ago, to 40 per cent males today), there are some teams which are single sex. A team is never formed with only one person of a particular sex.

While students are generally in teams of four or five, there also exists a bigger team made up of the whole class of twenty-five students. This is fostered through daily group meetings with a group teacher (who also teaches a number of other subjects). There is also the sense that there exists a bigger team, made up of all Year 7 or all Year 8 students. There are regular meetings with all students and a camp and excursions to reinforce the notion of a big team. The result is that Endeavour Hills Campus is seen by many to be a 'family'.

A common misconception about the Model is that students are always working on team projects. This is not always the case; often students are completing individual work, work in pairs, or work in another team of some sort, even though the room may be set up in team formation. On average, the students spend about 40 per cent of their time on specific team projects, requiring contributions from all team members.

The teachers

Participation in the Model is voluntary at Endeavour Hills. However, if staff wish to teach at Year 7 or 8, they are required to teach within the Model. This has meant that some staff have opted out of Year 7 and 8. This has only been possible because of policy support and a directive from the school administration. Those staff who choose to teach within the Model are making a commitment to teach almost exclusively at either Year 7 or Year 8, with perhaps one class at Year 9 or 10. The teachers in the teams are required to teach two or more subjects to one class of students, and are group teachers also.

Those teaching teams meet at times negotiated by team members. The meetings are non-hierarchical; there is no 'Chair', 'President', etc. Traditional meetings that most schools have – General staff; Curriculum; Faculty; Whole College meetings – still take place, so the middle years' initiative is taken on in addition to these other responsibilities. This is because we are developing a change on a school that already exists.

The Year 7 team meets after school on a Wednesday; the Year 8 team before school on a Thursday or Friday. The difference with these meetings, compared with other meetings in the school, is that they are purposeful and valuable. A team meeting is never held just for the sake of tradition. If no issue needs to be discussed at that time, or staff are too busy, the meeting is cancelled. The agendas for these meetings are organised by the Year Level Co-ordinators, and the items are placed on the agenda by any team member who has an issue to discuss. The meetings are informal in the sense that the team is meeting for a purpose and does not allow traditional meeting regimes to interfere with that.

There are generally two main focuses for the teaching team meetings: pastoral care and curriculum. The staff talk about specific student issues that may be a concern – misbehaviour; obvious alienation; family issues. They also talk about methods of engaging students in learning in active, relevant and purposeful ways by using an integrated curriculum where the students have some ownership.

Parents/community

The Endeavour Hills Campus works hard to have a partnership with community and specifically parents. There has been a conscious effort on behalf of the teaching teams to keep parents informed about the work their children are doing. In particular, the information the students are given is sent home to parents including outcomes from the CSF documents, and the assessment criteria. We also invite parents to help us with assessing the students' work, help their children complete their projects, and to come to the school to help out during project time.

The integrated projects have allowed tangible partnerships to occur between ourselves and the community, by having guest speakers, or by visits to workplaces, in order to use the skill of experts in the community when developing and designing our projects.

The curriculum

The curriculum within the Model is integrated in a number of ways:

- Informally, when the teaching team discusses what it is they are teaching and makes links with others during team meetings.
- More formally, with 'mini' projects which run for about one week, involving most of the Key Learning Areas (KLAs).
- Formally, when the teaching team uses National Schools Network money to buy time to plan major projects, which run for about six/seven weeks. There is one of these each semester for each year level.

The major integrated projects are worked on for about 50 per cent of the time. The rest of the time is spent on traditional curriculum work that is related directly to the project – the difference is that the students have a purpose for learning something, compared with learning it because they are required to.

In 1997, the Year 7 semester 1 project is a parody of the Cannes Film Festival – ours is Cans. In Year 8, the project is on the theme of Shelter. These projects involve aspects of every KLA with input from all staff in the team. Much time is spent developing the subject and assessment criteria, and makings links to the Curriculum Standards Framework or CSF (the state guidelines for all Victorian schools), because like all schools, we have our critics and we must prove that we are addressing the CSF outcomes, even though in the school, teachers using the traditional model, do not have to.

The integrated projects at this stage are developed by the teachers, but the plan is to have the students involved in the assessment of the projects this semester, and then next semester to negotiate the projects with the students. It is important to note here, that some projects work well with students; others do not. It is important to show the students that projects are relevant to them, that they have clear outcomes, and that they may be involved in their development.

Professional development

There is a complex interaction of people inside and outside the Endeavour Hills Campus. It is made up of the teaching teams' need for growth and expansion of ideas, and the need of educational communities beyond Endeavour Hills' to learn about the work we are doing.

The minimum Professional Development (PD) required to establish teaching terms with the TSG Model is at least two days. The five-day workshops run by the National Schools Network are preferable. There is a definite need for teachers to go through the same team building processes as the students. The optimum number for a TSG inservice is 20. It is also ideal to mix two or more schools together as this allows for a flow of ideas and experiences, breaking out of tried and true approaches.

There has been a major shift occurrence at Endeavour Hills, where previously (as still in some schools) there was the belief that unless teachers had writing on paper at the end of an inservice day, it was a waste of time. Now, however, the teaching team spends time reflecting on their teaching and learning practice. They often talk about their work and celebrate the events as they occur and use National Schools Network money to buy time to reflect critically on their pedagogy. This is a powerful form of PD as it enables teachers to articulate what they are doing and look forward to potential changes and improvements.

Teaching team meetings are also an excellent form of PD as they allow teachers to talk about their classes in a collegiate way and arrive at management strategies that make sense for the context they are in, and which are consistent as all teachers of the student or class have had a say in the way challenges are dealt with. The teaching teams not only attend inservices related specifically to the TSG Model but go to many about the Middle years: Alienation and Engagement; Behaviour Management; and Information Technology. The teaching teams' approach is that they nominate what it is they need to know as a team, rather than have someone tell them.

About half of the teaching teams have attended National Schools Network workshops, which have proved to be essential for the sharing of ideas and resources and accessing new information. The teaching teams are also linked with State Co-ordinators from the National Schools Network, who have provided much guidance and assistance for the teachers as they make their way through a regime of change. When a new teacher comes to the school, the 'experts' in the teaching team spend a great deal of time with them, talking through issues related to teamwork, until they are able to attend an inservice. The sense of empathy that can only come from participation in an inservice is essential for the teaching team to work effectively and appreciate what the staff and students are going through.

Teachers at Endeavour Hills run one-day workshops for staff from across Australia. A number of teachers from the Year 7 and Year 8 teams and administrative staff have run these, thereby providing a number of positive outcomes for internal school staff:

- increased teachers' ability to celebrate their work, by sharing it with others
- improved knowledge and communication about the Model
- increase in ideas that staff are exposed to, by sharing stories with teachers from other schools
- improve teachers' presentation skills
- change in focus of the nature of inservices, where now all staff have many things of value to add to workshops, and where there is no longer a division between 'expert' staff and 'followers'.

The demand for these workshops is very high and the teachers have nominated one day a week for the running of these. They are held at the Endeavour Hills Campus, where there is a Conference Room, with coffee machine and excellent lunches.

All staff have the opportunity to present at regional, state and national workshops, for example:

- Victorian Welfare Conference
- Various Middle School Forums, such as the Northcote Network or Schools; and National Middle Schooling Forum
- Cranbourne/Wonthaggi District
- National Curriculum Services
- National Schools Network, 'season' schools
- Australian Curriculum Services Administration in Melbourne, 1995
- University of Melbourne
- Victoria Department of Education.

External links

By sharing our work in such a way, we at Endeavour Hills have been forced to ensure that what we are doing can be adequately justified with respect to rigour and validity. We have to document as much of our work as possible and ensure our classrooms and meetings are open to scrutiny. This has been of enormous benefit to teachers at Endeavour Hills, as it has forced us to examine critically our everyday practice and seek improvements. This has led to us having open and often heated discussions about the future direction and prospects for the teams.

Of enormous benefit for Endeavour Hills staff have been the continuing links with colleagues at:

- the local level – The Werribee Grange
- the national level – the NSN, Sydney University, Deakin University, Central Queensland University
- the international level – our German counterparts from the Saarland where there have been opportunities for teachers to share and talk about their work. Additionally, Casterton Community College in England has provided opportunities for sharing experiences between both students and teachers.

The above links have allowed staff to keep up-to-date with recent education-related publications. These have provided many ideas and further contacts for the continual improvement and development of the Model. Staff have also been involved in writing a range of materials for journals and books based around the curriculum, professional development, collegiality, teaching and learning.

The staff at Endeavour Hills have also participated in a National Research Circle to produce samples of integrated curriculum, documenting the process to share with others. It was an exciting time and staff were involved in planning a number of workshops for people across Australia. Two of these were for the teaching community, the third for students. The occasion was a fantastic opportunity for showcasing and sharing the TSG Model and progress being made in schools. It was also an opportunity for educators across Australia to participate in exciting and dynamic workshops which allowed a brief insight into what the TSG Model is and how it operates. One of the important points that arose was that the Model in Germany had not been adopted in its current form, but rather was adapted to suit our specific needs. This has been the case for all schools that have adopted the TSG approach – the Model has been organic and taken on its own form within the setting in which it exists.

The infrastructure

For the Model to operate effectively, there is a need to have someone within Administration who has a commitment to, and working knowledge of, the Model. At Endeavour Hills, Principal Ian McKenzie is that person, who is considered the teaching teams' 'critical friend'. Without the ongoing support and injection of ideas, the teaching teams would have stagnated long ago.

As with any change, it is difficult to make a change effective and absolute, without a person in a position of authority constantly providing encouragement for that change. The change process has not been easy, and Ian is vigilant about the need to provide teachers with the opportunity to celebrate the journey as well as the final outcomes. He is alert to the need to give staff 'time out' to avoid 'burn out'. To do this, he has 'shared the load' among the teaching teams to ensure that one or two teachers are not left with the work all the time.

The Administration has also ensured that the Model is a priority at Year 7 and Year 8 and has not put in any staff who are not interested in teaching within the Model. This has only come about through Ian's vision of Teaching and Learning in the Middle Years. He has fostered the notion of sharing and celebrating work and involving students, parents and teachers in all aspects of education. This has meant that the Model at Endeavour Hills is an organic one – growing with each new development and change, yet still retaining the underlying philosophy of teamwork.

The timetable is still a traditional one, with separate year levels and 48-minute periods. The difference lies in staff teaching more than one subject to the same group of students, so that teachers are often 'blocked' for a double period, or even for a whole morning. There is flexibility within this arrangement to manipulate the timetable to suit the needs at the time. Teachers often 'team teach', or use the time to blur the traditional boundaries between subject areas.

Transition from Year 6 to Year 7

The staff at Endeavour Hills are seriously trying to address the issue of retention of students and alienation in the Middle Years. They are also trying to address the fact that students actually go backwards in the first two years of secondary school. By adopting the concept of close relationship with teachers and an integrated approach to the curriculum, the teaching teams are well on the way to doing so. To do this effectively, though, we work hard at keeping strong links with our primary feeder schools. This has been managed partly through a team approach to transition. Transition is seen as everyone's responsibility, and in an increasingly competitive environment, with an ever-changing image, all staff must play an active role in attracting students to the campus.

The Year 7 teaching team visits the primary schools in term two and takes with them an Endeavour Hills student who attended that primary school. The primary school students also visit the campus regularly to use the facilities such as science laboratories and technology resources. There are programmes for primary school students set up between teachers from the feeder schools and our campus. Regular meetings are held with primary teachers about curriculum issues to ensure smoother transition and to build on the student's experiences at primary school. It is a also a forum to share knowledge and resources to develop and present a better curriculum.

Projects

The Year 7 project was the 'Cans Film Festival' and the Year 8 project was 'Shelter'. These projects were developed by the teaching teams during meetings held in their own time and arose from the clear need to give students interesting, engaging work, with clear, relevant outcomes.

Evaluation

The evaluation for the projects comprised three main forms:

1 Student self-evaluation
2 Teacher evaluation
3 Presentation/celebration.

Students

The student evaluation required students to fill in sheets on a weekly basis; displaying their work to their peers and discussing and showcasing their finished products with their teachers.

Teachers

The teacher's evaluation required teachers to check against the CSF outcomes identified at the beginning of the project. The students were graded individually and as a team.

Presentation/celebration

The students from both the Year 7 and Year 8 projects were required to present their work to their peers, teacher and parents. They had to justify what decisions they made and the decision process they went through. The students also had to describe their finished product and explain how it linked with the outcomes determined at the outset of the project.

Each of the projects included a series of awards for presentation to the students, such as:

Year 7 as a parody of the Oscars

- Best Film
- Best Actor
- Best Comedy
- Best Special Effects

Year 8

- Best Design
- Most Economical
- Most Environmentally Aware
- Most Energy Efficient

Celebration

One of the essential outcomes of the TSG Model is the 'celebration' that occurs – on a number of levels. The first is an informal one, where the successes that are often overlooked in the classroom are shared and celebrated by the teacher and students. The second is the sharing of anecdotes during the teaching team meetings. The third is when the students display and share their work with each other and the broader community. The fourth is the teacher's own celebration with includes a congratulatory meal and also formal reflection time. This proves to be the most useful and beneficial for staff as they consider the work that has been done, look at what has been achieved with respect to the initial goals, and then decide on further directions. It is also an opportunity to look for, and seek improvements in, Teaching and Learning.

The future

The way ahead for Endeavour Hills seems clear:

- Negotiate as well as integrate the curriculum.
- Make a genuine effort to tackle assessment and reporting.
- Look at Year 9 and Year 10 and find a blend of the TSG Model and the rigours of the VCE.
- Continue to raise the profile of teaching and learning within the campus, by sharing knowledge and documenting existing practice.
- Continue to provide excellent PD opportunities for staff.
- Improve relationships with our community, particularly parents, perhaps by providing opportunities for parents to participate in forums where the students, parents and teachers discuss common goals and outcomes.
- Ensure that 'celebration' is included as an integral part of our everyday work.
- Continue to challenge traditional pedagogy and maintain enthusiasm for a Model that really does work!

References

Taylor, S. and McKenzie, I. (1997) in Davies, B. and West-Burnham, J. (eds) *Reengineering and Total Quality in Schools*, London, Pitman Publishing.

Ratzki, A. (1988) 'The remarkable impact of creating a school community – one model of how it can be done', *American Educator*, Spring 1988, pp. 10–43. Author unnamed.

14

■ ■ ■

The road to raising achievement

CARRIE SABIN-YOUNG

My work is the embodiment of dreams – William Morris

On 6 September 1996, a sudden and unexpected phone call from the assistant director of education resulted in my acceptance of a year's secondment. I had two weeks to clear my current caseload and make the necessary arrangements for someone to take over my post as team leader of a specific learning difficulty base. I had established the base from scratch, providing teaching and advice for 68 schools in our catchment area, in addition to running practical training sessions. Over the years, the quality and content of these courses led to a reputation and trading basis which allowed us to invite national and international speakers. The impact on the team was enormous. By the time I left, I had worked closely with seven of the most creative teaching and administrative personnel to be found and in many ways I felt as though I was deserting my 'baby', as well as my 'family'. I left for the chance to work at County Hall, as service manager. A chance, I thought, to work with some of the leaders within the LEA, and influence some of the decisions affecting special needs, at school and individual level.

Three *days* later, just as suddenly, everything within my world collapsed. I started my new post, with a new team, all of whom were facing major re-organisation. The prospect of working in different buildings, towns, or possible redundancy resulted in high anxiety and stress for all concerned. The same day, my husband announced our ten-year marriage was over. As

I grappled to provide emotional and financial support for our five children, driving a long distance to work, leaving my four-year-old daughter in tears with a suddenly appointed nanny, I genuinely didn't believe the friend who said that one day I would look back on all of this, and realise that it was all for the best. Alongside the trauma facing me as a Manager, four years previously we had moved to a semi-derelict watermill. That winter, as the roof leaked, the boiler packed up, and we were without water for a four weeks, I considered running away from it all myself. I wish we knew more about what makes some people fight through adversity and others despair totally. The same question must be asked of students – why do some flounder and yet others, with just as much emotional instability, academic failure and low self-esteem, fight through and win?

January 1997 resulted in an additional move, within County Hall, to work with another team, accepting an internal promotion to *area* service manager. However, my background in educational law, coupled with a desire to provide realistic school support for students with statements, frequently made me feel very uncomfortable. At the beginning of April, I telephoned a secondary school with regard to reducing support. What started as a flippant comment, 'find me a job', resulted with the senior teacher and myself producing a document – the sum total of many previous discussions. This was taken to the headteacher and governors, and I started a three-year project on 1 May, election day. The Raising Achievement Project (RAP) was born.

Success or failure?

When asked to identify the origin of my thoughts, on which the project is based, it becomes clear that it has its essence in my schooldays. Having been sent to a secondary modern girls' school, where we were told during every assembly that we were not clever, I had often felt that expectation was a significant key to learning. It is perhaps too easy to attribute any academic or educational success to date to the headteacher who wrote to my parents with the remark that 'she has no job prospects. She won't even find work at Woolworths'. However, it has left me with a desire to learn, and to facilitate learning with others. John Visser of Birmingham University often talks about students finding it difficult to invest any more 'learning currency' when they have already spent £99.99 of their £100 quota. How sad it is to recognise that many pupils have *felt what it is like to fail*, only one or two terms into their formal education. The 'Success for All' project in the USA provides greater insights into this.

The vision

Prior to reading works by Senge and Fullan, the vision had emerged. The challenge became that of transferring it from the authors' heads to the rest of the school, student and parent community. My role, as director of the Raising Achievement Project, was to bring about a significant change in the secondary school's philosophy and practice. The project was deliberately given a short time span, with the clear intention that Raising Achievement was to impact directly on *every individual*, and that every individual had direct *responsibility* for raising their own, as well as group, performance. Each teacher and faculty group had to be part of the vision and recognise their role within it. A whole-school collaborative approach was essential. Schools are good at identifying the needs of students, but however excellent the teamwork, programmes tend to remain fairly isolated. They may build upon each other, but with the RAP we attempted to build a philosophy alongside a wide and ranging raft of support. Clear targets were set for the three-year period. Within a five-year period, all students were to leave school with a minimum reading, comprehension and spelling age of ten. Somehow, even that target seemed educationally unacceptable, but with a near failing school, we had to start somewhere.

However, perhaps more crucial, the block in which the project was housed was to create and represent a pro-active demonstration of a commitment to lifelong learning. Training sessions for teachers, involving students from both the secondary school and feeder schools, were made very public. In addition, local industries and businesses were asked to take part in a particular approach to literacy. This would allow and empower all members of the community to build on whatever skills they already had. The argument was simple: everyone can improve upon their level of expertise, from the least to the most able.

Creating the possibility of learning

The majority of students not experiencing success have a cocktail of difficulties. For instance, there is a direct link between low literacy and low self-esteem. If students were to *believe* that they *could* learn, then they had to feel comfortable with the notion that they did not know an answer. If they could be led along a route whereby they could identify and recognise their body feelings associated with not knowing, they would then be willing to open themselves up to the *possibility* of learning. Programmes to enhance self-esteem and body language, identify learning and teaching styles, were to become a prerequisite of the literacy programme. High expectations for students, teachers and parents would come about through programmes of empowerment.

Endless possibilities seemed to open up in the form of art and drama. Trestle Theatre Company were booked to provide a day's practical work-shop for a group of Year 8 and 9 students. Originally, the students were chosen to represent two vulnerable groups of the school community, all of whom had low self-esteem – those who were passive, and those who might be termed 'aggressive'. It was financed through other professionals attending the training day, with the aim of taking ideas back to their own schools. Teachers from primary, secondary, EBD a special school, and an adolescent psychiatric unit provided further opportunities for networking of ideas. The day was based around body language and experiencing another person's character via the use of masks, which the students made. It immediately became clear that this work would be useful to all, students and staff alike. In addition, much of the group work centred upon games to inspire complicity and a sense of co-operation. Following the course, the drama and PE staff made plans to build directly upon this particular element, rigorously introducing the students to these types of activities, which we anticipated would have a direct result on pupil behaviour and classroom management. For the first time, some of the least able, most vulnerable students had felt themselves to be in control of the more assertive personalities. If this could be harnessed effectively, then more passive students could have the space to take control of their own learning environments.

Who leads, who follows?

At this point, it is difficult *not* to believe that some greater power was, and still is, steering several key elements in the direction of the Raising Achievement Project and beyond. There has been a succession of unintentional and accidental meetings with a number of innovative and creative individuals, who are rapidly building towards the creation of a team. It feels as though we are being manoeuvred like chess pieces, each piece or position crucial to the success of the game. Perhaps it began five years ago with a quote that I placed in the resource area of the SpeLD Base:

> From a moral standpoint, schools have to be fundamentally and obsessively concerned with providing children with the very best education possible ... It is difficult to conceptualise a situation where anything less than total quality is perceived as being appropriate or acceptable for the education of children.
>
> (West-Burnham, 1992).

In October 1997 I embarked on the International MBA in Educational Leadership. Quite unintentionally, the author of the above quote became my personal tutor. The term 'reengineering' had not previously entered my vocabulary, but it was already clear that the purpose of education is currently undergoing a phenomenal shift. The profound social, economic and cultural changes taking place across the world necessitate a quantum shift in the provision of education within the next five years. A 'paradigm shift' is occurring. Some of the literacy work documented later in this chapter has led to the notion of providing 'the big picture', *all* of the information required by pupils being *taught* at the same time. The provision of a linear educational input is fast becoming obsolete. In the New Year, work is to begin on the setting up of a new type of educational training establishment, possibly sited at the watermill, where any member of the community can 'learn how to learn'. The capacity for change, to provide practical demonstrations of futures thinking, is so exciting and stimulating that without doubt the work taking place is only the very beginning.

Learning styles

One intention of the project at the school was to demonstrate visually three possible learning styles to all concerned. Initially, the simplistic plan had been to identify and then tag with badges those students who learned from verbal or written instructions, those who required visual images or diagrams, and those for whom the experience or action itself was required in order for learning to take place. Visiting a student in the local MLD (moderate learning difficulties) school, I chanced upon an article entitled 'Teaching and style. Are you making a difference?' Visits to the assessment research unit at Birmingham University resulted in the purchase of an easy-to-administer IT programme. This was immediately introduced for use with all staff and students, starting with the senior management team. The nine learning styles identified (analytical verbaliser, analytical bimodal, analytical imager, intermediate verbaliser, intermediate bimodal, intermediate imager, wholist verbaliser, wholist bimodal and wholist imager) had a far greater impact on 'differentiation' than previously encountered. Initially students, and possibly staff, may have felt their styles validated only one possible way of learning/teaching – the 'take me as I am' principle.

Quickly, however, students began to realise that if a teacher was presenting a topic in a different style to their method of learning, they had to take responsibility for their own learning by paying more careful attention. The least preferred style required greater concentration from the learner, not less. In contrast, the teacher who may have been identified as wholistic verbaliser, must take responsibility for the intermediate imagers within the class group. Current plans involve an industry-financed day, students and staff wearing nine possible colours of T-shirt with pertinent slogans – 'verbalisers do it with words'? There are numerous possibilities here for the design students to take a lead. The intention of this very graphic display, with the emphasis on 'groups', will be to ensure that both students and teachers recognise the different dynamics within each class or setting, and harness the different strategies available to raise the learning profiles.

At the start of the assessments, I felt confident that a minimum reading age of ten would be required in order to access the typed information and questions. However, students who had the questions read to them while using the programme seem satisfied that the printed result truly reflects them. A variety of checks were undertaken to assess the validity of the results. Within the sixth form, Years 10 and 7, only five students felt that the two-page analysis did not reflect them at all. Interestingly, all of these students fell into bimodal categories. This could indicate that with a slightly different score, they could shift into other categories. The students repeated the assessment, and accepted the second print-out. One student produced the same category of style on four consecutive occasions. Eventually, through discussion with friends and teachers, he felt comfortable that if he was open to positive interpretation, rather than viewing each statement as a negative, the outline did reflect his learning style. In contrast, the most commonly received comment from students and teachers alike, was: 'How does it (the computer) know? This is exactly like me.'

From the very first assessment, and subsequent discussions, the notion of 'failure' seemed to dissipate. Terminology such as 'thick' or 'least able' disappeared from the language used by staff and students. During a special sixth-form event, students were organised into groups reflecting each specific learning style. As well as proving great fun, it was interesting to identify one almost totally male group, with students following career paths such as airline pilot, or hoping to join the RAF and Army, etc., joined by two females about to enter the police force. Within an almost all-female set anticipating careers such as children's nanny and veterinary work, two males were hoping to join the RSPCA and go into nursing.

The information collated to date will have a major impact on the delivery of the curriculum. The latest data available dictates that student performance benefits directly from being organised into learning style groups, rather than cognitive ability sets. It is the intention to provide a research opportunity based upon reorganisation of certain curriculum areas, such as maths or science, matching teaching and learning style.

It was not surprising that companies such as Roche, Marks & Spencer, the Water Authority and McDonald's attended an industry luncheon to decide ways in which we could support each other.

A new framework for the teaching of literacy

In the summer of 1995 I had invited Alan Davies, co-author of THRASS (Teaching Handwriting, Reading and Spelling Skills), to speak at a convention for teachers, assistants, educational psychologists, etc. This was to prove one of the most far-reaching decisions of my career. At the end of the first hour and a half, I had heard enough to declare publicly that this was exactly what I required in order to *teach literacy effectively*. The past 22 years had been spent providing an expensive resource, exclusive to the few with the severest learning difficulties, either via one-to-one or small group withdrawal, or in-class support. Pupils' rate of effort was rarely rewarded with the appropriate rate of progress. If they did begin to achieve, they were frequently 'rewarded' with a reduction in their necessary support. Sustainable progress was, at best, patchy, rarely transferring to the everyday world of the classroom. Within the specific learning difficulty team, virtually all available reading/spelling schemes had been trialled, further supported by individually devised worksheets, games, and the use of specific IT programmes, etc. Everything was directed towards the need for remediation. THRASS provided a multisensory framework which could not only remediate, but far more importantly, *prevent* failure. It provided an understandable method of teaching and learning all the 'rules' of the 'literacy game' which children and adults of any age could easily access.

With other schemes or programmes, the teaching and subsequent learning takes place in a fairly linear form. Building bricks of knowledge are cemented prior to moving on in a student's understanding and demonstration of knowledge base, within their individual work. THRASS presents the entire picture straightaway, and pupils are given the language and understanding to manipulate it correctly. Furthermore, key skills are rehearsed and overlearned, which are fundamental to any learning situation – the development of listening skills, following instructions, tracking, skimming, scanning, specific teaching in developing visual and auditory skills, developing memory and recall, training in asking questions, testing hypotheses, as well as inadvertently *always* achieving success. All these seem to be almost accidental benefits of THRASS. Self-esteem, and the willingness to invest in learning, are transformed. The framework lends

167

itself to the use of 'real' books, poetry and environmental print, as well as the myriad schemes already in schools. As students and staff have written in thousands of evaluations, 'it just makes sense'. Here was a key to the empowerment of students, teachers and parents alike. A programme of training for each teacher and assistant ensured that all staff understood and felt skilled in the teaching of literacy across their subject area. Parents who had previously felt disempowered with helping their children learn, attended introductory sessions and were quickly offering mentoring, buddying, and the possibility of starting weekend workshops, to bring their younger children, or indeed, young adults/grandparents, to learn alongside each other.

Having established a THRASS training centre at the school, with the consent of the authors, links with local business and industry quickly established a mutual method of support, whereby further literacy training could be provided by us for employees. This would ensure necessary funding for educational resources, as well as supporting the philosophy and public demonstration of lifelong learning. Company directors were becoming interested in the early identification of learning style and possible links with appropriate staffing choices. A further chance meeting was to lead to THRASS for the soul!

A quite bizarre set of circumstances ensured that I introduced a stranger to the concept of THRASS during a break in a course on behaviour management. He quickly enrolled his headteacher and staff in the possibilities of introducing THRASS, and a series of stimulating and creative meetings followed. It was during one of these that I was introduced to the Landmark Educational Forum. It is difficult to describe the events of the three-day course, alongside 160 other people, reflecting a complete cross-section of background and race. Delegates had flown in from France, Germany and Denmark to give themselves the gift of living completely in the present. Had I not been introduced to the concept by an articulate, intelligent professional who was also a friend, I doubt I would have undertaken the course. However, by the latter part of the third day, I indeed experienced the promised 'emotional paradigm shift'.

The group dynamic (gaining insights into yourself through listening to the experience of others), the simplicity of the materials presented, and the powerful, provocative yet respectful coaching of the course leader combined to produce a level of self-learning that I had never experienced in 23 years of 'traditional' education and management training. It can only be described as breakthrough learning. I wanted every relative, friend and colleague to experience the same, but more importantly, recognised a key element that had been missing from the Raising Achievement Project.

How could students be introduced to this concept in order to truly know themselves? How could they be introduced to a new vocabulary, which could allow them access to new ways of being? People go on to higher education and beyond to learn a vocabulary which allows them to become good business managers, doctors, traders, etc. The vocabulary taught in the Forum gave people access to becoming more effective and powerful human beings. Children need to be supported differently if they are to learn to live life fully, *now*, in the moment that is presented to them, rather than wait for the *tomorrow's* – how 'it ought to be'. The individual agenda that a pupil of any age brings to school forces a mismatch to occur between the curricula, educational agenda, and the personal one. Our tools for dealing with this are limited. We employ differentiation, enrolment (entertainment), use of learning style, counselling and pastoral support, to a lesser or greater degree. But does it work? I believe where good practice occurs, we can, at best, only alleviate the symptoms.

Experience since doing the Forum dictates that when you *are* present to how things are as opposed to how you want them to be (wishes and wants), a power and freedom is created to become more effective. One teacher told me of Jo, a Year 10 'average pupil', who was predicted to achieve five A–Cs following her mock exam results. During the summer vacation, she took part in the 'young people's Forum' and later achieved nine straight As in her GCSEs. She later confided that the Forum had allowed her to see just how much she was getting from making her parents responsible for her average performance in school. The Forum had not made her give up 'any of the stuff' she was doing before; in fact, she was going out more often. However, it had made it possible for her to see that she, alone, was responsible for her GCSE grades. She felt able to concentrate during lessons rather than think about relationships with her peer group and boyfriends. She was present to what was in front of her.

Jo's experience shows that like the pupils of any age, who grasp the whole picture of literacy through THRASS, teenagers are able to take on breakthrough learning. Alongside the tools with which we can equip each student for the necessary literacy understanding to access any subject, we now have the tools and vocabulary to equip us with the necessary insight and understanding to really know ourselves and therefore how we relate to others. The missing link.

The past two years seem to have provided a network of creative and innovative professionals who share in the notion that current education, in remaining linear, target-driven and knowledge-ridden, does little to equip students for life – *work and relationships*. The time seems right for a quantum leap in terms of what education can and should provide. Schools are at the centre of many communities, and with the necessary training and leadership, are set for providing life skills across the age and ability range. The dream, if not the vision, is to set up a training centre to ensure that a range of different professionals can act as trainers in their own communities. A true Raising of Achievement.

> *To believe what has not occurred in history will not occur at all is to argue disbelief in the dignity of man.*

> (Mahatma Ghandi)

References

Bane, G. and Rayner, S. *Support for Learning*, NASEN 1997, 'Teaching and Style Are you making a difference?'

Fullan, M. (1993) *Change Forces*, Falmer Press.

Landmark Education, 23 Gosfield Street, London W1P 8EA. Tel: 0171 580 1997.

Senge, P. (1990) *The Fifth Discipline*, Doubleday.

West-Burnham, J. (1992) *Managing Quality in Schools*, Harlow, Longman.

15
■ ■ ■

Reflection and the infant – a quality experience

LINDA WHITE

Eastwood Infant and Nursery School is located in a small former mining town on the Nottingham/Derbyshire border. A flavour of the town and what living conditions are like for its inhabitants can be found somewhere between a D.H. Lawrence (birthplace Eastwood) novel and a Channel 4 documentary on the effects of a pit closure on its community. Practical survival rather than spiritual reflection is the order of the day.

Conflict is often present. Conflict between children; conflict between families; conflict between home and what is commonly perceived to be authority. Conflict resolution is a feature of the school day. I have worked closely with a class of six and seven-year-olds to develop their own strategies for dealing with difficult situations. Self decision making is a priority.

Philosophy/approach

We always begin the day with a discussion about what is required and the best way to organise ourselves (me in particular) in order to meet these requirements. There is a genuine commitment to achievement and a pride in their environment from children who often struggle to find the appropriate language to express their needs and feelings. Therefore, it seemed to be a natural progression to create the space to reflect on the day's happenings in order to plan for the following day. This time for reflection then developed into a much more spiritual experience for all of us.

Background

In my experience there are many and often limiting assumptions made about what the young child can and cannot do and about what the young child can and cannot understand. I find it challenging to explode what I refer to as the 'they are only little children' myth.

As co-ordinator for professional development, I had previously developed a system for personal development planning which had the teacher, as a reflective practitioner, at its centre. As a result of this process, I firmly believe that the key to the improvement of skills and to the acquisition of knowledge, the key to job satisfaction and enjoyment – in fact, the key to learning – lies in the ability to reflect and change. If this is the case for me the adult, the teacher, the learner, then surely it must be the case for the child, the pupil, the learner. Although I did believe that it was possible to discuss reflection with my class of infants. I needed to create the necessary conditions for reflection to occur. I needed to set the scene.

I have always used music in my teaching. I have found it useful for a number of purposes ranging from story writing to the discussion of issues such as racism and sexism in a global society. However, the choice of music for a reflection time was crucial. I gradually introduced tracks such as the familiar and celestial chimes of Enya from her *Watermark* and *Shepherd Moons* albums to the totally unfamiliar and non-mainstream inspirational Tibetan temple chants from the Hanshan Temple. In this case I was attracted to the 'timeless chords' of the Buddhist meditative chants which the promotional literature assured would create a 'tranquil ambience'. However, not only did this music demand reflection, it also required candles. The scene was set. Something very mystical then started to happen.

Action

Reflection is certainly easier to achieve between late autumn and early spring. The atmosphere is better. Lights are switched off. Children sit in a circle in something we call a 'listening position'. A position reminiscent of meditation and The Beatles visiting the guru. A position invented to enable the infant to 'receive and share' as opposed to the temptation to become involved in hairdressing activities or rattling Lego pieces in the nearest plastic tub. The door is firmly closed. A 'Do not disturb' sign is attached, courtesy of Wallace and Gromit.

The day has been extremely hectic as usual. Too many subjects to teach. Too many children. Too little energy, on my part anyway. The corridor is already filling with parents struggling with the obligatory pushchairs and wayward toddlers. A scene reminiscent of the underground at rush hour. Inside the closed room all is calm; all is silent. The candle or occasionally the oil burner is lit. (I can recommend an oil aptly named 'Calm Balm' for this purpose.) A few words are sometimes spoken to guide thoughts, sometimes silence. The room is so quiet, a veritable oasis of calm. The feeling is spiritual and very special. The feeling is very much of a group who are together. Sometimes it lasts 20 minutes, sometimes five. Sometimes it follows a story or a wet and windy playtime, sometimes it stands on its own. It is always demanded and enjoyed. It certainly helps me to face the rest of the day, but what about the children?

Stacey: *'You look at the candle and you see yourself.'*

Makyila: *'You don't move.'*

Alex: *'When you look at the candle and close your eyes you can think about the day.'*

Christopher: *'It gives you peace.'*

Andrew: *'It changes yourself.'*

Shaun: *'You close your eyes and think about the day.'*

Donna: *'You see yourself when you look at the flame.'*

Edward: *'You can lie down when you feel like it.'*

Scott: *'I like it when all the circle is quiet and I can think.'*

Donna: *'It makes you calm.'*

Andrew: *'It changes the day.'*

Shaun: *'You need the candle.'*

Gareth: *'It stops you fighting.'*

Edward: *'The candle clears all the bad things out of your head.'*

Taylor: *'It's like when you look at the sun, when you close your eyes it's like the light comes through to you. It's resting when you are in a mess. It makes you calm and quiet again. When you've been scrappy, it makes you more calm.'*

Laura: *'When you look at the candle you can travel to another country if you think about it. When it's dark, the light makes you feel nice inside.'*

Andrew: *'It changes your body language. When you look at the candle, it gives you some control. The candle is like a sun.'*

I am now in the process of developing a mentoring system. Watch this space.

Part 3 – Reflection and review
■ ■ ■

1 When was the last time you conducted a fundamental reappraisal of the principles underlying learning and teaching strategies in school?

2 How valid are the benchmarks and 'bottom-line' principles in use in school?

3 Do we know how to listen to students effectively?

4 How open are you and your colleagues to new knowledge about how we learn?

5 To what extent are teachers learning?

6 On what basis are learning and teaching policies and strategies selected?

7 To what extent is the individual at the centre of all decisions about learning and teaching?

8 How much significance is attached to the emotional side of learning?

9 What opportunities exist for review, reflection and the creation of personal understanding?

10 How much *learning* is taking place in school and how do you know?

PART 4

■ ■ ■

Technologies of learning

The case studies in this section all include reference to the increasing importance of information and communication technology in facilitating effective learning. However, they all contextualise ICT in a broader range of approaches – learning strategies, community involvement, new approaches to managing resources – which indicate a willingness to question the fundamental premisses on which the student experience is based.

16

■ ■ ■

Jewels in a lead coronet

MAX COATES

Introduction

The Bourne Community College nestles in a small corner of West Sussex. The area consists of pockets of considerable affluence interspersed with agrarian poverty and stands cheek by jowl with Europe's largest municipal housing development. Many of the local villages retain a fierce individualism which would serve to inspire Steinbeck.

The college has served its community well, although a marketing campaign focused on a motif as a 'caring school' has resulted in a Warnockian excess of pupils with special educational needs. The numbers and the ability of the intake had been sliced by competition from two single-sex high schools still basking in the afterglow of earlier days as grammar schools. The loss of the sixth form eight years previously had conferred relegation status on the college in the eyes of staff and potential client group alike. Potential strategies had included the use of Semtex on the local high schools and the performing of frontal lobotomies on Years 10 and 11. The previous headteacher had been overtaken by the pace of change since the Education Reform Act 1988 (ERA) and had been granted an honourable discharge. There had been three attempts to appoint a new head, which prolonged the uncertainty of an interregnum. The context and circumstances of the college has led to a celebration of failure. More dangerous was the perception by many staff, and even some officers of the LEA, of the college as victim. A presentation on 'value added' had prompted one teacher to counter concerns over performance with the comment: 'What do you expect with these children?' At a stroke, this subverted the entire message of 'value added' and confirmed the member of staff in a state of professional emasculation.

Henry Ford is famous for his assurance that his cars were available in any colour so long as it was black. Less well known is his pithy observation that 'whether you think you can or whether you think you can't, you're right'. Of course, this strikes to the heart of most human enterprises, both individual and corporate. It was to be belief in potential that proved to be the springboard for a fast-track recovery. If all share a communal institutional death wish, the task of regenesis may be a resurrection too far. However, I was convinced that this headship was not a poisoned chalice and accepted the post from April 1996. My certainty was reinforced when I discovered a large number of key players who were ready to run with a new vision and who had the skills to turn dreams into reality. There were indeed jewels set in this lead coronet.

Dream-master

Mordja Amari Bradja
(those who lose their dreaming are lost)

(Aboriginal proverb)

Leadership is about becoming the dream-master; articulating a vision of the possible, painting a polychromatic future for those trapped in a monochrome present and dogged by a sepia past. The dreams of others must be drawn in and integrated into a single story-line.

Many discussions took place in the first few months of my headship. It became clear that there were a good number of excellent teacher practitioners, but three principal dreamers: one brought a passion for individuals and their achievement of personal potential, another a vision of the role of new technologies, and the third a belief about pupil performance and the place of education within the community. The core of our dream had been reduced to the following four key areas:

Teaching and learning

Two processes take place in classrooms: teaching and learning. Sometimes they are connected. There is a wealth of new insights into teaching and learning, much derived from our improved knowledge of the brain and its function. Alistair Smith (1996), in true Pareto style, asserts that 80 per cent of what we know about the brain and learning has been discovered in the past 15 years. This may, of course, be true of most areas of knowledge. Surely, then, this must serve to challenge much of our pedagogical stance.

I qualified as a teacher in 1970 and remember well the tension as I attended education lectures on Plato and undertook a teaching practice at the William Penn comprehensive school, nestling on the edge of Brixton. Clearly, the elder statesmen of the profession have missed out on key advances. I would contend that temporary entrants to teaching also lack a cohesive model of teaching and learning.

Our initial focus was finding more efficient ways of tackling literacy and numeracy deficit. The first discovery was that while there was a wealth of experience at the primary level, the secondary approach was not dissimilar to that of the Englishman in France; namely, shout louder and gesticulate wildly. The college did have a well established package of reading and spelling clubs, supported by special needs assistants and parents. This tended to assist pupils with special educational needs. Strategies were needed to reach the majority, especially boys who had achieved a state of arrested literary development as books were discarded in favour of Playstations and Megadrives. ERIC (Everybody Reading In Class) was quickly imported instead of tutor time, with the teacher reading to provide the role model. This proved a positive first step. Our subjective view is that there were significant gains through what is a self-differentiating process.

A group of staff continued to research for other strategies. The group was joined by the head of mathematics who was concerned to find a concurrent approach to numeracy. We became convinced that integrated learning systems (ILS) were the appropriate way forward. Visits to other schools, and a review of research in this area, brought us to several conclusions:

- A common front end was needed for all programmes – different operating systems for numeracy and literacy programmes could only serve to get in the way of the main event.
- In many of the situations we looked at, the deployment of these very sophisticated tools was haphazard and often restricted to pupils with special educational needs.
- It must be delivered through a network – the management by pupils on a stand-alone PC of a course carried on 32 CD-ROM discs was a disaster waiting to happen.

While it is still early days, our initial evaluation is beginning to pose some challenging questions and also show trends:

- Gains are being made and these range between .3 of a year to two years.
- The package is American-based and it is clear that in number work, as opposed to problem-solving, our national levels are lower than across the Atlantic.

- The most significant gains are being made by pupils of lower and higher ability; the middle ability range do not seem to make such significant gains.

- Although there is autonomous learning provided by the programme, different levels of progress are being recorded by groups supervised by different staff.

- Differential gains are being made by groups using the package at different times of the day – early morning groups are making the most significant progress.

- General IT skills are increased, displacing the need for specific teaching in this area.

As a college, we are taking our first faltering steps towards establishing new ways of working. Methods rooted in the forties and fifties cannot serve the educational needs of the 21st century with its demands to empower flexible learners capable of responding to jobs which have not even been invented. The college is looking at the development of a learning policy which will scrutinise practice in every area in order to enhance learning. Everything must go into the melting pot to be recast. This will include timings of the day, using ICT for registration so that the day can start with learning, flexible working patterns, the development of ILS into other areas of the curriculum, incorporating accelerated learning perspectives, the increased use of performance data in setting individual targets, whole-school mentoring by all staff, and changing the daytime diet and eating patterns. Teaching, as an esoteric art form, must go, and be replaced with a model which is based on research and not posture.

Resources

The buildings dated from that unlovely period of educational architecture, the fifties. It is possible that the architect had designed pill-boxes in the Second World War. Time had not inflicted a mellow desirability. Posters were structural materials and the technology department had been one of the last strongholds of the Luddites. Physical resources are nowhere near as crucial as good colleagues (note the careful avoidance of the term 'human resources'). Even so, there was an urgent need to secure improvement in key facilities and refresh the tired building. In an ideal world, such work would be undertaken by the LEA on receipt of an appropriate form issued in triplicate. In reality, hard pressed LEAs are still trying to replace outside toilets, eradicate asbestos, replace boilers and conform ageing buildings to the demands of a plethora of regulations.

Self-help may be anathema to many in education, but the alternative of battle-ship grey and Great Western green is too bleak. One particular governor accepted the challenge. He recruited a labour force from those directed to community service. The materials he collected in the course of his work from builders' merchants all over the south coast. Of course, the paint donated tended to be in colours spurned by the shopping public. In places, a term like vibrant would be generous.

More serious redevelopment brought us into the arena of 'the bid'. Currently, we have bids pending for sports hall funding with the national lottery, technology funding with the specialist schools initiative, and the second New Deals for Schools bid and industrial sponsorship. While the rewards can be great, the work involved in assembling bids is enormous, especially for a smaller school. Senior management, working closely with a complex and rapidly moving process, may well cope with the occasional hits, but the majority of staff find the process difficult to comprehend. The disappointment of the failed bid is keenly felt and all too readily leads to a lowering of morale.

Professional development

There had been a visionary commitment to initial teacher training with strong linkages forged with several universities and institutes of higher education. This had developed to a point where 50 per cent of the teaching staff were trained mentors. This, in turn, had promoted a reflective and evaluative approach to classroom practice and led eventually to 11 staff undertaking post-graduate degrees. The revenue from the ITT had been strategically reinvested. It is on this substantial foundation that we have now committed to Investors in People (IIP). Through this, we are seeking to secure a climate of continuous professional development for all staff. This must be the springboard to promoting a high-reliability organisation.

Our experience of professional development has led us to the following conclusions:

- professional development must be an entitlement for all staff
- it must be self-evidently linked to development planning
- significant amounts of the training should be delivered by 'in-house' staff which promotes a climate of dedicated training and fosters a team approach
- high quality training enhances pupil achievement, staff confidence and concurrently reduces stress.

Changing the context

Schools have traditionally operated within an LEA context. The officers of the local authority had usually served their apprenticeship in schools. There is still a shared educational world view at the heart of which remains a conviction that education is intrinsically worthwhile. It is seen as a master and not as a servant.

The contemporary context is very different: politicians and industrialists see an efficient education system as the key to delivering economic prosperity. The Tony Blair thrice-uttered mantra of 'education, education and education' as his political priorities show the extent to which schools have moved centre stage. Bourne Community College has sought to retain its valued partnership with its LEA by reorientating its context to stand in the midst of commerce and industry. Those involved in the hard-edged world of commerce are usually approached for small donations for library books or some cast-off piece of equipment. Our aim has been to convince them that we are in partnership. A school will usually be among one of the larger businesses in a locality. Certainly, in our area, 95 per cent of businesses employ 20 staff or less. This places the average school or college in the premier division of employers.

In striving to establish partnership, we have built heavily on personal contacts, drawn flies into the web using business breakfasts, lunchtime meetings. It is as these personal links have been established that opportunities have opened up. The college started with the Midbank initiative, and now has key contacts with more than 30 companies. Currently, we are working with Matra/Marconi (Space) to deliver courses in space-related engineering, backed by its far-sighted production director who shares our commitment to real-time education. As dialogue has progressed, partners from industry have begun to recognise the relationship as being two-way: ICT has become a focus for development, with key areas being training and the provision of internet facilities for small and medium-sized businesses. This will prove vital in changing the operational context of the college.

The experience of education for the secondary school pupil must reflect current commercial and industrial practice. Progression from school should be seamless and not provide a discordant jolt. It is no use delivering IT on Acorn machines and expect to see young people make the change to a PC environment where information is routinely disseminated via a network. Technology must go beyond yoghurt pots and Blue Peter, and provide experience of CAD and CNC machining. Communication with other countries must involve the internet and video-conferencing, rather than relying on 'pen-pal' initiatives.

The danger in dreaming

Dreaming is not for the faint-hearted. Most institutions arrive at a stage when maintenance is pre-eminent. Such a position is usually preoccupied with the urgent and important. The task of keeping going is overwhelming and, in the case of English and Welsh education, the process is exacerbated by the National Curriculum coming out in more versions than Sylvester Stallone's *Rocky*. Announcing the dream immediately produces two negatives. First, those in the 'hamster wheel' want it to turn more slowly and will believe that more change will cause the bearings to overheat. Second, the new vision will almost certainly be understood as writing off what has gone before. Calling for colleagues to work smarter and not harder can have an undesirable sub-text.

Dreams are about possibilities and not actualities. The future does not lie within the gift of any leader or manager. Of course, professional expertise tries to ensure that the vision is achievable. The very activity of beating a different rhythm transcends the status quo and carries its attendant risks. If the vision portrayed is delayed or does not materialise, the credibility of the leader is diminished or destroyed. At the time of writing, we are waiting to learn if we have been granted specialist school status. Failure to jump this hurdle will require some very nimble managerial footwork or a tanker of Prozac to avoid serious corporate depression and reduced performance.

Vision cannot be declared in a tentative, hesitant manner. It must be expressed with a considered confidence. The more the vision is communicated, and the more colleagues identify with it, the more teams must be entrusted with its achievement. The charismatic leader who leads the school out of Egypt and towards a pedagogical Canaan all too readily becomes the patriarch who must supply the answers. When a head steps into this role, he becomes too vulnerable to blame when setbacks come and, of course, inhibits the contributions and development of others.

Dreamers often find the routine does not hold their attention with the same intensity as vision and possibility. The urgent and important can be sidelined by the not urgent and unimportant. Maintenance at all levels can all too easily be relegated to a lower division. The management of the ordinary can all too easily be a response to crises or left for Belbin's body of completers and company workers to mop up in desperation. Certainly, there have been numerous occasions when present reality has broken into future vision. Recently, with the leadership team preoccupied with forward planning, we allowed a situation to develop where a combination of trips, Inset and absence resulted in inadequate levels of staffing with a loss of stability. Repeated fire-fighting is the domain of poor management.

Conclusion

Education is dominated by innovation and change, most of which has passed by too quickly to evaluate. So much of this change has been about reinstating former traditions. For many educational managers, simply keeping abreast with new directives is all-consuming. It is more important than ever to dream if we are to find new ways of operating which can be adapted to meet a changing society and new patterns of employment. In a structured educational environment, where so much seems to be prescribed, the dreamer can still find interstices in which to innovate and subvert.

References

Smith, A. (1996) *Accelerated Learning in the Classroom*, Network.

17

■ ■ ■

From vision to reality: learning at the centre

RICHARD S. FAWCETT

Removing the bifocals

'Man, I got vision where the rest of the world wears bifocals.' Butch
Cassidy and the Sundance Kid were on horseback riding along a river bed
planning their ill-fated get-rich-quick strategy to finance a life of luxury.
One man's vision is another man's myopia. So it is in the educational
world. What may seem visionary in one school may be yesterday's story
in another, and not even clearly seen on the horizon in a third, just a blur
through misty bifocals. Schools are all at differing stages of development.
So, too, are their leaders. What there is in common is the need to develop a
vision relevant to their strategic future, a vision which will promote success, not a shoot-out with fatal consequences as met by Butch and
Sundance in their Bolivian showdown.

In the 11th year of headship, the 25th in a senior management team, the
need to re-find a vision, to do some serious educational thinking rather
than the giving which is a focus of life in school, was an imperative.
Thurston Upper School needed to move on from the base it had established. A co-educational comprehensive school of some 1 350 students
aged 13–18, and serving more than 200 square miles of Suffolk countryside
to the east of Bury St Edmunds, refocusing the energies of the school and
the headteacher would hopefully, in a newly thought-out strategy, further
the aim of raising standards of learning and teaching.

Strategic management has become important for every school. A vision for years ahead is essential in a world where unpredictability is increasing. Drucker (1995, p. 296) has identified the response required:

> ... *the educated person of the future is somebody who realises they need to continue to learn. That is a new definition.*

Learning by school leaders which is relevant to the future of the school is of the essence. The stimulus to make the first moves to learn seriously began through the recommendation of a colleague, also a long-serving head in one school. He had found an educationally-based MBA uplifting when he, as he put it, had plateaued and did not really know where to go with his thinking or his career. The MBA had lifted him out of the day-to-day world into one which offered the opportunity to tease out the direction he and his school should take.

There is no doubt that losing a sense of direction is frustrating. There is also no doubt that it is very common. Charles Handy, a visionary thinker, felt that Britain had lost its way (1995, p. 266):

> *Sadly, she is more likely to be known as a museum than as a cultural centre, but the opportunity is there to find a second curve and to lift her people, to give her a sense of new direction.*

The second curve is the uplifting sigmoid curve which, if identified at the most appropriate time, will ensure continuing success for an already thriving school. Obtaining that lift on the second curve carries the obligations of both personal action and the need to involve the whole organisation in which one works. There is also the question of morality. Real educational benefit has to flow to the school from the changes that will come from new thinking. Senge (1990, p. 349) recognises the need for a moral underpinning:

> *Embracing change does not mean abandoning a core of values and precepts.*

He emphasises, too, the need for change to be creatively embraced through continual learning by whole organisations. Senge's fifth 'discipline' (a body of theory and technique to be mastered and applied) is systems thinking. Building on personal mastery, Senge stresses the need for shared vision and a shift of mind to recognise that it is our own actions, not those of others, that enable change to take place. Such views are easy to gloss over at school level, but ignored at peril. Staff and pupils are adept at identifying change for change's sake, change which is not well thought out but based on whim, not bringing real educational benefit.

186

Bringing about valued and valuable change requires not only a moral perspective but also a holistic one. Senge (1990, p. 14), in lamenting the small
number of learning organisations, defines one as

an organization that is continually expanding its capacity to create its future.

Remembering Lafontaine's fable, 'he who hesitates is lost', enrolment in
the International Leadership MBA at the University of Lincolnshire and
Humberside soon followed the conversations with my uplifted colleague.
But it also followed soul-searching that questioned the readiness individually and of the organisation to accept future change.

Into the digital sandpit

A second stimulus for re-evaluating personal leadership came from an
awareness that the information and communications technology (ICT)
revolution was washing into school, happening before one's eyes but not
within any personally-developed model that had a philosophical or practical base. The school had previously received finance under the
Technology for Schools Initiative. The investment in it had, at the time,
been forward-looking. Now, however, there was the pressure for even
more computing power. The expense of making further provision would
be great and would need to be justified, not only in pragmatic terms of
what would not otherwise be provided in school, but in terms of the educational future for students. The need to redefine the strategic aims of the
school with learning at the centre, making full use of ICT, was emerging as
a central task. But how to do it?

The MBA provided the framework. As part of it, a focused international
study was required. Using the network of the Secondary Heads
Association (SHA) in England, contact was made with colleagues in
Australia and New Zealand where it was known that ICT practice was
ahead of the field. In addition, a conference of the International
Convention of Principals (ICP) in Boston, USA, provided the starting
point for what was to be a life-changing experience. The conference outlined the world of ICT provision today and tomorrow, and Paul Kordis,
adviser to the American President, held the delegates speechless with his
futurologist's visions and descriptions of reality today. The ending of
genetic disease, the imminent ability to reverse the ageing process, blind
people using satellite technology to move along pavements, a chip the size
of a sugar cube holding all the books in the US Congress Library, a fully
automated McDonald's with the only people around clearing up, Olympic

skiers training on virtual-reality machines, medical surgery on eye patients carried out 100 miles away from the patient – these are realities in today's world. What place the blackboard?

> *On the horizon we can see virtual reality and a whole new constellation of surrogate worlds rapidly approaching. With them come a range of new and challenging problems. Not least among the latter are the misdirections inherent in commercially motivated material concerning such major issues as technology, violence and futures. So the task of creating new realms of meaning, of building culture, of exploring the mythic and celebrating it, lies heavily on educators.*

(Beare and Slaughter, 1993, p. 100)

There can be no doubt that with rapid change and an unfamiliar world encroaching on the 'digitally homeless', those for whom ICT is the concern of someone else, there is the need to think again, particularly for those involved in education.

> *... the prime task of imparting, checking and testing the retention of information need no longer be a main activity to be carried out in a school as we know it today.*

(Bowring-Carr and West-Burnham, 1997, p. 57)

But that is exactly what central government is demanding of schools. Indeed, the government has not yet reconciled the available learning technologies with the availability of resources. There is almost a breathtaking fear of encompassing new technologies, for

> *... sufficient to say that once schools are given the means and the freedom to respond to the vision of the twenty-first century, they will look and behave very differently from the ways in which they are constrained to behave at present.*

(Bowring-Carr and West-Burnham, 1997, p. 59)

Schools looking and behaving very differently from the present are difficult to define in detail, hence difficult to plan for. It is not surprising that lack of coherent action from government causes Stevenson (1997, p. 6) to say:

> *Our recommendation to central government is that they must make the act of faith and encourage the education sector to start using technology rather than talking about it.*

Paralysis by analysis? There is some sign of movement, but not of a coherent plan. So what do schools need to consider? Hardware is what usually comes to mind. But that brings its own myopia:

Many IT initiatives have focused on just one area, often the provision of hard-ware, at the expense of addressing more widely how computers can be fully integrated into education.

(McKinsey and Company, 1997, p. 1)

If the preparation of students for the future really is the central task for schools, then there is a need to come to terms with the reality of what lies ahead. For some things are certain. The digital revolution is just that, a revolution. In the view of Cummins and Sayers (1997) the central respon-sibility of teachers is to enable students to participate in the democratic process, the cornerstone of Western civilisation. Participation means inter-cultural learning, enabling students to live together in a multi-cultural human village, and to do so through long-distance teaching partnerships available through modern communications technology, in particular the internet. For Cummins and Sayers there is the need to enable students to have experience in intercultural collaboration and critical thinking. Education needs to be reframed around critical enquiry and collaborative generation of knowledge. There is a sense of the touchstone of truth in seeing for education that

global learning networks have the potential for creating, nourishing, and sus-taining the genuine learning communities so desperately needed if we are to confront the social, cultural, economic, and ecological challenges of the coming years.

(Cummins and Sayers, 1997, p. 16)

Putting it more specifically, they emphasise:

In the world of the twenty-first century, decision making and problem-solving in virtually all spheres – business, science, community development, government, politics – will depend on electronic networks that span diverse national and cultural boundaries. Students whose education has provided them with a broad range of experience in using such networks for intercul-tural collaboration and critical thinking will be better prepared to thrive in this radically different communications and employment environment than those who have not been provided with access to cross-cultural awareness and problem-solving skills.

(Cummins and Sayers, 1997, p. 12)

When confronted with these global perspectives, what importance has much of what we teach in today's overcrowded, subject-specific, acade-mia-protected curriculum? Quite bluntly, Stevenson (1997, p. 10) specifies something of UK need:

Developing students' competence in ICT is now an essential part of the nation's infrastructure and, in the national interest, central government cannot afford not to do it.

Given that the internet and other digital communication will be at the heart of the world of today's students, tomorrow's wealth-earners and social fabric-providers, what do we need in schools? Teachers who understand what is happening to the world of information technology are central. The realisation that teachers who rely on 'I know it all' will not be respected by students; that students do not have to go to school to glean all the facts they need to know; the possibility of developing higher order thinking skills at an earlier age; the need to work information and communications equipment hard as it will become obsolete before it is worn out; the distance developing between the ICT haves and have nots. All these are powerful forces alive and well today. However, it is the students and the retired who inherit the digital earth at the moment.

As the study tour in New Zealand and Australia made clear, what to buy (if you can afford it) is not the key problem, it is rather identifying a clear management framework and purpose for ICT. So here was the emerging focus, the vision to bring to reality: what is the required framework to support well managed and appropriate information and communications technology that enhances learning in school and prepares students for the future?

Peripatetic coaching: visiting the future

The two decisions – to study for an MBA and to carry out an international study of ICT provision – were key decisions on the road to creating a vision and translating into reality. The power of peripatetic coaching, visiting schools and colleges which have embraced ICT to student benefit, cannot be over-emphasised. Working alongside staff, understanding their decision making and looking at the progress being made by students where decisions have been turned into provision, is a powerful vehicle. Fifteen schools and colleges were visited, all different, none pedalling the 'we've got it cracked' delusion. Instead, it was possible to gradually piece together an ICT jigsaw that emerged as a vision for the future of ICT at Thurston. To some it will be a distant vision, to others old hat. At the time, and for the school, it became a target that was realistic but challenging.

The framework for supporting effective ICT owes its origins to the thinking of staff in many places. In particular, three key places contributed a great deal. They were Bendigo Senior Secondary College, Bendigo, Victoria; Appollo Parkways Primary School, Melbourne, Victoria; and Lanyon High School, Canberra. What can be gleaned by visiting schools and colleges? An example of the ideas and individual pieces of jigsaw may be seen in the example of outcomes of the visit to Bendigo College.

Bendigo Senior Secondary College

This school for students over 16 is a 'Navigator School', one of seven Victorian schools to model learning and teaching and administrative arrangements in environments where there is routine access to technology. The schools provide advice and professional support for other schools. Greatly enhanced funding from the Victorian State has been matched with the school giving financial and methodological priority to sustaining ICT developments. Two years of planning (1994–6) were followed by implementation in 1997.

The most outstanding feature of the school is undoubtedly the comprehensive planning and careful introduction of its scheme. Thought has been given to:

- objectives, strategies, responsibilities, timeline and costings
- the local area network which covers all rooms in the school
- the wider area network linking the school and homes to the world
- use of computers across the curriculum
- computer access for staff
- the professional development programme
- restructuring the school
- partnerships
- evaluation and benchmarking
- community involvement.

It was clear that the whole culture of the school, staff attitudes and skills had all been radically changed. There are signed learning plans between heads of department and the principal outlining what the departments will do. Students are very involved with their learning, taking charge of their enquiry methods.'Kids are fed up with going to school to watch teachers work' (the principal). For example, all students have access to the internet, and for $20 are given an e-mail address.

Key areas of interest are:

- The intranet: the school is putting publications and curriculum information on to the intranet and providing resources, including departmental time and money, to enable departments to do so.
- Research into the effectiveness of provision is carried out through student surveys.
- Teaching styles have changed – classrooms are more like primary classrooms (staff have visited primary schools extensively). They are seen as constructivist, active and experiential.
- Teachers are studying for PhDs and MAs which are technology-related.
- The technology planning committee includes staff representatives, outside consultants and students.
- Teaching and learning coaches (members of staff) teach one class less than normal.
- Laptops are sold to staff and later returned to school use. An upgraded computer is then issued for staff.
- IT friendliness is used as a staff selection criterion.
- Staff in positions of authority sign a document to say they support the direction the school is taking.
- Money has been created by not filling all senior posts and through a voluntary AU$200 levy each year on parents specifically for technology. A 15 per cent levy across departments raises AU$75 000 which has been earmarked for maintenance and software for on-line services.
- The library spends 50 per cent of what it used to on books.
- Twenty-five per cent of the support staff budget is for ICT.
- Student have wide ICT access including:
  - their own network storage
  - the internet and intranet
  - the library: there is always someone in the library to show students and staff how to use the internet
  - e-mail
  - chat rooms
  - real-time document collaboration
  - the college is developing software which will allow all students to have access from home.

- Digital photos for the student records.
- The librarian is a person with extensive skills and, for example, leads professional development.

Appollo Parkways Primary School

Appollo Parkways Primary School in Melbourne is a remarkable place. Funded as a Navigator School and one sponsored by Apple – an Acot school (Apple: Classrooms of Tomorrow) – the 23 classrooms are well equipped with computers and other ICT equipment. All the staff have undergone a great deal of professional development. The head of the school was emphatic that for every dollar spent on hardware you needed to spend at least two on staff development (a policy echoed by many other schools) to change the school culture. What had happened was that classrooms had become the place to focus on developing learning strategies using ICT.

It was clear that high expectations in the application of ICT can result in very high quality work that stems from motivated learners. Children as young as five took laptops to field work; seven-year-old students were able to scan documents and pictures as a matter of course; the same age students were regularly integrating their own text with art material and video excerpts in production of finished work. For example, excellent work focusing on poems written by the students, where a wide variety of ICT resources were used, produced outstanding end results.

Lanyon High School

Lanyon High School in Canberra operates outside national agreements on curriculum and staffing. It is open seven days a week. Teachers operate flexi-time. Each member of staff has a responsibility for 18 students. The school day for seniors is 8am–2pm and for juniors 10.30am–4pm. There is no lunch break. An activities programme runs between 8am–9am and 3pm–4pm. Students are placed in one of three 'home schools' and in a tutor group (called a 'home group'). They go to three curriculum banks a day (each with a minimum of 90 minutes). They leave the teacher when they have completed work to continue with other projects. The curriculum banks are:

- maths/science/PE/health
- English/humanities/Japanese and other languages
- art and technology.

In Years 7 and 8 this structure operates; in Years 9 and 10 every second day students have an electives session. Teachers operate as a team within the curriculum bank and manage a budget for classroom use, professional development, and relief teachers. There is a 'drop everything and read' session for 15 minutes each day when silent reading takes place and there is one-to-one tuition for reading from trained students. All students are tested for literacy and numeracy progress every six months. Every day they do mental arithmetic (80 questions) and use a published mathematical support package to identify and remedy personal mathematical problem areas. A 30-minute, daily intensive reading programme for the least able between break and lunch has achieved up to a 12-month reading age improvement in eight weeks.

The curriculum, accounts and administration of the school have three servers that talk to each other. The school has received sponsorship from Fujitsu to install 'thin client technology'. A superserver is networked to lower performing PCs, for example 486s. The power of the superserver is so great that relatively low individual computer power does not matter. The school is now looking at the 'anaemic' client scheme, a development on from thin client technology. The school has a local area network with 280 voice and data outlets. All classrooms have four computers; there are also three computer laboratories and computers in the library. Laptop Pentiums are rented out to students. Every area of the school has access to the information on the local network. Staff have their own folders on the local net.

There is great emphasis on negotiating the curriculum with students who also meet to discuss learning strategies. In an interesting and full professional development programme, teachers learn alongside students, for example on the internet. There are also classes targeted at teachers who have themselves identified particular needs.

The ideas from the visits to the 15 schools, made over a three-week period, gradually distilled into a framework which could be used as the basis for formulating a whole-school development strategy at Thurston Upper School. Students were to be at the core of the plan. Supporting their learning was the main rationale for investigating the ICT role in raising standards.

From future to present: the application of research

The study visit to New Zealand and Australia enabled the identification of appropriate ICT strategies for the future, both at Thurston Upper School and in the field of secondary education at large. Good practice gleaned from other institutions and cultures has to be treated with caution in its introduction in a school or country of another nation. However, with a shrinking global education community and common challenges in learning and teaching, there is much which is transferable. On the return to the UK some conclusions were possible and are set out below.

Philosophy and practice

Core thinking needs to focus on the place ICT holds in learning and teaching. The schools visited did not all express this focus, but those with the clearest vision of their future, such as Bendigo College and Appollo Parkways School, certainly did. Supporting students' learning in school requires an ICT management structure, confronting personnel issues, refocusing the budget, and acquiring hardware. Beyond school the possible links with home, other schools and organisations (such as businesses and the local education authority), and with increasing reason the internet, all need defining.

A management plan must underpin ICT. The plan needs to be flexible enough to take into account future ICT developments. Changing technology will, for example, provide geostationary satellites creating 'information radiation' on earth: the internet will be available everywhere; the UK government is interested in facilitating an ICT community to which all schools will be linked; and the ICT industry is expanding and creating ideas faster than the available manpower to sustain them. Therefore, any planning with an over-tight time frame is going to fail. If ever there were a place for the application of the concept of strategic intent, it is in ICT. High levels of understanding are required to balance the high levels of turbulence in the developing ICT world.

ICT, the student and the school

'I am one of the last of the school's ICT illiterates'. So said an upper sixth student at Thurston Upper School four years ago in a frank discussion with a journalist writing for the *Independent*. We now have a younger generation to whom ICT is just a normal part of life, not even a subject to get excited about in a wide-eyed way. To the digitally homeless members of the teaching force and of society, quite the opposite applies. There are plenty of ICT illiterates; many teachers have yet to make the cultural and practical leap to integrate ICT into the normal practice of the classroom.

Forty years ago classes moved out of their classrooms to watch a film in the film theatre. A technician ran the equipment wearing the mystic white coat. The theatre required booking. The event was special. Today, much of the use of ICT, and in particular the use of computers, resembles the days of the film theatre in the eyes of many teachers. To many, ICT is not a part of everyday life in classroom learning and teaching: it is seen as a facility to be used on special occasions. Forgetting that the car, the telephone, the watch, the radio, the signal for the change of lesson, the payslip at the end of the month, the book used in the classroom, the clothes worn – all rely heavily on ICT, many teachers still do not articulate ICT as important in today's society, nor as an integral part of learning and teaching. Basically, schools need to reflect today's needs and tomorrow's skills in learning and teaching. Too often this is not the case.

What ICT provision should a school have? The idea that a library equals a room of books is out of date. It should be a resource base accessible throughout the school, from other schools, and from student homes. A start could come from spending 50 per cent of the budget allocated to the library on ICT sources, as at Bendigo. Just as a traditional book-based library has been central to learning and teaching, so today is a digital library. Thurston has an emerging digital library. There is a network on which information is held, but the concept of a whole-school intranet is in its infancy. Publications and curriculum information for every school department should be on the intranet, accessible 24 hours a day, 365 days of the year. Schools such as Bendigo College and Lanyon High School have made great strides in this direction.

Students need skills to handle ICT sources and checks need to be put into place to monitor their activity, just as in the management of a book library. Clear procedures are needed, from deciding when particular skills should be taught to issuing students with a licence to use the internet once skills are evidenced. The skills to use internal and external e-mail must also be learned. The role of students in managing the school network needs to be reviewed. Their expertise should be harnessed now and their skills developed for a future wider role. They could be paid ('Kentucky Fried Chicken wages' according to Ron Lake, principal at Bendigo College) for work during the weekends and holidays. This is one of the antipodean ideas that has travelled well and since been implemented at Thurston.

The internet

The internet represents a great challenge to learning. Access for all students at any time from home and school should be the aim. It should be a prime means for students to obtain information. The librarian should download data on to the school intranet. It should be the vehicle for video conferencing, where there are many opportunities emerging for linking students with students, staff with staff, and staff with students. Interesting applications will come from the linking of Thurston with the three contributory middle schools to joint teach, perhaps starting with the most able students. Such developments are envisaged within the short term.

There are many implications. The librarian should have a central ICT role. The internet will increasingly have an important part in the learning and teaching of the school. Access needs to be fast and open. The opportunity for increasing capacity as demand rises is essential. Within school, fibre optic cabling is necessary.

Professional development

The message from the head of Appollo Parkways to spend twice the amount of money on professional development as on hardware is a realistic one. To develop teachers professionally requires a strategy that is well resourced. From providing a 'digital sandpit' to specific courses, a strategy is needed to support changes to learning and teaching. Allocating a lighter teaching load to a member of staff in a department looking to make moves forward with ICT could, with agreed focus, be powerful; introducing ICT 'teaching and learning coaches' in a department should be a priority. Teachers should also be required to have personal ICT targets and to acquire further qualifications which are technology-related.

An enthusiastic librarian with leading edge skills for running a digital library is essential. To have the skills of the Australian and New Zealand teacher librarian should be the aim. Students in their initial training year should develop the skills of school students by teaching and supporting them as part of their training year. The training of school students alongside teachers, possibly supported by student teachers, should be in the culture of the school.

The budget

ICT and related professional development is expensive. There is the need for money to purchase equipment and fund a replacement budget as well as day-to-day expenses. Some schools have generated moneys from such initiatives as the Technology College programme. However, much can be done by giving technology a priority within the school budget. Schools have top-sliced departmental and central budgets to support ICT. At Thurston, all areas of financing are being considered, but above all the school will need to become more entrepreneurial if money is to be found.

The management structure

Central to the successful implementation of future plans is the ICT co-ordinator. He or she will need sufficient time and a clear brief. He or she will need to be supported by staff – possible roles for network adminis-trator, coaches, library technician, and student technicians should be investigated. The ICT co-ordinator should be supported by a manage-ment group to give strength and direction to the school. Outline plans for the future should initially be worked up by staff, but a group to determine detailed strategy should be formed including students, par-ents, members of the community, consultants and governors. The group should be charged with planning for the future, and monitoring and evaluating developments. It will be crucial to keep the governing body informed of developments.

The hardware

Thurston has computers available on a network, but there is a need for more, certainly so if greater emphasis is to be put on ICT as a source of information. Future planning will have to balance the need for computers in 'laboratories', in classrooms and as a resource to use at any time else-where in the school. The servers to drive the system will need to be easily expandable and a further review of the cabling system will have to be car-ried out. Laptops have potential at Thurston. There is a clear need to have them available for use, both to support students and as a resource to take home, particularly for those students without a computer. Having four or six computers in each classroom as a longer-term goal is sensible. Philosophically, it is an imperative. Practically, with current levels of expertise, it would best be implemented gradually. But a start should be made with staff who wish to have the facility and will use it once opportu-nities for integration have been identified in schemes of work.

The personal availability of computers to teaching staff is essential. More difficult is the mechanism. Either purchase or rental could be used. Investigation is needed both of the legalities and the means of fulfilling such a policy.

Links with home, schools and other organisations

Once the intranet and internet have been established, students should be able to have access from home at any time. There should be the facility to send work to staff using the internet; all staff should have an e-mail address. Primarily a learning resource, the internet should also make school information available to parents and others. Coursework, the calendar, notices about events, the newsletter, opportunities in clubs and societies, all should appear. Schools in the pyramid (middle and primary) should have access to the school's resources and the librarian should have a brief to provide for all schools' curriculum needs. There would need to be funding agreements for such a venture. Joint teaching using video-conferencing through the internet should be used. The school should become a web site for the entire catchment area. Every primary and middle school should have its own web pages; businesses, community groups and organisations should be able to subscribe to the web site.

Conclusion

The opportunity exists to make great strides quickly. The world of learning and teaching is changing as are the related needs of students. ICT can increase motivation to learn, give a feeling of ownership of work, and widen horizons. All will lead to higher standards. Not to take the steps outlined would be nothing short of an abrogation of responsibility. Opportunities for changing the culture of learning and teaching are real and available now. Thurston Upper School needs to continue to develop, providing the adults of tomorrow with the skills they need for success.

Success through planning?

Headteachers of schools in England and Wales are likely to agree that

> *The scope and pace of change in education at the start of the 1990s are nothing short of breathtaking.*

(Caldwell and Spinks, 1992)

Indeed, leaders of schools in the late nineties require the acceleration of a sprinter, the stamina of a marathon runner and the manoeuvrability of a slalom skier. In such an environment careful planning is essential. Stoll and Fink (1996, p. 64) appropriately stress the need to sustain balance between increased school autonomy and national, provincial or state government controls in the continuing educational race to raise standards. As they correctly state:

> *In essence, they (the schools) must know where they are headed, which in school effectiveness terms and improvement terms is towards better learning experiences and outcomes for pupils.*

School development planning provides the opportunity to bring together the school's thinking in looking ahead. Balance, purpose, and a breadth of involvement and understanding can bring positive learning and teaching benefits. Strategic change is, perhaps, the most difficult type of change to bring about. Leading a learning organisation requires thinkers at the helm. Information-literate and with organised information about the environment in which schools operate, school leaders need to think strategically

> *to keep abreast of trends and issues, threats and opportunities, ... set priorities and formulate strategies ... ensure the attention of the school community is focused on matters of strategic importance ... facilitating an ongoing process of review.*

> (Caldwell and Spinks, 1992, p. 92)

All are clearly important, but maintaining a real focus for the whole organisation is difficult. School development planning can provide that focus but planning to keep ahead of the pack is, even more challenging:

> *If the baby's cry is to be heard by your people ahead of your competitors, it must be significant to them. Successful leadership understands that everyone needs to share the corporate vision, from their own perspective and for their own, personal reasons. That is the real challenge for today's direction-givers.*

> (Sworder, 1996, p. 93)

So, how to go about introducing the ideas learned? A combination of means came together to help. The first was the bidding procedure for technology college status. The processes of thinking about the future were in place on return to the UK. A bid team looking carefully at the school's future, led by two of the deputy heads and drawing in key heads of department, meant that some of the fear of looking ahead had been overcome by exposure to the possible benefits. Second, the decision had been made by the senior team and governors to reflect on the future of the school, the bid being an integral part, but the opportunity a wider one. Injecting some new thinking was important and the consultant came with a track record of being able to promote fresh thinking about change, with a focus on changing school structures to facilitate individual student learning improvements. Discussions between the governing body and the senior team on two separate occasions during the afternoon and evening, supported by the facilitator, developed a new strategic intent for the school. Five priorities emerged:

1 The development of learning experiences which will maximise opportunities for individual learning, development and success.
2 Leadership and management by all which focuses on the quality of learning and teaching and empowers individuals to maximise the effective use of resources.
3 The creation of a school which is in active partnership with local, national and international communities and the business and voluntary sectors.
4 The organisation of learning through reviewing school structures and systems to promote a focus on the individual student's learning, differentiation, and pattern of the school day and the academic year.
5 The deployment of information and communication technology to support learning and management strategies.

From these a plan was developed to introduce change over a period of time. The existing school development plan required some revision. While the five identified threads that emerged were very specific, the school had been making some moves in their direction previously.

What of the staff? How could they be drawn into the flow of thinking? Was this an entirely top-down model? The consultant was able to help. Taking on the role of critical friend and person to blame or argue with was all part of the bargain of his working with the school. An 'infiltration'-model was adopted rather than a 'flash flood' of ideas. So the consultant began to hold meetings with the heads of department who had the greatest stake in the technology bid and whose work might be first changed by an emphasis on ICT in learning development. He also worked with the staff in a middle management group which had been formed to support those who held middle management posts or who aspired to one. This was an important influence group in the staff. Work with other staff members was to follow, with an emphasis on integrating ICT and the learning process inside and outside school.

An added bonus came out of pyramid liaison. For two years Thurston Upper School had hosted a 'Pyramid Bash', a dance involving jazz, folk and popular music organised by schools in the pyramid. At a planning meeting for the third such occasion the headteacher of Thurston Upper sat next to a new member of the planning group. He was from the PTA of a small primary school. He explained that he was a director of a company which, among other things, created central government department sites on the internet. The two discussed the head's vision for the future of the school's ICT provision. An offer to create the intranet between all the pyramid schools and to enable Thurston to offer a service to local schools, businesses and community groups in putting their information on the internet followed and was eagerly embraced.

Expenditure ahead of any possible technology college status began. Planning for a Thurston Learning Centre (the head liked the initials) began in some earnest. The very friendly county architect, who had been associated with the school for a long time, drew up plans for adapting and enlarging an existing computer room near the library and at the centre of the school, and putting the learning development department (special needs department) next door with direct access. Funding came from the school capital account which had been established by the governors for such developments. SuccessMaker was installed (following a long period of investigation into its applicability) and training undertaken by some staff. A beginning had been made. The internet was accessed under an offer by a computer company with which the school had been involved for some time. From two lines with access the school now had ten. Another beginning.

Curriculum planning the previous autumn had led to the planned implementation of a course which did not lead to a GCSE but enabled students to develop their learning strategies and key skills at the same time as supporting their GCSE coursework. Accreditation for their work was under the aegis of the ASDAN project. They, along with particular students coming to the school in Year 9 the following September, would be the first to use SuccessMaker.

By involving the governors and senior staff in systematic strategic planning, and by the use of a consultant to work with influential groups of staff working to a future point where all staff would be drawn in, an 'infiltration' model (seen as positive infiltration like steady rain) rather than a 'flash flood' attempt to convince all staff (a strategy which, in the culture of the school, would have failed immediately) was proving successful. Staff liked the idea of thinking about their work in the new framework set out for the school. The notion that the initiative was in the hands of the professionals rather than the DfEE was appealing and strong. Change was acceptable. After all, pride in your work is what is at the heart of all teachers' reality, and if you can be a part of shaping the vision, then change is of your own making.

References

Beare, H. and Slaughter, R. (1993) *Education for the Twenty First Century*, London, Routledge.

Bowring-Carr, C., and West-Burnham, J. (1997) *Effective Learning in Schools*, London, Pitman Publishing.

Caldwell, B.J. and Spinks, J.M. (1992) *Leading the Self-Managing School*, London, The Falmer Press.

Cummins, J. and Sayers, D. (1997) *Brave New Schools*, New York, St. Martin's Press.

Drucker, P.F. (1995) *Managing in a Time of Great Change*, Oxford, Butterworth-Heinemann.

Handy, C. (1995) *The Empty Raincoat*, Sydney, Arrow Books Limited.

McKinsey & Company (1997) *The Future of Information Technology in UK Schools*. London, McKinsey & Company.

Senge, P.M. (1990) *The Fifth Discipline*, London, Century Business.

Stevenson, S. (1997) *Information and Communications Technology in UK Schools, An Independent Inquiry*, London, The Independent ICT in Schools Commission.

Stoll, L. and Fink, D. (1996) *Changing Our Schools*, Buckingham, Open University Press.

Sworder, D., (1996) 'Hearing the baby's cry', pp. 84–89 in Garrat, B. (ed) *Developing Strategic Thought*, London, HarperCollins.

18

■ ■ ■

It takes a whole community to raise a child

STEVEN HALES

'It takes a whole village to raise a child' provides the framework for a partnership model which enables the global village to be used as a network of skills, resources and points of reference to support children's learning and allows the whole community to grow in terms of values, attitudes, knowledge and understanding.

This case study will describe how the leaders of Beaupré Community Primary School, a small, rural primary school, have created a community partnership model which supports and enhances the children's learning. It will show how the model has developed with the advent of new technology. The practice of this community primary school has gained national and international recognition, as the children have achieved success by improving their communication and problem-solving skills and have grown in terms of self-confidence and self-esteem. The model has contributed to the raising of expectations and standards across the school's community. In conclusion, the case study will show how the model is a critical part of the school's approach to 'future thinking' and 'management of change', in giving children every possible chance to meet the demands of the 21st century.

Background

Beaupré Community Primary School is situated in the village of Outwell on the Cambridgeshire-Norfolk border between Wisbech and Downham Market. The community shows many signs of rural deprivation, with limited opportunities and services. Parts of the community are isolated and there are subsequent effects on family and community life. This background, and its related challenges, have been recognised by the school management as well as Cambridgeshire Local Education Authority. The school was designated as a 'community primary school' in 1972 and is the main meeting place within the village. Over the years, the school has become 'the heart of the community' and was recognised in 1992 and 1997 by the Schools Curriculum Award for its achievement in this dimension. Currently, there are 184 children in the school, with seven teachers, including the headteacher, and ten support staff.

The partnership model

The school leaders have developed the philosophy of 'it takes a whole village to raise a child' as a framework for developing a network of community partnerships to support and enhance the children's learning. This framework provides a strategy to meet the challenges of the 21st century which focuses on improving the children's skills in communication, teamwork and problem-solving, while increasing their self-confidence and self-esteem, their cultural understanding and their love of learning. There is an important commitment to lifelong learning and the whole notion of community development through partnerships. Above all, the model supports the viewpoint of Etzioni (1993), voiced in the preface to *The Spirit of Community*, that

> Communities are social webs of people who know one another as persons and have a moral voice.

The model is represented by concentric circles – 'villages' – which spread out from the child at the centre through the family, the school, the local community, the district, the country, the continent and the world. For the children of Beaupré Primary School, the 'layers of village' spread from the child through their own family to the school, Outwell, East Anglia, England, United Kingdom, Europe and the rest of the world. This network of people and places provides a rich plethora of skills, talents and resources which can be used to support the children's learning. The Beaupré children find one-to-one contact a prime motivator for acquiring and developing knowledge and understanding. Consequently, accessing the network can be through personal contact or the school's database or through telecommunications or internet research. As teachers plan their various subjects, they can access the network for themselves or facilitate the children making their own connections. Beaupré has moved steadily towards being *'a community of learners'*, as described by Sergiovanni (1994, p. 154):

> *Becoming a community of learners is an adventure not only in learning but an adventure in shared leadership and authentic relationships. It requires a certain equality and a certain willingness for individuals to know themselves better, to be open to new ideas and to strive to become. It is an adventure in personal development.*

The model is supported by important values, which were originally identified by Cambridgeshire LEA as critical values for community development – opportunity, participation, entitlement, community, progress, continuity, worth and evaluation or reflection. For some, the model is seen as an example of curriculum reform, but this is one of its strengths, as supported by Fullan and Hargreaves (1992, p. 16):

> *Curriculum reforms can be adapted to the needs of one's own school. They can be used as opportunities to reflect on, reconstruct and even reaffirm one's values and purposes as a school community.*

The development of these values becomes an important part of the school's work because, for the children, the values form an important framework upon which they can become citizens of the 21st century. This practice is confirmed by Etzioni (1993, p. 266):

> *While it may seem utopian, we believe that in the multiplication of strongly democratic communities around the world lies our best hope for the emergence of a global community that can deal concertedly with matters of general concern to our species as a whole; with war and strife, with violations of basic rights, with environmental degradation, and with the extreme material deprivation that stunts the bodies, minds and spirits of children. Our communitarian concern may begin with ourselves and our families, but it rises inexorably to the long-imagined community of mankind.*

It has to be said that there have been educators, such as some OFSTED inspectors, who have found the model difficult to understand and are unable to see its value and relevance, particularly to a small, rural community. However, Fullan and Hargreaves support a rationalisation of this way of working (1992, p. 17):

Our schools need the growth and learning that comes from individual diversity and creativity from within and outside themselves and their LEAs. We must experiment and discover better ways of working together that mobilise the power of the group while at the same time enhancing individual development. We must use collegiality not to level people down, but to bring together strength and creativity.

The model in practice

It is important how the model works in practice and this can be shown through some examples. The community, which comprises a network of people and places, must be recognised as a resource to support and enhance children's learning. There is some comparison with a London taxi driver, as the approach does need to have the 'knowledge' – the knowledge of the whole community, from local to global, and the kind of support that can be available. There are some important people in this process. On the one hand, there are well established members of the school community, such as the school secretary, the nursery assistant and the vice-chair of governors, who have important, almost unstated roles, in making connections. On the other hand there are the 'newcomers', such as the deputy head and some parents who have moved into the village from other parts of the country, who bring their own connections. The head-teacher plays a lead role in developing this ethos. One of the parent governors does keep a database of volunteers, but in many respects the 'knowledge' is within people's memories. The critical role for the school management team, when monitoring and evaluating teacher's planning, is to ensure that the community is being used and can advise on the connections that are possible.

As has already been said, the model is based on the African proverb 'it takes a whole village to raise a child'. The practice can be best described by using examples from the various 'layers' of village:

● **The 'school' as a village**. The day-to-day organisation of the school can be seen as a true community, as all children, particularly when they are Year 5 and 6, help the smooth running of school by undertaking a range of tasks and responsibilities, such as answering the telephone at break and lunchtimes, collecting the e-mail daily, keeping the libraries tidy, helping with the parent and toddler group, and organising the school council. All are significant roles within the school's community and can be seen as an opportunity to develop skills in citizenship.

- **The 'village' as a village**. The business and economic community within the local area is an important resource for developing the children's awareness of the outside world. This process starts in the pre-school group, who visit Outwell post office, the fish and chip shop and the local supermarket. As the children move through the school, geography visits are arranged to businesses like the Old Mill Hotel in Upwell and Tesco's Superstore and Paragon Garage in Wisbech. Each of these businesses has connections with the school as they are run by parents or friends of the school. Beaupré has been recognised by Greater Peterborough Chamber of Commerce and has been encouraged to disseminate good practice across the region, nationally and internationally.

- **The 'United Kingdom' as a village**. Being in a rural community, access to a range of facilities is difficult, so it has been an important strategy to enable the children to experience a range of creative arts experiences from across the cultures. The children have worked with the National Trust Youth Theatre, the Norwich Puppet Theatre, the Classic Buskers, black storytellers from Lambeth, the Peterborough Arts Theatre Samba Band and a paper sculptor, to name but a few.

- **'Europe' as a village**. The school has an active European Education Partnership with a school in the Netherlands and a school in Denmark. Using EEC funds, the schools have collaborated to produce a tri-lingual chain story, 'The Big Red Balloon', a photographic exhibition which reflects upon the similarities and differences in the way the three communities celebrated various festivals and a creative arts project based on the theme of 'circus'. The partnership is developing links with Finland, the Czech Republic and Greece.

- **The 'world' as a village**. Beaupré has developed a 'family' of link schools across the world, from the UK to Finland, the Netherlands, Denmark, Greece, South Africa, Australia, the USA and Canada. A technology project, in which children collaborated with each other to produce designs for their 'classroom in 2020', has just been completed. Communication was by fax and e-mail, and as pupils received information, they increased their global perspectives. For example, it was interesting to observe the discussion between pupils in Finland, South Africa and Beaupré about optimum learning environments, especially considering the climatic differences.

These examples give a flavour of the innovative practice that is undertaken. In some cases, it is similar to work undertaken in other schools, but it is the holistic framework of the partnership model which is different.

The Beaupré model matches Whitaker's summary of the primary class-room of the future (1997, p. 80):

> *The future will demand that we continue to seek ways to help pupils to develop a whole range of skills and abilities not traditionally regarded as part of the curriculum for schools. Not only are these vital life skills that will be needed later in adult life, they are the very skills that will enable pupils to become more committed and responsible learners while they are at school. It is in the primary school classroom that this process should begin and it is vital that we develop a curriculum which includes management skills; planning and goal-setting; choice and decision making; co-operation and involvement; and accountability.*

The impact of technology

Similarly to the way that the model has evolved, resources supporting and enhancing children's learning have also changed. The school leaders at Beaupré view learning resources in three categories: books, information technology, and people and places. Originally, spending was focused on books. However, recently there has been a more even balance. Books and libraries are still important, but the range of information that can be accessed through CD-ROMs and the internet is critical to all parts of the primary school curriculum. The tight financial scenario for primary schools has meant that the culture of enterprise and partnership with the community is necessary for schools to keep abreast with technological change. Likewise, the linking with people and places costs money, and budgets have to be allocated.

The impact of technology on Beaupre's community partnership model has been significant. The improvement in telecommunications has enabled connections to be made in a variety of ways. Children are particularly impressed with the fax machine. They regard it as 'magic' that their questionnaire can be sent across the world and back again with comments written on it. Children consider the speed of e-mail important, while video-conferencing is an exciting way of talking and seeing people. It is important that children have equal access to this kind of technology.

Beaupré has established itself as a centre for innovative practice in information technology and, accordingly, attracts resources which may not be available to all schools. It is important that schools capitalise on the use of these resources and take responsibility for sharing their newly discovered knowledge with other schools. An example of how this works in practice is the development of video-conferencing. Cambridgeshire's Education

Information Technology Centre (EDIT) worked with the Beaupré staff at the beginning of a pilot project for developing the use of this technology in primary schools. The school has two years' experience of using the technology and has found enterprising ways to integrate this work into the curriculum. At the end of a Key Stage 2 history module, children video-conferenced with students from Samos, one of the Greek Islands in the eastern Aegean. Beaupré children were able to check out with their counterparts what they had learned about the Ancient Greeks and whether it was the same as what the Greek students knew. The children were able to show their models of the Greek Gods, their clay pots and their masks for the Greek theatre. In almost all respects, the learning was similar. But it went further than that – the English children had managed to learn a few words of Greek, while the Greek students, who were aged 14 to 16, knew more English. However, one of the Greek teachers was talking to one of the Beaupré children and asked if they knew how to say 'hello' in other languages. They managed 'bonjour' and 'Guten Morgen', and then the Beaupré child said he could teach them 'hello' in Chinese. This he did, but the Greek teacher said she had visited China and was able to share impressions with the child. And so the learning continued.

This is the challenge for primary school leaders – how do we keep abreast of new technology with ever-diminishing budgets? Initially, there needs to be acceptance across the school community that information technology is critical to supporting and enhancing children's learning. Second, there needs to be an opportunist approach to making best use of the technology that is already available – how many schools let children have access to the office fax machine? Third, there needs to be a spirit of enterprise among school leaders to find curriculum opportunities for technology and to encourage community partners to be involved for mutual benefits.

The raising of expectations and standards

In considering the raising of expectations and standards, it is important to note that Beaupré Community Primary School is placed in the group of schools with the highest socio-economic need in Cambridgeshire. Undoubtedly, this is because of the rural deprivation within the community and the many associated factors such as the lack of facilities and services. As education moves into an era where data are critical in measuring school improvement, there is evidence in the target setting in literacy that the Beaupré model is making a difference. Against the national and county benchmarks in English for similar schools, Beaupré falls into the upper quartile, both at Key Stages 1 and 2. As more data become available, this improvement trend will become more evident. Recognition for the work of the school, and the community partnership model in particular, has come in the form of Schools Curriculum Awards and a European Curriculum Award. These are important markers for the school community, as they show parents and governors that Beaupré is special and worth celebrating.

Representatives of the school community, including children, have presented case studies of the school's work in the UK and internationally. These are important events for the school community, but also in the wider community, who may ask what a small, rural primary school is doing presenting at an international conference in Toronto or Trondheim. The response can be twofold: first, it is an important strategy to raise expectations, awareness and horizons across the school community and second, it is critical for educators to share practice among educators. The external perspective of Beaupré's work is important because it is not always understood just what this community partnership model is doing for the children within the school. In the booklet prepared by the school in 1996 for the 3rd International Partnership Conference in Toronto, the following comments were included:

- Paul Springford, deputy director of Cambridgeshire's Centre for Information Technology in Education, an OFSTED inspector and an educational consultant for British Telecom:

  What always impresses me about Beaupré's approach to community partnerships is the enthusiasm with which they are developed and nurtured. Those at the school are always willing to provide information and ideas to assist the work of teachers and pupils in other communities. Equally impressive is the almost instinctive impulse to turn to their international network and use them as a resource to inform and enrich the curriculum. It seems to me that the Beaupré children are privileged to learn from the whole community – locally, nationally and globally.

- Liz Wade, business education partnership manager for the Greater Peterborough Chamber of Commerce:

  Beaupré is at the leading edge of business education partnership work. The whole philosophy of curriculum delivery leads each teacher to consider resources for learning in a different way – how can I use information technology and our local community, including employers, to enrich the children's learning? It does not come as an accredited after-thought. The young people develop opportunities to learn from everything around them in school and in the outside world. How better can you prepare children and motivate young people to enjoy learning for all their lives?

Conclusion – education for the future

This case study has sought to explore how a community partnership model supports and enhances children's learning. There are two fundamental principles upon which the model is based. First, primary schools need to consider that they are preparing young children for the future. What are the values and skills that these young people will need when they enter the employment market in 2010 and beyond? The viewpoint of Fitch and Svengalis (1979), as cited by Hicks and Holden (1995, p. 3), emphasises the importance of a future dimension:

> By adding a future dimension to the learning process, we help to provide direction, purpose and greater meaning to whatever is being studied. By integrating past, present and future, we act to strengthen a neglected link in the learning process.

Second, primary schools need to be flexible – a key skill in the leadership and management of the change process. However, this can be difficult, as Whitaker (1997, p. 26) points out:

> We are now part of a profession whose raison d'être is learning for change.

He continues by arguing that it will be necessary to stop regarding change as an event that will require strenuous efforts from time to time, but to see change as a process of continual modification and adaptation. Whitaker (1997, p. 27) reflects that

> The primary schools of the future will need tight control of their values, visions and principles of their work, but individuals within the system, both pupils and teachers, will need greater authority to work with trust and integrity within their spheres of influence.

Whitaker sees that there will be a reworking of traditional roles and responsibilities, spreading authority throughout the school, including giving pupils a much greater part to play as co-managers of the process. He concludes (1997, p. 27)

> The principle of subsidiarity – ensuring that decisions are taken at the lowest possible level – will form a key part of the primary school of the future.

At Beaupré Community Primary School, the school leaders have been prepared to take a major step in considering future needs and being ahead of the change process. The community partnership model is an important part of this process as a pathfinder, which can be applied to any school in any community. Whitaker (1997, p. 164) quotes the psychologist and writer, Sam Keen:

In every society, there are extraordinary men and women who, for a variety of reasons, stand outside the social consensus, shatter the norms and challenge the status quo. Their qualities of exploration, courage, a sense of wonder, self-awareness and fun and joy are especially significant.

If the work of Beaupré Community Primary School can be seen partially in this light, then the journey into the 'school of the future' has begun with the recognition that 'it takes a whole village to raise a child'.

References

Beaupré Community Primary School, 'It takes a whole village to raise a child'. Brochure prepared for the 3rd International Partnership Conference, Toronto, April 1996.

Etzioni, A. (1993) *The Spirit of Community,* London, Fontana Books.

Fullan, M. and Hargreaves, D. (1992) *What's Worth Fighting For in Your School?* Buckingham, Open University Press.

Hicks, D. and Holden, C. (1995) *Visions of the Future: Why We Need to Teach For Tomorrow,* Stoke-on-Trent, Trentham Books.

Sergiovanni, T.J. (1994). *Building of Community in Schools,* San Francisco, Jossey-Bass.

Whitaker, P. (1997) *Primary Schools and the Future: Celebration, Challenges and Choices,* Buckingham, Open University Press.

19

■ ■ ■

A seriously happy place

PHYLLIS HARRIS

I dwell in possibility.

(Emily Dickinson)

There was never a time in history like this one. World and national economics, people and population migration, culture and fear of cultures influence what happens in our schools. That influence is evident in public policy initiatives, funding and budgetary priorities, and in the public's perceptions of schooling. While some despair about what's wrong with the world today – how much harder it is to just teach, and maybe it is – society's problems can offer us an opportunity to recreate ourselves and a piece of the world. This is the story of my two years as a school principal (1995–7). But I have been a catalyst for change throughout my life. This means that I'm used to being in trouble. I'm used to listening to a different drummer, and I've been known to have already moved on before Godot has had a chance to arrive. I like to write new chapters and close old ones. I believe that as educators, we are doing important work even though it is work that few people want to do. We deal in global issues, such as who will be free and who will not. We deal in human rights, such as who will have voice, who will have just language, and who will not be heard (Freire, 1970, 1993). Some of us work in war zones and deal with those who are visibly and invisibly scarred. We confront life situations that most people consider uncomfortable to discuss in mixed company. We do important work that few people want to do. In order to do this work well, we need to know what matters and what does not matter and we need to understand it in such a profound way that this understanding is evidenced by our behaviour.

Background

Washington Accelerated Learning Centre (WALC), in Pasadena, California, became my opportunity to recreate a piece of the world. By leading a team of kindred-spirited teachers, our philosophical convictions and beliefs about learning were used to mould an ordinary school into one that demonstrated the seminal theories of minds such as Paulo Freire, Thomas Sergiovanni, and Lev Vygotsky. The task represented to all of us a level of challenge and opportunity that we couldn't resist. Dreams of equity and access – quality schooling for every person to know how to know – became our world. This wasn't easy work, easy was not an option, but it was important work and we wanted to do it and we wanted to do it together.

The school's six guiding principles were adapted from the work of Thomas J. Sergiovanni (1992):

- **Learning community**. We, as educators, are committed to developing a spirit of curiosity, inquiry, and reflection that touches students and adults alike.

- **Equity**. We, as educators, believe that every student will learn and we dedicate ourselves to that belief. Learning conditions that impede learning, no matter what their origins, are viewed as problems to be solved rather than as conditions to be accepted.

- **Holistic learning and the ethic of caring**. We, as educators, seek to provide for the whole student. We will not shrink from our responsibility to do everything in our power to attend to the developmental, physical, and social needs of our students.

- **Respect**. We, as educators, acknowledge and honour our professional commitment to our own continuous study and growth. We believe in demonstrating a model of mutual respect for ourselves, other teachers, students, parents, and other adults within our community of learners.

- **Partnership**. We, as educators, believe in the reciprocal and interdependent rights of students, teachers, parents, and other adults in the community to participate and benefit, to support and assist the school and the community. Between the school and the parents there exists an exchange of constructive, meaningful advice that enhances and makes possible the enriched educational experience of our students. These actions represent a relationship of mutual trust, mutual goodwill, and mutual benefits.

- **Confidence and access**. We, as educators, believe that confident students engaged in challenging work will get smart, and that everyone will become lifelong learners as well as informed citizens leading personally satisfying and socially productive lives.

These principles were not only powerful but also complex and required a moral style of leadership weighed by action not rhetoric. Purpose-focused action plans to mount and sustain these principles often consumed 15-hour days, seven days a week, especially in the first year of my assignment. With a committed staff who put in hours beyond the imagination of any contractual agreement, these hours were filled not just with rigorous work but with joy and laughter. The work became, for most of us, a state of 'flow' which Mihaly Csikszentmihalyi (1990, p. 71) describes as

> ... a sense that one's skills are adequate to cope with the challenges at hand, in a goal-directed, rule-bound action system that provides clear clues as to how well one is performing. Concentration is so intense that there is no attention left over to think about anything irrelevant, or to worry about problems. Self-consciousness disappears, and the sense of time becomes distorted. An activity that produces such experiences is so gratifying that people are willing to do it for its own sake, with little concern for what they will get out of it, even when it is difficult, or dangerous.

The educational philosophy behind the principles and the philosophy followed by the team at WALC came from a strong and unshakable belief in the principle of efficacy. It is the notion that serious effort plus hard work builds self-confidence and creates or develops intelligence or smartness. Importantly, self-confidence is not an ephemeral or illusory intangible. Self-confidence develops when a person has achieved a significant level of skill or knowledge in some activity or field. Undergirding this is the issue of access – a person must have access to the ways and means of getting work or practice or instruction that is effective and meaningful for them. Achievement, therefore, requires an opportunity and a chance to take advantage of it. Critically, without actual achievement, self-confidence cannot develop and informed and intelligent progress will not happen. This integrated concept of building self-confidence through the achievement of challenging goals was at the heart of the operating principles at Washington Accelerated Learning Centre.

We believed and behaved according to the idea that all children have the capacity to become special, gifted or talented learners. WALC's business was thinking, learning, and academic discipline. We transformed every aspect of the school site into a brain-compatible facility. We had classical music in the cafeteria; reading alcoves were located in entrances, hallways, and stairwells; baskets of apples and books were placed everywhere. Additionally, the three Spanish-style 1923 classroom buildings were called 'think tanks' and the lawn was known as the 'quad' (used for football, soccer, meditating, talking *and* reading). There were large pots of flowers outside every class and office. A soft and surreal mural (called 'Steps into Knowledge') covered 60 ft of the think-tank wall at the top of the sloping quad. Children gathered and worked in every area of the campus. Here, we benefited greatly from the California sunshine and good weather. Fathers and guardians sometimes dropped by during recess and lunch to coach soccer and football. The children's latest enthusiasms – projects, original plays, academic contests, videotaping – went on in hallways, the little theatre, and the gardens. Posters, advertisements, and newspaper editors' calls for work and participation jumped off the walls. Fourth grade student editors corrected work contributed by sixth graders. Age didn't matter – talent, interest and effort did.

Our major goal was to find and build upon the strengths of each person who worked or studied at WALC. We knew that we could do that best in an emotionally and physically safe environment. Consequently, we did our best to reflect a universe for person-to-person harmony and to min-imise the institutional effects of schools. One example of this was the constant presence of the 'WALC bear'. A large, soft, furry brown bear (a toy) managed to reassure children experiencing acute or chronic emo-tional upsets. The bear was often borrowed as a personal companion by a child or a class for hours, days, and sometimes weeks. When not being hugged or talked to, this bear sat in a chair in my office. It helped me calm down parents going through their own traumas and was once held by an applicant on her lap throughout her interview. She was hired.

As an accelerated school, we moved students quickly and thoroughly through the regular curriculum, with opportunities to deepen learning through research projects, exhibitions, debate, intensive reading and writ-ing. Students spent more time on academic activities both at school and at home. Teachers expected serious academic work from *all* students and used a variety of strategies (discussed later) to help students increase their potential. An accelerated school programme is often greatly misunder-stood by the teachers, the parents and the students as well as by the community. The programme was for all students and not just the identi-fied gifted. It was designed to stimulate the forward movement of learners through a body of knowledge work utilising and emphasising the devel-opment of cognitive skills, and it did so by any means possible.

Instructional strategies that encouraged thoughtful answers and, by the very nature of the questions, created periods of frustration or academic challenge to force out that next level of thinking and understanding (cognition) were expected parts of acceleration. If students and, for that matter, teachers were working in class completely in their comfort zone, they were not accelerating; they were not entering their 'zone of proximal development' (ZPD). This is a Vygotskian theory (Vygotsky, 1978) which states that what someone can actually do alone (ZAD, or the zone of actual development) is not necessarily all that they *could* do. Ever greater skill and knowledge is increasingly developed through mediation and scaffolded learning experiences. This is what is occurring when a student is pulled forward into the next level of development by intelligent modelling, adult demonstration, peer tutoring or demonstration, mentoring or coaching. Think, then, of learning or the theory of the ZPD as a construction site (Newman *et al.*, 1989) where learners are building a knowledge base and continuously being assisted to move forward on their own personal cognitive time track. To advance in skill, in knowledge base, and in the art of living, one needs to operate at the edge of one's competence for a part of each day. The longer that part of the day gets, the more exciting life becomes for the learner.

Implementing this philosophy meant that every student at WALC in Grades 4–6 was assigned a research project that reached for depth and complexity on key concepts in one core curriculum area every three to four weeks. Teachers decided on this by collaboration and shared outlines, formats, research, and personal expertise. They considered and formulated one basic rubric (an objective criterion for assessment) and reviewed reports, graded other classes' student work, and used the student work for grade level discussion meetings and assessments. Some teachers taught rubrics as a subject to the students and the students then created their own objective criteria for assessment. These student-created rubrics were often significantly more difficult, complex, and demanding than the assessment criteria the teachers had anticipated and envisioned. This was an excellent example of students' real desire for challenging work, high expectations, and self-imposed targets.

Metacognition – the art of thinking about your own thinking – was essential for WALC students to learn how to study most effectively. This required teachers attending to each student and trying to identify his or her area of strength in terms of multiple intelligences and learning styles. Note-taking and note-sharing, reciprocal questioning between students, making presentations and answering academic questions from researched knowledge, tape recordings of text to assist limited readers, and peer tutoring were all strategies that sought to mediate the learning process. We needed to note those strategies that were most effective, and for whom. General, short anecdotal notes (mere phrases) helped each teacher keep track of their students but, more importantly, the students needed to keep track of their study effectiveness as well. This meant there was a constant flow of communication about what and how things were done between the students and other students, between the students and the teachers, between the teachers and the supporting staff members, and often most critically among the students, teachers and parents.

In terms of site leadership, WALC was a constant pull on my learning curve. It was like a great roller coaster ride with steep inclines and deep, scary runs, but it was worth it. The school was a throbbing and relentless learning community. Every now and then, I would do an observational drill that I designed for a teacher training course. You simply take five minutes of your day spontaneously and do nothing and say nothing and simply look at what is happening – no notes, no interruptions, no intervening. Five pure minutes of seeing without acting and without deciding and without judgement. You must suspend disbelief long enough to forget what you think you know – then you learn by watching how people are learning and doing things. To understand *my* role in the web of inclusion (Helgesen, 1995) that WALC encouraged, the following passage is an excerpt from an instructional memo (a four-page discussion of teaching and learning – I produced eight such memos throughout the year) dated 27 November 1995:

> ... *questions? concerns? ... This Instructional Memorandum is meant as a resource if you will ... a kind of revisit to what we are trying to create as a model public school ... we aren't there yet ... we are a work in progress ... actually, we always will be ... I'm here to suggest, guide, demonstrate, and support you in any way I can. Please let me know what is happening so I can help you in whatever you need. Remember, I already believe in your ability and skill. Implementation is the most difficult piece in any plan. My most sincere advice is not to work alone, the age of teacher isolation is over – we can do well alone but we pursue excellence when we do it together.*

> *Thanks, Phyllis*

WALC was unique within the school district (the American equivalent of a local education authority) in a number of ways. The school was located in the segregated, inner city quadrant of Pasadena. The area was known for high poverty, high crime, gangs, little commercial development and a difficult and often dangerous environment. For example, the school was across the street on two sides from crack cocaine houses (drug selling and using) and a halfway house for prisoners out on parole. The statistical profile for WALC's 300 students in Grades 4–6, included African-American 48 per cent, Latino 32 per cent, White 17 per cent, Asian 2 per cent. About

17 per cent of students were limited in their English language proficiency and 50 per cent were eligible for free or reduced lunch. A great many of our students were living with caretakers (foster homes/foster parents) or were members of non-traditional family structures.

The school site had been closed down 12 years before but increasing community interest for a school that developed from and met parental needs for higher quality public schooling gave birth to the idea of WALC as an accelerated learning centre. WALC functioned as a neighbourhood school at Grade 6 (ages 11 and 12). This meant that if you lived in the surrounding area, you would be zoned to go to this school for Grade 6. In 1995–6, it was also a school of choice for Grades 4 and 5 (ages eight to ten) only. This meant that all our students were originally assigned to other schools but had to select WALC and get a district permit to come to WALC. Two-thirds of the students actually came from other catchment areas by parental request and by providing their own transportation from other parts of the city. An indicator of success for the school was the permission to add a multi-age class for grades 1, 2 and 3 to the options for parental choice for the 1996–7 school year. The major reason for opening these grades was to offer an option for parents who had to take younger siblings to different schools in the city. Significantly, within days of the announcement at the end of June 1996, all 32 pupil spaces were filled and a waiting list was established for the first time. Owing to the class size reduction initiative in California for 1997, this class became a combination Grade 1 and 2 limited to 20 students, and a separate third-grade class was added.

There were significant proportions of high- as well as low-achieving and under-prepared students at WALC. Class sizes were normally between 30–35 and all classes had children who were identified within special education categories (the American version of 'statemented'). However, test scores were consistently above the district average in maths and reading.

The job required of you is hard, that's why you must support each other.

The faculty was notable for its collaborative spirit, with regular time set aside for training, sharing best teaching practices, and common planning. Ninety-five per cent of the students and their parents had signed home-school contracts agreeing to give the extra effort that WALC expected, including students doing two hours of daily academic/reading work at home (including weekends) and three to five hours of monthly parent volunteer service. This was a requirement to get into WALC, which did not have any other selective admission requirement. Special programmes included NASA's Youth Enhancing Space, a national grant won by classroom teachers for the school. The following is from an interview by Jenny Singer in the Pasadena Weekly:

...one of WALC's fifth-grade classes was selected as one of three test sites in the nation to join Kid Satellite. Working closely with JPL (Jet Propulsion Laboratory), the class will be in charge of operating the space shuttle's camera which will be launched in March 1996. The students are now in the process of constructing an operations room from which they will develop their mathematical calculations of the planet's trajectories, select the points to be filmed, speak directly to the astronauts and guide the camera's shots.

In order for this project to succeed, everyone had to be willing to help at some point. The number of classes involved expanded in the second year of the shuttle launch and the project allowed many parents to see what their children were learning on serious computation work, map and radar image matching, teamwork, and public relations. It was an important exercise in authentic learning and again demonstrated the initiative of committed teachers.

Additionally, there was a school newspaper whose student editors, regardless of their grade designation, won their jobs by submitting anonymous but coded work samples to a body of sixth-grade student judges who sponsored the paper's organisation by running it during their lunchtime and after school. Two computer labs with full internet access were manned and opened after school hours for anyone's use. The lunchtime Cognition Club for chess attracted the most unlikely candidates for an intellectual exercise; these students (previously thought to be not high achievers) ran serious schoolwide chess championships and had an afterschool club as well. Order on the campus was assisted by a student Peace Patrol (prefects), and there were additional programmes and community partnerships interconnected with district programmes. We were eager, we were busy, and we thought excelling was okay. It was often a case of '*...run, don't walk to class ... there's so much to do...*'

Academic programmes

What matters most about education happens inside the classroom.

All WALC students had access to a rigorous, challenging curriculum. Staff, students, and parents worked together to increase time-on-task, encourage academic pursuits, and demonstrate the benefits of doing serious, challenging work. The particular features of the implementation of the curriculum at WALC were:

Mathematics. We were particularly proud of how teachers restructured the maths programme in grades 4–5 to accelerate learning and build on teachers' strengths. Students were grouped by achievement across grade levels, with a smaller class size for a recovery group of under-prepared students. Students moved in and out of maths groups, often based on need and topics covered. Parents worked with independent subgroups in the advanced maths programme and in the recovery class. Teachers analysed student work and collaborated on homework assignments and grading at grade-level meetings which replaced faculty meetings twice a month. Important information in the subject area was added to teachers' weekly newsletters to parents to keep them involved in academic progress and work topics.

Language arts. We instituted daily writer's workshops through peer training of teachers in all classes. This focused on a five-step writing process – pre-writing, draft, revise, edit, publish – using individual student-teacher writing conferences during the workshop time, and brief (ten minutes or less) whole-class instructional introductions, with student collaboration on editing and revision.

Literature circles. Small groups of students used Wonderfully Exciting Books (WEB) to study and write about literature, and students borrowed chapter books for home reading through a teacher grant for a Bag-A-Book programme (lunchtime paperback book borrowing on the playground from the 'library on wheels'). This borrowing programme was in addition to the normal class library visits to the local city library and class library books and principal's library books. Reading was permitted everywhere on the campus including the lunchroom, office, nurse's office and hallways. All waiting areas had stacks and baskets of books nearby and the walls were covered with print (what we called 'thinking quotes') to create a properly stimulating environment and reasons to read. One of our favourite quotes was: 'Think for yourself. Your teacher may be wrong. Prove it.'

Students from all grades wrote and edited the school newspaper, the WALC Times, under the direction of a sixth-grade teacher and several parent volunteers. Two sixth-grade classes had a six-month language arts through fine arts programme funded by a special district grant, and two resident artists spent Fridays at the school shared between the two classes. This programme went to the newest teachers to give them deeper support and to enrich their classes.

Enriched academics. Students and parents worked in after-school teams voluntarily to participate in Odyssey of the Mind competitions. There was also a Saturday Scholars programme in Science and Computers and Maths from 9am to noon on the campus. Additionally, there was a Cognition Club used as an optional activity during lunch and break time, supervised by a parent volunteer, that offered chess, advanced puzzles, Scrabble, and strategy games for those who wanted an alternative to the playground or independent reading.

Special independent maths groups existed for those students who competed in districtwide Math Field Day (a mental bloodletting sport in this district). The academic challenges were encouraged. WALC won championships in district Spelling Bees, African American History, and Odyssey of the Mind, where all six teams (twice as many as any other school) gained winning positions in our first year. All Grade 4 students studied the violin and roughly 75 per cent of the children participated in instrumental music, orchestra, and/or marching band. Seventy-four children (out of a population of 300) were selected after trials for the WALC Chorus.

Research. In all classes, as one part of the work, students were expected to do a major research paper/project in one core curriculum area each month. This reinforced information retrieval, reading, presentation skills, writing, and work planning for all students while allowing especially ambitious students to pursue their interests in greater depth. Teachers set up criteria with students in advance, with student-created rubrics for grade attainment. Students often made the criteria significantly harder than the teacher had anticipated. They met their own targets; they usually beat their own targets. For the students it became a game, a challenge, a triumph. They didn't feel the competition except with themselves. They felt emotionally safe.

The students understood that learning was a process of making mistakes on your way to self-confident action. They were guided in learning how to do this by studying student work exemplars and discussing this work at length with their teachers. The rubrics were often developed through small group discussion at the beginning of a unit of study assignment. These projects accounted for some of the work done at home.

Homework. We believed that rigorous homework was essential for developing the habits of mind that lead to success in life after formal schooling. Importantly, academic discipline and the basic literacies will be required to maintain a successful and satisfying life in the next century. WALC students were required to spend two hours on academics every night including weekends. This included 30–60 minutes of reading for assignments or pleasure. We encouraged meaningful assignments that extended over time, utilised libraries and computers, and engaged family members with the work of the school. Teachers often shared and co-operated as well as co-ordinated their assignments. This occasionally included drama, music with voice or instrument, and very often included fine arts integrated with core academic curriculum.

Teaching strategies

The work force is the student body.

WALC placed a great deal of emphasis on staff development and the sharing of effective teaching strategies that maximised the skills of both faculty and students. Some examples of our approach to professional development follow:

Higher order thinking skills

Students were required to analyse information, compare and contrast, predict outcomes, summarise text, and debate ideas in all subjects. They were encouraged to offer thoughtful responses and alternative interpretations with supporting evidence from textbooks, literature, historic events, or mathematical and scientific experiments. The faculty was supported and trained for a minimum of 15 hours with county consultants who were experts at instructional strategies normally used only with identified gifted students. Stipends were paid for training hours outside the teachers' regular work schedule.

Reciprocal teaching

With this method of teaching, two students work together and choose to take the position of either the teacher or the student. They read a selection together and follow steps to draw out questions, summarise the passage, clarify meaning, and write their own predictions or ending. Each step in the process is carefully taught with immediate oral feedback shared by all the smaller groups within the larger classroom. Four WALC teachers volunteered to be trained in reciprocal teaching techniques by the school district's division of instruction. This was done on release time for three full days over four weeks to encourage classroom use, peer mediation, and follow-up before advancing. These teachers then trained the rest of the faculty for one half-day, with peer follow-ups for those willing to actually use it. Many teachers found this method highly beneficial for literacy development and the study of history.

Peer mediated learning

With this method, the teacher acted as a coach or facilitator while students guided each other through a task and constructed answers jointly. The 'academic talk' enhanced understanding of the material and nurtured understanding and sensitivity. Teachers used this method in the district's model science 'inquiry'-based programme (through Grade 6). The idea was to transfer those training skills to other curriculum areas. This had limitations depending on the teacher's personal style. Essential to the success of the method was teacher monitoring of small groups, flexible and brief revisions, good organisational management, and clarity of directions. Other important instructional attributes were creative or active listening to student answers; asking deepening and complex two-step-plus questions; and acceptance of divergent answers and strategies.

Recovery versus remediation

This was perhaps the heart of the matter in the education we offered the children. The concept of recovery was based on the overarching principle of finding and building on a person's strengths rather than focusing on a deficit (as in what we would call the 'medical model') in order to overcome learning problems. This method particularly addressed concerns of under-preparation. Since a lack of preparation was often caused by exclusion from previous classroom learning or by a total lack of outside supervision with cognitive stimulation, the academic emphasis and the attitude of rigour plus joy in learning were very beneficial to those under-developed students in need of recovery in one or more areas.

Recovery was usually done in consultation with the full-time and part-time specialists assigned to the school out of compensatory federal programme funds. We encouraged a *pull-in* system of coaching and guiding students whenever possible rather than the stigmatising pull-out system that has been used in the past without much evidence of success (Reynolds, 1990; Ysseldyke, 1990). Most often the specialist teacher used a co-teaching model with the classroom teacher and worked with a virtually unidentifiable and flexible group within the larger class. It was that group that included a fluid selection of students targeted for special assistance. Specialist teachers ran one faculty meeting a month which were actually break-outs for teacher assistance teams. These same specialists (whether part-time or full-time) were available for Inset as requested by the teachers. In areas of literacy and numeracy, where cross-class or cross-grade grouping had created a recovery class for under-prepared students, the specialist co-taught that class as often as the schedule allowed.

Teacher collaboration

Everybody is involved in decision making, everybody is informed about what's going on in the community and in the school. There's a feeling that everybody's thoughts count.

In order to meet the challenges that WALC presented to the faculty, teachers needed to work together co-operatively in an environment where they were free to try out new ideas, explore strategies, take risks, and fail. A culture of collaboration was reflected in how we solved problems and met self-imposed goals. We accepted challenges and even some challenges that actually appeared impossible at first. We examined critical feedback from whatever source it emerged from, which could be students or parents. We learned from our experiences and remained fluid and flexible in our approach to our work. There was a climate of support, camaraderie, and collegiality among teachers and between the classified (non-teaching support) and certificated (qualified to deliver instruction) staff that helped make WALC a good place to work and learn. This excerpt from an ordinary note to me helps demonstrate how teachers not only thought but acted on their own initiative:

October 5th, 1995

Dear Phyllis,

Proposal:

We would like to try multi-graded, achievement grouped mathematics across the fourth and fifth grade. We have bounced the idea around for several days and finally met on Thursday, Oct. 5th to see about arranging children into classes and trying to even out class sizes and still meet the needs of each learner.

Possible guidelines:

I   *Offer a special contract to the students who are in the fastest achieving groups so that they and their parents can decide if they are up for the extra challenges that these classes will offer.*

II *Class size in slower achieving groups will be smaller and will cater to the special needs of student learning styles.*

III *Each will encourage divergent thinking, problem solving and higher order thinking skills.*

IV *Homework will be assigned nightly by the instructing teacher.*

There were several other ideas that we'd like to try and we will run our other ideas by you as they come up. Please let us know what you think. Your experi-

227

ence and vision for WALC is important to us and we want to make sure that this type of learning approach is consistent with our (WALC's) goals.

Cynthia, Anne, Elaine, and Gillian.

This particular project was so successful that the Grade 6 teachers eventually incorporated it with their studies, and variations and extensions were done in literacy as well. Teachers shared their knowledge of a large number of students and collaborated with each other in parent conferences and co-operated on homework co-ordination.

Teachers had many opportunities within the day-to-day life of the school to talk and learn from each other to enhance their skills. Besides conferences and staff development days (there were eight pupil-free training days permissible per year under state law), the other opportunities for teacher talk included:

- teacher-directed or facilitated faculty meetings
- grade-level planning meetings – banking time possibilities
- weekly support groups for new teachers and student teachers
- team teaching with shared planning and grading in areas of special personal interests such as art, computers, sports, literacy, history, etc.
- daily shared teacher duty-free lunch time
- exhibits on staff development in the faculty lounge
- exemplars of student work and teacher assignments in the faculty lounge
- a Burning Issues Board for general graffiti and serious messages between staff members
- teacher-led special groups and a scenario solving approach to sticky problems
- site-based management and school leadership teams
- communication flows that were a web of inclusion and without hierarchical 'niceties'.

WALC teachers trained their colleagues in teacher assistance teams, reciprocal teaching, mainstreaming and inclusion, maths activities, writer's workshop, computer technology and bilingual education planning and ordering of resources. Additionally, teachers had important and respected input on the spending of school funds for materials; an open stock room; faculty lounge housed learning materials with an honour system sign-out procedure; and total control over the spending of any grants which they bid and won (most effective).

Parents – getting them involved and keeping them informed

Perhaps the greatest social service that can be rendered by anybody to the country and to mankind is to bring up a family.

(George Bernard Shaw)

As an accelerated school with high expectations and homework requirements, WALC depended on parent support for academic discipline and achievement. We paid attention when a Princeton professor once said: 'It's always an advantage to not know what can't be done.' Thus, we required parents/guardians to sign a contract between the home and the school. It had to be read and signed by both the student and the parent/guardian. This contract, signed by 95 per cent of WALC families, formalised the relationship with our parents and students. Parents agreed to give at least three to five hours of volunteer service to the school each month. This was a different approach for a public school to take on the parental involvement issue. Individual and group conferences were often required with me or the teachers in order to engage the parents fully. The key to the success of our type of parental involvement in the school was the number of entry points available to parents and the specific directions offered to the parents on their initiation into this involvement process.

For many parents, school was not their favourite place, nor was it a happy memory. In fact, for many of the parents of the most difficult-to-reach students, school was a place of shame and failure, a place where somebody may have made them feel inferior and/or not valued. For these parents, special considerations in tailoring their entry into school participation was critical for the successful implementation of our home-school contract. For us as educators, we needed to constantly remember to ground our vision and our expectations in the remnants of other people's personal realities. Consequently, I would have several parent/guardian questionnaires, surveys, and one-to-one conferences done throughout the year in order to bring hard-to-reach and reluctant parents and families into the WALC community as valued members.

This was almost like a process to 'keep the pot boiling' and keep the interest and enthusiasm levels percolating through the community. Almost to a person, I discovered that it is quite true that no matter who the parents are, when you are discussing their child, you have their undivided attention. It was always at that critical moment of attention that miracles could be sought and secured for increased levels of participation. It was possible to do this through time and perceptive listening to what these adults were feeling and were thinking. If WALC stood for the principle of developing human capital by finding and building on individual strengths, the very core of the school was at stake every time. That was a strong motivator to not give up, no matter how many interviews were required to get people working with WALC for the increased potential of their child.

Family training institutes were held for parenting and homework assistance skills as well as English classes for Spanish-speaking parents. Parent classes were held at two different times for each session to accommodate working families/guardians and babysitting schedules. Thus, each training institute had an 8am session and a 6pm session. There was a special parent room for meetings, counselling and assistance, with an outfitted playroom (The Kid's Place put together by parent volunteers and donations) that opened on to it so that all children in the family could be accommodated at the school at any time of the day or evening when the school was open. Older children and teaching assistants provided coverage for special meetings; otherwise, the parents were in attendance physically and directly in visual control of their children.

Parents assisted and sometimes took charge of certain general classroom activities as well as special projects that complemented and enriched the curriculum, especially in their particular strengths and talents. Examples included:

- French classes twice a week
- NASA Space Program and Shuttle Missions – supervision, sleepovers, transportation
- newspaper writing and layouts
- sign language instruction
- independent maths study groups in or for algebra, recovery maths, Math Field Day
- lunchtime supervision of the Cognition Club and chess instruction
- visual arts workshops on an ongoing basis throughout the school year
- theatre skills instruction (voice, movement, costume, scenery building)
- computers (repair, teacher training, programming, run the technology committee)
- mentoring for troubled, disaffected, or difficult-to-reach children
- grant writing
- football and soccer coaching or just playing
- WALC drill team
- scholastic book fairs and book and game exchanges

- field trips and community service project participation and supervision
- lunch room and playground support
- campus and classroom refurbishing projects – hallways, flower pots, gardens, etc.
- the Little Theatre Project: refurbishing, painting, fund-raising for equipment.

Teachers worked closely with parents to keep them informed and to resolve problems. Some classes held regular monthly pot-luck meal evenings; one dinner theatre production for fourth and fifth year students brought in 250 parents to the school on a Friday evening. Each teacher sent home a weekly letter and as principal I did a biweekly WALC TALKS (news, notes, recognitions and education tips) newsletter that kept parents informed and feeling part of the school community. The bilingual teacher ensured that Spanish-speaking parents received all school communications in Spanish.

Conclusion

It so happens that to every understanding, sooner or later an action corresponds. Once man perceives a challenge, understands it, and recognises the possibilities of response, he acts. The nature of that action corresponds to the nature of his understanding …

(Paulo Freire, 1983)

My two years at WALC with the students, parents, teachers and supporting staff were great learning years for me. In terms of professional goal-seeking, principle-based actions and successful synthesis of practical and theoretical knowledge, I was definitely pushed to the edge of my competence. Moral leadership works. High expectations coupled with an unrelenting and resilient academic discipline work. Flowers, plants and classical music work. Parents, freely moving through the school, helping to not only create the school but also to sustain it, work. Whether these were school effects that set the proper preconditions for a learning environment or direct effects on variance in student achievement, the *cumulative* effect of these things was that they worked at WALC. It was a place where everybody was a potential leader; where everybody was responsible for not only themselves but for all of us; and where everybody was expected to be part of the action that flowed through the campus.

231

... he assumed a role more characteristic of the periphery – that of a gadfly, persistent doubter of conventional wisdom. Thus by his actions he linked the centre with the periphery, building tendrils of connection that established a true web of inclusion. The process was unscripted, unpredictable; it evolved as it went along.

(Helgesen on Socrates, 1995)

References

Csikszentmihalyi, M. (1990) *Flow. The Psychology of Optimal Experience*, New York, HarperCollins Publishers.

Freire, P. (1970, 1993) *Pedagogy of the Oppressed*, New York, The Continuum Publishing Company.

Helgesen, S. (1995). *The Web of Inclusion*, New York. Doubleday – A Currency Book.

Newman, D., Griffin, P. and Cole, M. (1989) *The Construction Zone: Working for Cognitive Change in School*, Cambridge, Cambridge University Press.

Reynolds, M. (1990) 'Classification and labeling', doctoral seminar session with prepublication chapter presented by Professor Emeritus Maynard C. Reynolds, Fall 1990, at California State University, Los Angeles/UCLA Joint Doctoral Program in Special Education.

Sergiovanni, T. J. (1992) *Moral Leadership. Getting to the Heart of School Improvement*, San Francisco, Jossey-Bass Inc.

Vygotsky, L. S. (1978) *Mind in Society. The Development of Higher Psychological Processes*, Cambridge, MA, Harvard University Press.

Ysseldyke, J. (1990) 'Classification of handicapped students', prepublication paper, University of Minnesota. Presented during doctoral seminar at California State University, Los Angeles.

20

■ ■ ■

Preparing students for a new reality

KATH LEE

The constant reference in the media to a rapidly changing world where our students are told that

> *within ten years you will probably be doing a job which has not yet been invented ... you will endure the disruption and uncertainty of having to change your career three or four times to adapt to the demands of a global economy*
>
> (Lepkowska, 1997)

> *new patterns of employment are making self-reliance and flexibility increasingly important*   (Warwick 1996)

and facts such as 60 per cent of students will be using technologies not yet invented ... have an increasing impact on the way we, as educators, must prepare our students for their adult life if they are to feel secure and be able to respond positively.

Individuals will need, out of necessity, to acquire skills and the ability to apply them to new situations so that they can take an active and fulfilling part in a world which will see continuous change. As a direct result the educational experiences offered must include an expansion of the basic three Rs to include problem solving, creativity and a capacity for the three Ls – Life Long Learning. This is well established rhetoric now, but the implications for schools, indeed any educators, are profound – we must continue to be flexible, responsive, adaptable and be prepared to evolve a new model for effective learning both for ourselves and for our students. We need to prepare our young people for a reality which at present does not exist.

Scene setting

What follows chronicles the beginning of the journey upon which we at King Edward VII Upper School, in Melton Mowbray, have embarked. Some seven years ago the impetus for changing the way we managed student learning took place. During this time there were several contributory factors that merit mention:

- the advent of a new headteacher with a visionary aim that has changed the ethos of the school
- IT across the curriculum, the demand for lifelong learning and learner autonomy
- curriculum initiatives – supported study and associated developments
- technology college status.

King Edward VII Upper School is a 14–19 rural school situated in Melton Mowbray, Leicestershire with a catchment area of some 186 square miles. We are part of a pyramid of 27 primary schools and four high schools. We have a population of 1450 students, including 490 in the sixth form.

How we started

An appreciation of a rapidly changing future where there is 'no job for life', the recognition of different intelligences and the need to cater for individual learning styles that can be used to help students learn most effectively for them (after Gardner, 1983) and the emphasis on the skills of 'how to' learn formed the starting point for us in 1989. Planning for a change to more flexible teaching strategies and learning styles began with their inclusion in the stated aims of the school, led by the then new headteacher who stated that 'student autonomy and flexibility is a secondary school educational goal'. We wanted to encourage the view that responsibility for learning lies firmly with the individual and the development of autonomous learners who are armed with transferable skills and the knowledge that they know how to learn. This becomes central to our school learning policy. Extracts from our development plan over several years recognise and demonstrate our commitment (Figure 20.1).

In a rapidly changing world in which technology and the growth of knowl-edge constantly demands new skills and flexibility, we must place increasing emphasis on teaching young people to acquire the skills of critical and independent learning.
School Development Plan 1990–1991

Priorities 91/92 and beyond ...
Promote the philosophy of flexible learning approach and subsequently adopt the policy of independent learning within our institution. Agree a strategy to implement the policy with respect to independent learning and with Year 12 and 13 but subsequently all students.
School Development Plan 1991–1992

The following practical measures should be adopted across the school in order to improve the quality of learning. Flexible and open systems of learn-ing which acknowledge and value the students' own ideas and contributions and help the development of self-management, self-confidence.
School Development Plan 1991–1992

And subsequently:

The school's learning policy states that we must encourage students to be independent learners. External pressures, including the NC and employers, require students to be flexible and able to apply existing skills so they can adapt to changing situations. It is unlikely that any young people of today will be required to do the same job for all their working life as technology and the pace of change is increasingly affecting our lives.
School Development Plan 1992–1993

Fig. 20.1 Extracts from the school development plan

First steps......

Post–16 developments. In 1990, a working party, with voluntary member-ship, was established. This policy-making group investigated the teaching and learning styles experienced by students, using classroom observation and through discussion produced a learning policy document for inclu-sion in the 1991–2 development plan. It was recognised by the policy makers that to change teaching and learning styles was a long-term process and several phases of development were required.

An independent learning centre within the sixth form was established. Mindful that 'it may be realistic to provide students with not only materials to meet their individual needs but also essential tutorial support' (Rainbow,

1989), funding was made available for Inset and part-time ancillary help, a member of staff with responsibility for the oversight of the development was appointed, successful bids to NCET helped to provide the resources to support the initiative, time within a training day was used to inform staff, and outside agencies (Leicestershire Flexible Learning Project) were invited to raise staff awareness. Inset was used to support enthusiastic staff, who formed a cross-curricular working party. Their specific objective was to develop materials to support independent approaches to student learning. Essentially these were generic study guides which were trialled within different subject areas to evaluate their effectiveness, both from student and staff viewpoints. In addition, several small clusters of resources based in curriculum areas were set up during 1991 to promote the acceptance of individual approaches throughout the institution.

Further steps

A cross curricular model for whole-school IT delivery. A concurrent theme running alongside the need to develop student autonomy was the acquisition of IT skills that are essential to support the development of lifelong learning skills. IT was identified as the vehicle to focus our attention on effective learning of students. To emphasise transferability of skills, a cross-curricular model was implemented. Our philosophy was one of integrating relevant IT experience into specific curriculum areas with the aim of enhancing student learning and developing teacher expertise at the same time. We embarked on a five-year plan in which specific curriculum areas were targeted on rolling yearly development. IT specialists worked collaboratively with subject specialists to develop curriculum activities prior to implementation in the classroom.

Our model allowed the curriculum specialists to 'own' the developments which we felt was a key to the initiative working successfully. Staff and IT specialists delivered the activities together through a team-teaching approach. Through this model, teacher Inset was achieved while immediately giving relevant learning experiences. Over the years, as staff have gained more expertise and confidence, IT has become central to teaching and learning (with a move to incorporate communication technology through video-conferencing in the past year). IT Inset is in demand and since being granted technology college status this year, all staff are involved in organised programmes with the intention to accredit information and communication technologies expertise. To this end we are working with the Technology College Trust and intend to pilot its proposed framework for ICT accreditation. Other avenues we have explored are the use of NVQ accreditation and the possibility of accreditation in association with the Open University or Leicester University.

Moving forward

Innovation in the 14–16 curriculum – supported study. As a school we were determined that our moves towards more independent approaches and student autonomy would not be stalled, despite the demands of a National Curriculum that, 'replicates the regulations for secondary schools dating back to 1904 and Key Stages reproduce the pattern of the 1944 act where it appears we are determined to meet the challenges of tomorrow through action replay of the past'. (Warwick, D., 1996) and although 'the sheer pressure to teach to the syllabus under the National Curriculum has restricted the scope teachers have had to develop new courses and explore new learning approaches. At King Edward VII a team of teachers, working across a well established subject timetable, have introduced a course which is acting as a catalyst for change. The continuing debate over differentiation, use of national Record of Achievement (to be renamed Progress File), student profiling, coupled with the arrival of new information and communication technologies, are having and will continue to have an impact on the way teachers view and carry out their task' (Collins, and Lee, 1994).

To explain further, changes in the curriculum on offer in 1993 resulted in core delivery that satisfied the National Curriculum. The Curriculum Development Board (comprising all heads of faculty, co-ordinators, the librarian, headteacher and deputy in charge of curriculum) decided that the 100 per cent National Curriculum could be delivered in 90 per cent of the time, thus allowing a ten per cent option time. Choice within this option block was not to be limited to choose a new option – that of supported study. This was seen as a practical and focused way of introducing a pilot group of 14–16-year-old students to independent learning and to support them in their studies (Figure 20.2).

Supported study is a course in which students, in association with a study tutor, identify their own needs, direct their own studies and take responsibility for their learning outcomes. It is an achiever course that caters for students across the ability range. The course accounts for 10 per cent of each student's time. Students use the time to develop their study and independent learning skills which are transferable to all other subject areas. In addition, students have the opportunity to consolidate and extend their other studies across the curriculum. The approaches adopted allow individuals to work at their own pace, select the most appropriate way of working on a task and learn at their optimum level.

Fig. 20.2 Supported study

Supported study is a cross-curricular option in which students, in association with a study tutor, identify their own needs, direct their own learning and take responsibility and independence for their own outcomes. We stressed to both staff and students that it was not a course for the less able and also was not just somewhere students did their homework. Presently, for around 250 Year 10/11 students (25 per cent of the total cohort), the straitjacket of the timetable has been relieved as they are allowed to follow individualised programmes of study within timetabled periods, become familiar with information handling, and learn study skills. All other students opt for an additional GCSE with the exception of students with specific learning difficulties. The term 'supported study' is applied to a style of learning which enables students to study largely by themselves or in small groups with the added support of a tutor. It incorporates elements of other styles such as 'independent', 'resource-based', 'individualised' and 'open' learning, (Rainbow, 1989). As Collins and Lee (1994) explain: 'It is our contention that the skills of self-organisation, target setting, information handling, problem solving and self-evaluation need to be properly taught if students are to become confident users of the tools and resources, both physical and human, that schools make available to them. The supported study course became a focus for innovation and a training ground for teachers interested in exploring new approaches.' The course helps students to identify their own effective learning styles, supports the core curriculum in an individual way with the emphasis on raising expectations, self-esteem and the development of the habits of the independent learner.

Supported study – course organisation

The first weeks are structured to allow for the effective development of the study tutor/student relationship. The focus is on identification and acceptance of individual learning styles and the delivery of a range of study and IT skills within relevant subject frameworks. Throughout the course activities are contextualised and the transferability of skills across subject domains is emphasised, e.g. before all students take their module examinations in science, students are introduced to all the various methods of revision and allowed to decide the most effective for them based on their individual learning preferences.

Increasingly, students have a responsibility to organise their own time. This is achieved in a variety of ways, such as individual interviews with the study tutor which are held regularly to identify the focus for further work;

using targets identified in profiling sessions with subject teachers; or subject teachers feeding back extension or consolidation work from specific subject areas. Tasks may focus on generic or subject skills. The whole emphasis is on encouraging the student to gain the confidence to do their best.

The supported study tutor takes on the role of facilitator and supports the individual activities of the students in their care. In each supported study lesson there is a variety of modes of working and students are encouraged to find their own preferred learning styles that bring them success. Over time supported study students may work as a class, in small groups, individually or in pairs. Student activity is monitored lesson by lesson and students plan and log their work and present the record to the study tutor for signature and comments every lesson, thus ensuring the student of some attention each lesson. It also provides an ongoing record of each student's progress against identified targets.

Supported study – measures of success?

The customers: students. Evidence from student comments would suggest that they clearly value the time and assistance they are given to help them succeed and achieve their best. We assume students talk positively about supported study with their peers judging by the number who wish to opt into supported study after the first few weeks of Year 10 and from hearsay such as 'I wish I has done supported study, instead of …'. Also, students in the sixth form who have had experience of supported study are requesting similar support in the post-16 curriculum. There is a demand from other post-16 students who feel they should have access to a course which focuses on 'how to learn' effectively.

The customer: parents. With so much emphasis being placed on subject examination results, convincing parents of the merits of a non-examination course was an early challenge. However, feedback suggests they are pleased with their children's progress. Increasing numbers opting for the course, after the initial 80 in the pilot, lead us to assume that we have met the challenge. Indeed, parents go further. 'Shouldn't all students have access to this option to help them with their studies?' At our selection evening for the new intake of Year 10 students, we are regularly asked variations of the question. Our response is unequivocally: 'Yes, we agree.' Our future developments, under our Technology College initiative, due to be implemented in 1998, will give all students in Years 10/11 access to a subset of the supported study activities through a remodelled (reengineered) tutorial programme. Post-16 developments, due to be implemented in Year 12 in 1998 through an accredited key skills development, will ensure progression through to age 18/19.

In addition, since the opening of our ILIAD centre (*see* later section) we have many enquiries from parents for out-of-school access for their children and indeed, there is a demand for parent workshops. Parents clearly want to know what is going on in their child's education and to develop their own skills. This has led us to investigate, in association with the Open University, an accreditation for parents in ICT as a future initiative. Although still at the discussion phase, we are confident of a positive response from parents when this is implemented in the future.

OFSTED inspection. The OFSTED registered inspector came with a preconceived idea that supported study would be 'a nightmare of organisation' and, in his view, 'a recipe for disaster'. However, OFSTED observations and comments from the report suggest that supported study is highly successful:

> *Students are responsive and responsible in supported study at KS4. Learning is of good quality ... the innovative course of SS of which IT forms a part ... where... students are able to discuss their work in depth and with understanding ... Use of IT is good, particularly searching and utilising information in SS ... There is a high level of expectation of all abilities and classes are taught well ... Teaching is good and the supported study team is adept and extremely competent in developing work appropriate to individual students ... the school wishes to extend this provision further, which seem sensible given its good quality.*

The comment that 'supported study should be offered on a school-wide basis' is something with which we are grappling because of the huge resource implications in terms of management and co-ordination, curriculum, staffing, Inset and access to ICT facilities and learning resources. Our proposed model for school-wide implementation (as explained previously through our remodelled tutorial programme and post-16 key skills programme) requires all staff (in their tutor role) to deliver components of the study skills programme in Years 10/11. The model for post-16 delivery allows for a broadening of curriculum experience, but exploiting a more independent learning style with a tutorial at fortnightly intervals to monitor progress through target setting, action planning and review. These approaches not only require more teaching hours, they demand additional support from para-professionals. We have employed a learning resource co-ordinator, two full-time assistants and part-time assistants on a flexible format to ensure that the learning centres are staffed throughout the school day, into evening and holidays.

During the summer term, a programme of Inset and resource generation is to take place in preparation for implementation. There has been much debate about how to find additional time in the school day to pursue the 'supported study for all' opportunities. At present, time will be gained from the existing school day pattern, but it is our intention to pursue a more flexible and responsive model for the school day to provide greater access to human resources. Access to learning and technology resources have, to some extent, improved with a successful Technology College bid which has reduced our workstation-to-student ratio. However, we fully expect demand for access to resources, whether human or physical, to overcome supply in the future. An extended school day, with opportunities to work from home, at any time, and in the school holidays, is ultimately the model to adopt where the school becomes a learning centre for all.

Impact of our experiences

It became apparent as the IT cross curriculum programme progressed and the supported study programme became established that both have been effective as tools for introducing changes in teaching and learning styles. There have been far-reaching consequences outside of what we originally perceived at the outset.

Changing role of the teacher

On our journey we have needed to rethink our roles as teachers. With an increased emphasis on independent approaches and the role of technology to support learning we have had to change our perceptions of ourselves. Traditionally, we have taught what we know and managed learners. Instead of the 'font of all knowledge', we needed to accept a role which has been typically described as the 'learning facilitator', 'learning coach', 'the guide on the side' or 'the learner mentor'; in essence, a manager of learning. This is especially true in supported study lessons where study tutors are not specialists in all subjects in which students may need support. It also occurs where staff may find students with more advanced IT skills than they currently possess.

We have overcome this in several ways, and each has merits.

Teacher collaboration. We have adopted several models of collaborative working:

- Timetabling different subject specialists as study tutors in supported study at the same time allows them to teach. Students benefit from access to support and teachers from access to fellow professionals.
- Inset activities within the supported study team rely on different subject specialists 'leading' the team so that teachers can learn from each other.
- Inset activities to gain IT expertise are of two kinds: either all faculty members take part with a specialist leading them; or an individual team member is trained and then cascades expertise to colleagues in their subject teams.
- Informal 'corridor consultancy' or 'on the hoof' training occurs between colleagues.

Teacher collaboration has:

- provided access to different styles and techniques employed by fellow professionals
- a notion that *all* are learners within the school
- strengthened the team ethos, particularly in supported study
- created a climate of reflective practitioners who provide mutual support
- provided an appreciation of the demands of the whole curriculum on students and the need to stagger deadlines across the curriculum at Key Stage 4
- given us (teachers at the school) many an insight into how students can be motivated to organise and study at their own pace
- encouraged a breakdown between traditional subject boundaries often prevalent in secondary schools.

Teacher and student as collaborative learners. Study tutors may be asked to carry out unfamiliar activities and must have the confidence to do so. This has value for the student as they see the techniques and strategies employed by the study tutor in their efforts to help individuals. This can be seen as a positive strength as the tutor can refer to this experience the next time the student asks for help and encourage them to apply the strategies – really showing them by example 'how to learn' for themselves. This approach has the added advantage of placing the student and teacher on a similar footing, thus reducing the 'superior position' of the teacher in the teacher-learner relationship (Bowring-Carr and West-Burnham, 1997).

Student as 'expert'. Teachers may find themselves in a situation where there are students who have a greater expertise and knowledge than they possess. This is a potentially threatening position for teachers if they have not changed their perceptions of their role. However, there are many staff (although not all, yet) who are only too willing to accept help, thus placing themselves in the position of learner and handing over the role of teacher to the student.

Students as collaborative learners. We have found that another option to support student learning is to exploit the other experts – the students or 'consultants' in the class or room – and encourage peer support and collaborative working. I would support the view expressed by Harris and Russ (1994) that 'learning is strengthened ... where teachers encourage pupils to work together to develop their own esteem'. This is particularly evident in the independent learning areas where students work with their peers in groups and engage in peer-to-peer tutoring models of learning. These are powerful ways of enhancing student learning and increasing student autonomy.

Using para-professionals. We also discovered the importance of access to help from para-professionals such as support staff and learning resource managers. They provide help as and when requested by the student and support their self-directed learning. In addition, teaching staff rely on their expertise in aspects of information handling, resource generation and effective use of technology to enhance learning, both for themselves and for their students.

Tutoring models

Our experience shows that the success of supported study relies heavily on the positive student-supported study-tutor relationship. The most important aspect students value is the relationship they form with the study tutor. The most effective learning is achieved where the teacher gets to know the whole student well and supports them in their learning. The process of regular meetings with the study tutor is powerful and provides an ongoing picture of the whole student. This holistic view of the child is the basis of effective tutoring and the holistic approach has become central to our thinking.

We are considering more creative ways of using time to allow us to implement an academic tutoring model through the pastoral system. Pilot systems are in place for Years 10, 11 and 12. Each tutor (in pastoral teams Years 10–12) has feedback on generic approaches (attitudes to study, behaviour and attendance) and subject-specific performance on a regular basis from subject staff. Traditionally this has been available at reporting once or twice a year. With the advent of computerised recording of assessments and attendance, data are collected from subject staff and disseminated to tutors efficiently. The feedback forms the basis of a one-to-one dialogue for all students with their tutor for target setting, action plan and review. Tutors gain an overview, progressive over time, of each student in their care. Not only does the tutor have the knowledge of where each individual is but importantly, also the opportunity to celebrate success and promote positive self-esteem, which we know, from our experience in supported study, helps students to succeed .

Catalyst to involve others

Where students and staff have used IT successfully, their example has acted as a spur or catalyst to get other students and staff involved in using IT to enhance learning. This has been achieved by several means: teachers demonstrating to their colleagues during Inset; students encouraging their teacher to allow them to get involved during lesson time by referencing how their friends were using IT to enhance their studies; and students exchanging expertise with each other informally.

Transferability of skills

Through the IT programme not only did students use IT in subject-specific boundaries, they also realised its potential application for other studies. The same is true of supported study students. They are able to transfer the skills and adopt the approaches in other subject areas to enhance their learning, giving them control and the ability to manage their learning.

Reengineering the use of school accommodation

Our school, like many others, has been built with a particular type of education in mind – a classroom with a closed door with a teacher teaching – so to achieve our aim of focusing on student learning and responding to student demand for access to facilities, we needed to rethink our use of classroom space. This inevitably meant carrying out alterations and putting in place the range of technologies which students need to exploit to prepare them for their future (an obvious implication of this is the continual acquisition of new and emerging technologies and upgrading of existing resources to service the demands of learning for the future).

Accommodation has been redesigned (reengineered) to provide appropriate facilities to support increased student and staff demand as and when finance has allowed. Such was the success of the sixth form Independent

Learning Centre that a similar independent learning centre was established during 1993, for the 14–16-year-old students. By extending the existing library to become a well resourced central base which includes a wide range of facilities, information technology workstations specifically for information retrieval, audio visual equipment, an area for small group work and individual work was established. The area is staffed at all times by a technically competent member of staff to ensure that students are supported in their studies. This gives the opportunity for everyone to have access to the facilities that encourage and support student-centred approaches. A further extension of the main Independent Learning Centre, into traditional classroom space, took place in 1995 to service increased demand. Cluster centres have been established, in specialist areas, as more staff encourage students to work autonomously.

Open access policy

Demand from students for access to facilities and expertise to carry out independent work led us to formulate an open policy in which students are encouraged to use the ILCs to use IT (and latterly communication technologies) to support their learning outside of the classroom. The open access policy has changed the way students approach their learning, and their perception that learning is an activity solely for the classroom. They are able to be pro-active and direct their own studies.

Time – in school in the holidays

We became victims of our own success because, despite providing additional facilities, we were still unable to meet the demands for access to support the self-directed learning of our students, and for subject areas to use IT to enhance and enrich the curriculum they offered to students. Creative timetabling of facilities went some way to meeting the demand, but it presently outstrips supply.

Encouraging independent approaches to study and focusing on student learning empowered our students to demand additional access to expertise and facilities. Initially this was in the form of after-school sessions and then expanded to include some weekend and holiday openings. Our initiative is called SAS (Supporting the Achievement of Students) programme. It is staffed voluntarily at present, such is the commitment of staff. We created headlines locally and nationally when we provided access for students to study during holidays. Why? Because as a school, we were challenging the widely accepted norm that learning takes place in schools between 8.45am and 3.30pm for 40 weeks of the year. Access will be significantly enhanced in the future due to our Technology College developments.

There is no doubt that exploiting IT has been a powerful means of promoting student autonomy and enhancing student learning. I would agree, from our experience, that 'IT is the single most powerful change creator in the history of humankind' (Bowring-Carr and West-Burnham, 1997, p. 114).

The next few years

As a recently designated Technology College (September 1997), we are able to build on the strong foundations laid over previous years. As a Technology College we will continue our pursuit of the goal to prepare our students for independent and lifelong learning. We aim:

- to make independent learning central to all students' experience, equipping them for employment and lifelong learning (ILIAD)
- to continue to re-design (reengineer) classroom spaces across the curriculum to allow students to develop lifelong learning skills
- to use new technologies to reorganise (reengineer) and extend the time spent on study in school and at home.

(King Edward VII Upper School Technology College bid, (1997, pp. 2–3)

Further reengineering of accommodation

As I write, a further stage in our reengineering of school space is nearing completion. Owing to a successful lottery bid we were able to build a new sports complex. As a result the old gym has been completely refurbished as part of our Technology College programme to become the ILIAD Centre. Our Technology College submission outlines where we intend to be in the Year 2000. It emphasises our continuing commitment to the development of independent and lifelong learning through the exploitation of information and communication technologies. Already we are encouraging students to use their information handling and IT skills to give access to global information using the internet and video-conferencing.

As a school we are responding to the demands to help our students to learn how to learn and attain their full potential through:

- access for *all* to key parts of the supported learning through the tutorial programme
- an accredited study skills programme for *all* within the sixth form
- the provision of resources, human, physical and electronic (school intranet, TCTrust net, UKNet Year, NCET Virtual Teacher Centre)
- the provision of co-ordinated programmes of Inset for staff
- access to resources, both physical and human, at all times and via electronic media.

I must stress that our journey is ongoing. We are prepared to pioneer approaches and challenge traditionally-held views in our quest to provide an enriching educational experience for all, staff and students. Our involvement in new initiatives such as NCET Virtual Net, Technology College Trust Intranet project and European projects clearly demonstrates our commitment. As a school we are excited by the challenges the learning society presents to us. It is an exhilarating time preparing students for reality that does not yet exist but knowing they will have the skills and attributes to cope and respond positively. We are determined to give individuals the opportunity to learn in their own time, at their own pace, when they wish and at any age.

References

Bowring-Carr, C. and West-Burnham, J. (1997) *Effective Learning in Schools*, London, Pitman Publishing.

Collins, B. and Lee, K. (1994) 'Independent flexible learning', *FORUM*, 36(2).

Gardner, H. (1983) *Frames of Mind*, London, Fontana.

Harris, A. and Russ, J. (1994) 'Pointers for prizes', *Times Educational Supplement*, 23 September.

Lepkowska, D. (1997) 'No jobs for life in a flexible future', *Times Educational Supplement*, 12 November.

Rainbow, B. (1989) *Supported Self Study*, NCET.

Warwick, D. (1996) 'Learn from the future not from the past', *People Management*, 26 September.

Part 4 – Reflection and review

■   ■   ■

1 How clear and confident is your vision of how your school *should be*?

2 What is the status of ICT in your school?

3 How aware are you of the possibilities and potential of ICT?

4 Do you have 'the knowledge'?

5 What are your school's links with the local, national and international community?

6 In what ways does your school invite learning?

7 Walk around your school. In what ways are learning, achievement and community expressed through the physical environment?

8 Scan part 4 – code your responses to the strategies described:
   ✓ = we are doing this
   x = we are not doing this
   ? = I'm not sure if we could or should do this.

How does your school compare to those in the case studies?

PART 5

. . .

Creating a learning culture

21

■ ■ ■

Creating a learning culture

JOHN WEST-BURNHAM AND CHRISTOPHER BOWRING-CARR

At the heart of every case study in this book is a process of change. The success of the various innovations described is directly proportionate to the extent to which a significant shift in attitudes, perceptions, values and behaviour has been achieved. These in turn lead to a reconceptualisation of the nature of roles, relative status, the allocation of resources, levels of authority and responsibility and, in the final analysis, a reappraisal of the core values and primary purpose of the school.

Perhaps the greatest myth with regard to innovations in schools is the notion of the *rationalistic fallacy*. Successive governments, governmental agencies, LEAs and governing bodies, and senior management teams have sought to impose change on the basis of their perceptions of the obvious need for change and the 'fact' that they have discovered the optimum solution which is so obviously correct that no debate is necessary: the solution lies in unquestioning implementation and any challenge to the new orthodoxy is misguided if not actually mischievous. This culture has prevailed for at least ten years and might explain (at least partially) a teaching force that perceives itself to be undervalued, under stress, under-paid and under threat.

The rationalistic fallacy is axiomatic to any 'top-down' view of educational reform or change. It is derived from the confidence that comes from diagnosis and prescription based on a hierarchical model of policy making. One of the most significant features of the case studies is that in many instances they are exemplified by caution, if not actual diffidence, and are the result of the aggregation of multiple perceptions at all stages of the change process. The case studies offer a powerful antidote to the notion of improvement through the imposition of right answers, and reinforce the principle that *true* change (i.e. that which is real, profound and lasting) has to be institutionally based and has to focus on the perceptions of the individual and in particular on the emotional response to the innovation.

In the final analysis the case studies in this book are about changes in the behaviour of classroom teachers. Although changes in policies, school structures, etc. are important buttresses, it is the internalisation of the change by individuals that is the most significant criterion for the success of any innovation. This is made even more complex when the topic under review is classroom practice. The culture of most schools, from a teacher's perspective, is highly individualistic. Most teachers achieve personal and professional understanding through the habituated patterns that define their classroom practice. Such practice is the result of an immensely complex set of variables: the teacher's own experience as a student, the nature of professional training, their perceptions of the status of their subject, reinforcement through different types of success, etc. What is clear is that after a number of years of successful practice (and longevity may be a major criterion) it is very difficult to separate the teacher from the practice. It is not a matter of replacing one set of techniques with another; in a very real way the teacher *is* the practice. Therefore, any attempt to change classroom practice will strike at fundamental, if not elemental, issues of self-image, coping and survival strategies, personal models of success and effectiveness, and a complex sense of self.

The cases studied in this book all represent a significant shift in the perception of the role of the teacher, what constitutes learning, and how achievement is to be defined. Each of these factors represents a significant challenge to those who would seek to introduce change. Quite apart from the perceptions of individual teachers are the cultural norms which serve to reinforce the historic patterns of operating in schools. It is not too much of a caricature to argue that schools are fundamentally and profoundly archaic organisations. The hierarchical structure, the organisation of the school day, the relative status of student and teacher, the deference accorded to knowledge, the control over resources all point to an organisation that is fundamentally and profoundly at odds with its environment. It is, therefore, all the more remarkable that the schools represented in this book, and many others like them, have broken free from the chains of history and the dead hand of externally imposed policy to find creative and appropriate strategies that actually make a difference to pupil and adult learning.

At this stage of the discussion, it is perhaps worth revisiting the orthodoxy of the factors which make managing change such a problem in any organisation, and in schools in particular.

252

Problems of managing change

1 The first issue is the very concept of managing change – this is, in essence, an oxymoron. Management is essentially a static activity; important and necessary but concerned with maintenance, not innovation or improvement. As we will argue later, change requires leadership.

2 All too often change is seen as an event rather than a process. This is a classic manifestation of the rationalistic fallacy where the promulgation of a new policy or strategy is seen as self-legitimating, or is imposed with the threat of accountability-based sanctions. This approach ignores the reality of organisational life, i.e. a complex interaction of variables which rarely, if ever, allow a plan to be implemented as first postulated. Most importantly it ignores the need for people to adjust and learn and the possibility that the proposal might be improved during the process of implementation.

3 Although vision and values are fundamental to any change strategy it also has to be planned and executed. Many valid projects fail, not because they are unworthy but because the organisational details are ignored, the plans are not developed, the resources are not committed and the time is not made available. Most importantly, the relevant information is not communicated.

4 If there is one key factor that militates against the successful implementation of a change in schools, it is the failure to recognise the impact on the people who will be responsible for implementation. Most change challenges the status quo, yet the status quo represents personal histories, years of dedication and the investment of energy and resources. Coupled with this is the fact that many of the current reform initiatives are externally determined, producing a perception of imposition and overload which in turn is seen as a primary cause of stress and burn-out leading to cynical rejection.

5 Even if a proposed change has total professional validity and integrity it may fail because its implementation depends upon an unreasonable expectation of altruism. Two factors reinforce this view. First, it is rare for school-based changes to be accompanied by an appropriate level of training which is designed to create both confidence and capability. Second, there is also, often, a failure to recognise the importance of rewards associated with the successful implementation of change. These rarely need to be financial but do need to include recognition, reinforcement, celebration and praise.

What is significant about this list of the problems of enabling change is that they are exactly the same as the problems of enabling learning. A crucial feature of the case studies in this book is that in a variety of ways they are all demonstrations of individual and organisational learning. To learn any-thing is to change – learning is a process involving changing, an individual cannot acquire new knowledge or develop a new skill and stay the same person. Therefore, to change is to learn. If the five barriers to change are reinterpreted as barriers to learning, then every effective teacher would see them as examples of inappropriate practice. Unfortunately, policy makers (at all levels) have yet to understand the importance of the symbiotic rela-tionship between what is required to be changed and how it might be changed. The *how*? will often determine the *what*?; there has to be a high degree of alignment between the desired outcome and the processes identi-fied to achieve it. The end does not justify the means – to argue that it does is a form of moral pragmatism that is inappropriate in an educational con-text. It also fails to recognise that 'do as I say' rather than 'do as I do' is the quickest route to generating cynicism, scepticism and ultimately rejection.

If a school is to replace a knowledge-based culture founded on the pri-macy of teaching with a learning culture, then the processes involved are vital as they will be powerful signifiers. Meaning will be extrapolated from the messages implicit in the strategies as much as from the explicit purpose. Drawing on the principles of effective learning established in Part 1 and the range of insights available from the case studies, it becomes possible to postulate a range of principles for the introduction of success-ful innovation which are compatible with, and reinforce, the principles of effective learning.

Creating a learning culture

Leadership is in danger of becoming a bland cliché, the last refuge of the educational polemicist. However, what is clear in every example in this book is that leadership is a crucial determinant of success if it meets the following criteria:

- it is concerned with futures thinking, values and the quality of social relationships
- it is distributed across the school and is not the monopoly of one individ-ual – it is found in the whole school, every team and every classroom
- it is prepared to challenge the status quo to maintain the integrity of the values and core purpose of the school
- it is focused on action, making things happen
- learning is seen as a fundamental and essential characteristic of the role of the leader.

Prior to any initiative is a detailed situational analysis which sets the school in context not only in terms of its own community and statutory requirements but in a far broader view of the changing world that schools will inhabit. Such an analysis needs to be aware of:

- social, economic and employment trends that will determine the nature of the world that pupils will inhabit as adults
- research into theories of learning, neurological functioning, cognitive psychology and the impact of information and communication technology on the learning process
- research, especially school-based research, into effective leadership, management and organisational practices
- international trends in educational practice.

One of the outstanding characteristics of the individuals whose narratives appear in this book is their awareness of the 'broader picture'. This raises the issue of the learning and development of leaders as a fundamental precursor to organisational change. Implicit to all the case studies is a desire to change based on broader understanding and an intellectual perspective on the nature of learning and the role of schools. Coupled with this awareness is the capacity to generate unique solutions and to translate those solutions into practice.

Closely related to the process of situational analysis is the development of strategic thinking. The schools involved in this collection all demonstrate the ability to think and plan in the longer term. Although the school development planning movement did much to improve short-term management, and in particular prioritisation and deployment of resources, it did create a limited perspective and inhibit strategic thinking. There appears to be a consensus that the most effective organisations, and individuals, are able to think in an extended time frame. This is not to diminish the significance of the development planning approach but rather to argue that it has to be set in context.

Given the numerous short-term imperatives found in schools, it requires a significant conceptual leap of faith to spend time talking about the school in a five- to ten-year time frame. The combination of externally imposed short-term imperatives and the historic management cycle in schools inhibits moving outside operational thinking.

It could be argued, and this book provides examples, that a key function of the senior management team and the governing body is to push back the boundaries of strategic thinking. In other words, to set the school in a far broader context than is normally required by statutory or organisational imperatives. The development of strategic thinking helps to provide a school-focused context through which to interpret statutory requirements and, perhaps more significantly, to create the flexible response that a fluid, complex and dynamic environment requires. However, it would be wrong to underestimate the psychological and cultural changes necessary to regard time spent on long-term strategic timing as relevant and valid. The problem is one of the most fundamental in the human psyche – replacing short-term gratification with a long-term perspective.

Closely coupled with the notion of leadership outlined above is the importance of an innovator or change-agent in bringing about change. The case studies show that such a person may be the headteacher or another senior member of staff but can equally be a middle-manager or classroom teacher. It is also possible that such a person might be an external consultant. It is obviously much easier to initiate and sustain change if a person has formal organisational status and control over resources but this does not appear to be a fundamental prerequisite (although support is).

What does seem important is that the change-agent has qualities which might not always make them the easiest of colleagues:

- a high degree of confidence and convictions that what they are seeking to do is 'right'
- personal enthusiasm, often almost to the point of obsession, for the initiative
- the ability to translate principle into practice
- the capacity to adopt, change and learn from others and through experience
- the ability to negotiate resources, influence decision making and create alliances
- the capacity to think creatively.

Every organisation, and every team, needs at least one of these 'eagles' who can soar above the routine and mundane, spot a new opportunity and target it. This implies a culture of innovation which recognises and respects this role and, perhaps more importantly, actively cherishes it.

The role of the external change-agent is equally complex. Although there are many advantages in using a consultant (for want of a better term), not least the existence of a scapegoat if things go wrong and someone outside the organisation to absorb the inevitable anxiety and hostility, there are also problems. The advantages of using a consultant might include technical knowledge and expertise; broad-based experience; skills in managing innovation; and lending a notional authority to the project. All of these can be outweighed, however, by the danger of perceived external imposition and a lack of ownership. External consultants are probably useful only to the extent to which they support a pre-existing and coherent strategy.

Given the fact that the learning of young people is all about change, challenge and innovation, it is bizarre that schools as organisations are often so cautious about experimentation and change. This is partially explained by the sheer weight of prescription and the prevailing models of accountability. However, as the case studies demonstrate, it is still possible for schools to adopt radical, alternative, approaches which reconcile accountability with creativity.

However inspirational the leadership and compelling the hero-innovators, no reform will work unless it secures the commitment of all. Therefore involvement and communication are fundamental. A distinctive feature of most of the examples cited in the case studies is the very high flow of information and, equally significantly, the avoidance of any notion of a clique or élite. A range of strategies are employed by the schools in the case studies:

- maximum dissemination of information through documentation, meetings, etc.
- regular opportunities to contribute to the evolution of policy
- delegation of decision making to the most appropriate level, especially with implementation strategies
- open meetings with regular review and opportunities for feedback.

It is this final point that provides one of the most significant opportunities for creating a learning culture – comfortable with change and committed to improvement. Institutionalised review of every aspect of the school's life, lessons, meetings, projects and events is one of the most powerful means of creating genuine involvement, stimulating valid feedback and demonstrating a commitment to learning in every aspect of organisational life. Genuine and systematic review is at the heart of all learning.

A further crucial element in securing commitment is the area of professional development. One of the key factors in the opposition to any change is the anxiety generated by fear of the unknown, in particular the challenge to long-established ways of working. Professional development in the form of conventional training is unlikely to alleviate such concerns. An essential prerequisite to the acceptance of any new strategy or technique is the capability to work within the new situation with confidence. This means that professional development has to focus on the work itself, which requires high levels of monitoring, review and reflection, with coaching as the primary means of developing capability. It is significant that in many of the case studies there is reference to the individualisation of learning and this needs to apply as much to adults as to students. There is an overwhelming consensus that supported reflection which is developed through coaching is one of the most powerful ways of enhancing capability and so changing behaviour. This in turn implies a radical review of how roles are described, in particular reconceptualising leadership and management functions in terms of monitoring, review and coaching.

However inspirational the leadership and powerful the vision, no reform or change will work unless it is underpinned by effective management. This is the process of translating the principles, vision and values into the practical outcomes that will make a difference in every aspect of a student's experience. This means a range of specific outcomes being managed, i.e.:

- short-term, focused development planning most appropriately expressed through target setting
- delegation of resource-management to the appropriate level of operational decision making
- high-quality communication through well organised meetings, notice boards and newsletters so that all students, staff and parents feel that they are wholly informed
- careful and systematic management of data and the organisation and presentation of that data in a way that can inform decision making
- specification of key operational procedures in such a way as to encourage consistency in all aspects of the school's work.

One of the characteristics of the case study schools is that most of them place significant emphasis on the physical environment. The creation of a learning culture requires attention to the way the school is presented to its community. There seems to be a high connection between raising pupil achievement and working in a stimulating and supportive environment. For students to care about their work, the school itself must be cared for. Equally, the school must manifest in physical ways its core purpose and serve as a medium for the emphasis on achievement, celebration of success and the creation of a sense of community. Paint, flowers, decoration, etc. may be just as significant as a learning policy and the environment in which computers are to be used as important as the number of computers.

All these factors combine to produce a purposeful culture which has a clear focus on learning, improvement and achievement. It is the focus on standards and the consistent articulation of expectations and aspirations that appears to be a crucial catalyst. All the schools in this book have changed their culture through changing their common vocabulary and developing common aspirations. Although not always explicitly articulated, the focus on learning and achievement in the case study schools is clearly derived from a fundamental belief in children's entitlement to effective education.

The changes that have been successfully implemented are the result of professional wisdom, willingness to learn from failure and mistakes, optimism and enthusiasm, and a focus on the centrality of the actual experience of every student. Perhaps the most important factor is the creation of a learning culture in the assertion of a student's right to learn and to be successful and the subordination of everything else to that fundamental principle.

PART 6

■ ■ ■

The future

22

■ ■ ■

Meeting learning needs in schools of the future

TREVOR MALE

I am much taken with the comments contained within the editors' preface that refer to the ability of teachers and leaders in the schools reported in this book to move away from the restrictive compliance of the current regime of education in favour of practice that meets the learning needs of students more effectively and seriously addresses the implications of the future. Much of the recent history of educational legislation, central government directives and local responses has contributed to schools becoming confused and confusing organisations, largely because of a lack of clarity over purpose and role.

Confused schools

Central government can claim much of the responsibility for schools being confused, largely through the imposition of an accountability model which has led to the instrumental and reductionist domain of schooling we can witness today. If we had a 'great debate' about the purpose and intended outcomes of schools in the late seventies that manifested itself into a raft of legislation during the next two decades, then the great debate of the current era is rapidly forming itself into a question of whether schools are actually places of education.

Schools have always struggled to identify their key purpose as expectations of them are so great. They fulfil more than one major role on behalf of society including, in the eyes of Reimer (1971), childcare, social role selection and indoctrination. The ills of society are laid at their door, together with the inadequate resources to deliver salvation. The call for higher standards is frequently set against the need to deliver short-term, partially designed and underfunded responses to the latest political hot potato. And, even when the shrinking (and ageing) teacher workforce is offered something by policy makers that partially relates to the education of children, it is overlaid with excessive bureaucracy or riven with conceptual flaws.

The messages from the research into school improvement are very clear in that the future success of schools will require a concentration on teaching and learning, particularly the enhancement of teachers' pedagogical skills, an expansion of ICT provision and capability to match the information age, and a serious attempt to provide meaningful learning opportunities that extend beyond the boundaries of the school working day. Thanks to government actions, however, we are obliged to see the processes of school improvement through the heavy gauze of target setting and league tables and hear the messages of alternative approaches to school organisation through the deafening cacophony of school inspection.

The vision of school effectiveness based on increased academic attainment on standardised assessments has implicitly become the preferred model of central government in its drive to raise standards. Nowhere do I see a definition of school effectiveness in any of the government documents, but the creed is clear in the press statements and the actions of ministers and civil servants. School effectiveness is all about results. Yes, we have moved on from league tables based on raw results, but the education service is still plagued by the need to demonstrate gains in easily measurable outcome measures. The algorithms of attainment may have become more sophisticated, as Dr Steven Davis indicates in 'Reengineering the classroom', but the message is the same.

The response to this demand for higher levels of academic success has created a model of school improvement which is short-sighted and divisive of the school population. There is clear evidence of schools engaging in the practice of targeting (Fitz-Gibbon, 1996) whereby students on the margins of 'success' receive additional support and guidance designed to elevate them into the appropriate category of performance. It is an approach to improvement that reduces the support for students at either end of the performance spectrum, as Kevan Bleach argues in 'Total quality provision for able children in comprehensive schools'. It is a short-sighted approach in that the law of diminishing marginal returns has to apply sooner or later, perhaps as demonstrated in the figures provided by the National Advisory Council for Education and Training Targets (NACETT, 1995), which clearly demonstrate a slowing down in the rate of improvement for Foundation Target 1. The target calls for 85 per cent of young people under the age of 19 to achieve the equivalent of five GCSEs at Grade A*–C by the year 2000. The Department for Education and Employment (1998) claims that just over 70 per cent have now reached the target, but NACETT show a decline in the *rate* of improvement which throws the potential for reaching the targets into serious doubt.

Sadly, the response from central government has been to label the original target(s) as overly ambitious and to commence work on a different set of targets. It is sad because targets based on outcome measures tend to encourage contrivance by teachers to adopt approaches that guarantee success in those terms, rather than reengineer their approach to teaching in support of learning for all. There is a wealth of current anecdotal evidence to support the claim made much earlier in the century by HMI Arnold (1910) that teachers tend to teach to the test:

> *The school examinations in view of payments by results are ... a game of mechanical contrivance in which the teachers will and must more and more learn how to beat us. It is found possible, by ingenious preparation, to get children through the Revised Code examination in reading, writing and ciphering, without their really knowing how to read, write and cipher.*

In fairness to the central government agencies, however, information is emerging that will help to militate against the drift to coaching that can be determined from the evidence of recent times. The production of benchmarking figures by the Qualifications and Curriculum Authority (QCA) is already identifying schools which were previously deemed to be successful as actually underperforming. Similarly, the move to publish secondary school league tables in terms of overall student performance, both on grades achieved and an average per capita points score, will also help to ensure all students receive attention and not just those in the middle of the bell curve of performance. This new data will be of vital importance to schools, such as the 'promenading school' described by John Versey in 'Raising standards in schools', which are complacent despite their inability to satisfy the learning needs of all their students. Certainly this factor has been the principal driving force in the attempt by the senior managers of Longsands College (p. 121) to 'move the college from comfortable complacency towards educational excellence'.

It is clear that the real process of school improvement requires a more substantive and in-depth attempt to meet the learning needs of all students than the provision of a centrally determined curriculum and assessment process can offer. Richard Fawcett addresses the difficulties offered by an 'overcrowded, subject-specific, academia-protected curriculum' in his excellent analysis of futures thinking in 'From vision to reality', particularly the likely impact of computer technology on the learning process. As we move into what Drucker (1995, p. 197) terms the Information Age it becomes apparent that the world will need what he calls 'knowledge workers':

> *The newly emerging dominant group are 'knowledge workers' ... the new jobs require a good deal of formal education and the ability to acquire and to apply theoretical and analytical knowledge. They require a different mindset. Above all they require a habit of continuous learning. ..... But knowledge work – and a good deal of service work, such as direct selling – is not **experience**-based, as all manual work has always been. It is **learning**-based.*

Such workers will need the skills to access information when it becomes relevant, rather than be reliant on a body of knowledge which bears more resemblance to the past than to the future. They will also need the ability to problem solve and the flexibility to reshape and reform as the world changes with increasing rapidity. We can expect children being born today to still be in the workforce in the year 2050, working with technologies yet to be invented (Davies, 1997) and to have four to five different 'careers'. This scenario requires school leavers who view learning as a lifelong activity and not as a means to an end. Such students will need to know how to learn and have a love of learning.

Such a vision does not appear to have entered the purview of government policy makers who, despite the mantra of 'Education, Education, Education' we heard during the 1997 General Election campaign, still appear committed to a model of schools which places students in direct competition with each other and their counterparts from overseas on archaic measures of academic capability. It would seem that it is more important to finish high in the international league table of certain subject specialisms than it is to produce a capable workforce. The Confederation of British Industry (CBI) is obviously concerned and voiced doubts at its 1998 conference about the capability of school leavers and graduates to enter the workforce. It is ironic that one of the major driving forces for this demand for higher achievement on academic subjects came in the wake of unfavourable comparisons of our students with those from the tiger economies of the Pacific Rim countries. With their economies now in tatters as a result of too rapid and unsustained growth, it places huge question marks over the strategy of higher levels of academic achievement in the school population as a means of ensuring economic prosperity.

As I have argued elsewhere (Male, 1998), what we need is a school system that strives to meet the learning needs of all students, helps students learn how to learn and provides them with the information retrieval skills necessary for the electronic age. To that we can add the need to inculcate a love of learning so that it has intrinsic value to the adult of tomorrow.

Confusing schools

If central government can take the bulk of the 'credit' for schools being confused, schools can take much of the responsibility for being confusing organisations, particularly for the student body they are intended to serve. Slavish adoption of curriculum models designed by external committees and reinforced by subject barons within the school, and adherence to objectives designed by politicians and reinforced by OFSTED henchmen, have all too often created divisive and ineffective internal learning environments at a time when the very opposite model is the one we need for success.

It is encouraging to see examples in this book of schools that have taken the time and energy to consider and, if appropriate, choose alternative models of curriculum and organisation. Kath Lee's description, in 'Preparing students for a new reality', of curriculum mapping in King Edward VII School provides one example of how schools can adapt internally to provide greater levels of support for individual student learning. Similarly, Dr Steven Davis' 'experiment' with Year 7 ('Reengineering the classroom') illustrates how much can be done to reduce confusion and concern within the student body, particularly in the early days.

Schools can be frightening and intimidating places which, as a consequence, can generate barriers to learning. Anything that can be done to provide confidence and stability within the students has to be welcomed. That is why the work of Linda White ('Reflection and the infant') is so important. I can imagine some of the sneers her sojourns to tranquillity will engender among the more belligerent of our colleagues who seem to prefer to meet aggression with aggression, but there are important messages there of huge significance within the field of school improvement. Frightened and worried children cannot learn, so any means by which we can establish trust and security have to be valid components of a strategy for encouraging learning. This point is further illustrated by Phyllis Harris ('A seriously happy place') who, apart from the substantial triumph of creating a highly effective learning environment in her neighbourhood school, makes good use of a soft, furry brown bear as a means of providing reassurance to children experiencing acute or chronic emotional upsets.

It is worth borrowing from the tenets of the Total Quality movement, as Kevan Bleach and Eric Tope do in this book, when establishing and maintaining a school environment that is conducive to learning. What does it feel like to be the student? Are we implicitly, through the organisation of the school, placing student needs lower in priority than the curriculum and the status of teaching staff? Certainly the abusive classroom practice by teachers that George Thomas ('Timetabling to enable change') has striven to eliminate from his school is all too common elsewhere. Furthermore, there have been many studies of student life, particularly in secondary schools, that demonstrate a semi-nomadic existence further embellished by a variety of different 'rules' and expectations in different classrooms. One easy study to conduct which tends to throw this confusing picture into relief is to ask students with more than one teacher how many different ways they are asked to set out work. Alternatively you could investigate the different ways in which formative assessments are conducted throughout the organisation. The answers are generally revealing and usually overly demanding of the student. An approach based on TQ principles would seek to make the processes as common as possible in order to enhance the learning environment for students.

The messages from this book

Central to the purpose of schools, argue all the writers in this book, is the education of the student, and they set about that task with rigour, inventiveness and enthusiasm. Each has presented a picture of school life that is supportive of student learning and each seems to adopt the laudable view that education is the primary purpose of their organisation. In their way they have reduced the external pressure for conformity to a model of government-sponsored schooling in favour of the promotion of student learning. The studies reported here represent a variety of approaches that will jointly win favour with advocates of a process of school improvement that exhibits equity and with advocates of a vision that extends beyond the current milieu.

Such a system of schooling would not only be more impartial, but would lead towards a more effective model of school improvement. A focus on meeting the learning needs of all students brings with it the need to develop curriculum planning and delivery that is contextually relevant to the learners. Also central to this approach will be to move the development of teaching and learning to the forefront of school priorities, as Graham Harrison suggests in his opening statement in 'The management of teaching and learning at Queen Elizabeth's Grammar School. There is, as Max Coates suggests in the beautifully titled 'Jewels in a lead coronet', a growing realisation that there are:

> *two processes that take place in classrooms: teaching and learning. Sometimes they are connected.*

The process of improvement that leads to learning demands advanced pedagogical skills, that semi-forgotten art form to which British teachers briefly subscribed before the National Curriculum reared its ugly head. The net result of such an approach should be a differentiated approach to learning that is learner-specific, and one that takes account of preferred learning styles and intelligences other than those measured purely on the academic/cognitive spectrum. Such an approach to differentiation is investigated excellently by Carrie Sabin-Young in 'The road to raising achievement'.

The demand to help students learn how to learn should foster and produce students who are intrinsically motivated and independent learners. And the need to provide students with information retrieval skills, as opposed to prescribed quantities of 'approved' knowledge, should lead, in turn, to the development of learners who know how to access knowledge as and when it is relevant, a vital skill for members of a workforce in the 'information age'.

New models of school organisation

If we see this agenda as the 'real' process of improvement, it will require schools to adopt the fully collaborative culture described by Fullan and Hargreaves (1991) and adopted by the Ratton School in Eastbourne (described in 'Putting learning first' by Ann Cockerham), which draws upon the full range of professional skills and expertise to be found among the members of the organisation. Such management cultures move us away from the individuality that characterised schools of the previous generation, heavily dependent on the headteacher as the leader, towards the high-performing organisation (Sawatzki, 1997, p. 147) distinguished by teams in which each member is a 'self-led, growing and dynamic individual, prepared to contribute to the greater good of the team and the organisation'. The underlying principle of the high-performance organisation (Katzenbach and Smith, 1994, p. 15) is the creation of teams which

> *... are more productive than groups which have no clear performance objectives because their members are committed to deliver tangible performance results. Teams and performance are an unbeatable combination.*

Such organisations, argue Sims and Manz (1996, p. 56), will be run by 'superleaders' who rely on the knowledge, creativity and experience of all their human resources, the day-to-day heroes, to improve performance. Howard Kennedy provides us with such a model in 'The never-ending story' when he describes the vision of 'corporate headship' in operation at Holy Family school which has seen the removal of the traditional management pyramid in favour of defining roles and responsibilities for teams and task forces. Such organisational models fly in the face, however, of the rubric from central government agencies, including OFSTED and the Teacher Training Agency (1998), which tend to describe schools as hierarchical structures with a clear focus on National Curriculum subjects. The OFTSED inspection process, argues Bolam (1997, p. 270), reports on outcomes and contributory factors which, *de facto*, have established a model of operation and management to which all schools must subscribe. Schools in this study, however, have worked hard to provide an organisational structure that matches their context and thus, in many ways, stand apart from the standard OFTSED model and in favour of their learners.

Conclusion

The messages from the body of research on school improvement provide us with a clear vision of how to structure schools and manage an equitable learning process that enhances achievement for all students. We know that schools will need greater clarity in their role as places of learning and that teaching staff will need to grow beyond their need to establish individual fiefdoms if they are to develop the fully collaborative cultures needed to support effective learning environments. Such growth is relatively uncommon at present, particularly in England and Wales where the powerful influences of OFSTED and other agencies of central govenment tend to militate against models of internal organisation that differ from a hierarchical management structure based on subject divisions.

The ability to provide a clarity of purpose and to investigate alternative models of organisation is what makes the schools reported in this study such exciting places. In addition, these schools have managed to make the life of students much simpler by reducing the levels of internal confusion in favour of enhancing their opportunities for learning. This book is laden with examples of the ways in which teaching staff, in conjunction with other adults associated in student learning, have worked collaboratively to place the interest of the student body ahead of all others. In short, these schools have provided us with working examples of the components of school improvement that enhance learning and lead to greater levels of achievement for all students. I look forward to the days when this model of schooling is the norm and urge all readers to learn from the examples in this book when working to that end.

References

Arnold, M. (1910) 'Reports on elementary schools, 1852–1882' in Fitz-Gibbon, C. (ed.) (1990) *Performance Indicators*, Warwick, BERA.

Bolam, R. (1997) 'Management development for headteachers: retrospect and prospect,' *Educational Management and Administration*, 25(3), pp. 265–283.

Davies, B. (1997) 'Rethinking the educational context: a reengineering approach' in Davies, B. and Ellison, L., *School Leadership for the 21st Century*, London, Routledge.

Department for Education and Employment (1998) *Targets For Our Future*, available online: http//www.open.gov.uk/dfee/ntargets/pg2.htm

Drucker, P. (1995) *Managing in a Time of Great Change*, Oxford, Butterworth-Heinemann.

Fitz-Gibbon, C. (1996) *Monitoring Education: Indicators, Quality and Effectiveness*, London, Cassell.

Fullan, M. and Hargreaves, A. (1991) *What's Worth Fighting For in Your School*, Buckingham, Open University Press.

Katzenbach, J. and Smith, D. (1994) *The Wisdom of Teams: Creating the High-Performance Organization*, Singapore, McGraw-Hill International.

Male, T. (1998, April) *The Inappropriateness of Patriarchal Leadership Models to the Process of School Improvement*. Paper presented to the annual meeting of the American Education Research Association, San Diego, California.

National Advisory Council for Education and Training Targets (1995) 'Report on progress towards the national targets', London, HMSO.

Reimer. E. (1971) *School is Dead*, London, Penguin.

Sawatzki, M. (1997) 'Leading and managing staff for high performance', in Davies, B. and Ellison, L. (eds.) *School Leadership for the 21st Century*, London, Routledge.

Sims, H. and Manz, C. (1996) *Company of Heroes: Unleashing the Power of Self-Leadership*, New York, John Wiley.

Teacher Training Agency (1998) *National Standards for Subject Leaders*, London, HMSO.

Index

■ ■ ■